Presents

BLACK EYE ON AMERICA!

A Real Story of American Life

By DEXTER CLAY

Black Eye World Publishing,
Beverly Hills, CA, 90211

Black Eye World Prod.

Special Thanks to
The Black Eye World Production staff

Senior Editor: Olinda Clay
Assistant Editor: Carolyn Richardson-Wells
Art Director / Cover Designer Shou Peng
Graphic Designer-2 Bit Studio.
Greg and Sandy
Photographer: Kevin Rolly

ISBN: 0-9665444-0-4
Library of Congress Card Catalog Number: 98-93142

Printed in the USA by

MORRIS PUBLISHING

3212 East Highway 30 • Kearney, NE 68847 • 1-800-650-7888

Acknowledgements

There are countless individuals that I would like to say thank you to; many of whom I have never even met. In writing a book such as this, there are people I want to thank, past and present. Americans of all colors that helped to make this country what it is today, whose names have been lost in the winds of time. The one true element that reminds us of their struggles is that this nation is at peace today. It is within this peace that I used as a backdrop to write this book.

I believe that the spirit of love and understanding which this country created its foundation, will never leave us. I feel that somewhere, somehow, it will find its way into our lives.

The names you find below (in this acknowledgement) may not mean anything to many of you; but, to me they are the light, the hope, the warmth and kindness by which God chose to shine his love in my life. To these people, past and present, I thank you from the heart.

To:

Mattie Hudson (Grandmother and my inspiration)

Quincia & Carolyn Clay (Mother and sister that I am proud of)

Reginald & Carl Clay (Two brothers whom I love)

Olinda & Family (The First Family)

Abraham Lincoln (An example of a true leader)

Joe (Homey) Cammarata & Family (Best friend)

Martin Luther King Jr. (The man I wanted to be like when I grew up)

Lee Andress (My godfather)

Susan Rich (Helped me to build the foundation for love)

Cricket (companion & best friend for twenty years)

Otis Carl Clay (Best dad a stepson could ever have)

Coach Smallwood (Eye to Eye)

Coach Hill (Very special teacher)

John Osteen & The Lakewood Congregation

Shou Peng (Artist)

Mr. Thomas Grey (Jr. High Principal)

Miss Rape (My second grade teacher with the great legs)

Bruce Hudson (Older brother I never had)

Missy Alford (Friend)

Jani Wheelock (Real person)

Father Chester Ball (Parish priest)

Frank Harvey (aka. Family angel)

Joe Spiegel (Softball coach/wonderful human being)

Mr. Cecil (Friend of the family)
Gerald Warren (Taught me how to pray)
Kevin Rolly (A real photographer)

These names helped to create my character, as a human being, a man and an American.

INTRODUCTION

In the midst of America's hope for greatness lies reality. It is with great enthusiasm that I present to you the contents of my book, *Black Eye on America*. I am proud to be an American! It is a blessing and a privilege to be a citizen of this country. I am truly thankful for my existence in America, at this time in history when a Black man can give a very candid and nonprejudicial look at this nation and say, " I have been an important part of this nation's past, I am part of its present, and I will be an integral part of its future! " This book is about the greatest country on Earth.

My purpose in writing this book is to give you a closer look at our nation without the crutch of political propaganda or the querulous attitudes that often discolor America's point of view. I hope that by reading my book you will have the ability to evaluate and understand the issues at hand. The eleven chapters of this book will help you take a closer look at the different facets of this nation; a country that in all its greatness is allowing herself to come to a complete standstill! At a time when Blacks have achieved greater access to education and jobs, our country is still grappling with many racial issues. I hope that this nation will listen to what one Black man has to say!

At some point in our lives we all wish that we could do something that would help to better the world we live in. I have often heard many of us wish that we could find a cure for world hunger or create a vaccine for cancer.

I believe that there is a need within all of mankind that inspires us to improve the decaying conditions of this world. Regardless of whether it's sympathy, empathy or pity that stimulates us to overcome the world's challenges, it is refreshing to know that our good intentions will somehow resurface over and over!

Oftentimes, society's lack of resources prevent us from making any attempt towards trying to make a difference in the lives of those who lack the spirit to move forward. In an attempt to reach out to my country, I have created this book, *Black Eye on America!* In a way, I consider this to be my opportunity to give back to this nation. My hope is that many of you will embrace this book with an open mind and heart and that it will make you aware of the challenges that lie before us. Each chapter depicts issues that are vital to the future progress of America. As I set forth to record my words on paper, I refuse to compromise my candid feelings and thoughts regarding this country. Whether or not you agree with my views, it is important that you realize that I never allowed any animosity toward the White man to taint the substance of my thoughts.

I did this on purpose, in order to give my readers an opportunity to see this nation exactly the way it was created.

As you begin to read this book, I hope that you will recognize the importance of an honest evaluation. It is this personal awareness that will allow us to pursue a change. Change is the vehicle that will enable us to move this nation towards greatness. Let's push for a change for the better, not for the worse. At times, we find ourselves walking through life accepting the past, hiding from the present and lacking hope for the future. If it were not for the reality that is forcing us to be aware of this state of mind, many of us would continue to go through life buried in darkness. It is my purpose to shed a ray of light on a race of people that has learned to shine through this nation's darkest moments.

Black Eye On America!

Table of Contents

I

III

INFLUENCE

I could tell where the lamp lighter was by the trail he left behind him.

HARRY LAUDER
Scottish music hall singer / comedian

CHAPTER ONE

AMERICAN LEADERSHIP
LIVE OR LET DIE

I thought it would be important to begin my book with this chapter on the status of America's leadership.

I believe that the importance of this country's leadership has to be burned into your hearts and minds. All the chapters in *Black Eye on America* are equally as important; however if we continue to ignore the quality of our leadership, we might as well compare ourselves to the nation of Israel at the time of Moses, when his people wandered helplessly without direction or purpose. Whether we choose to accept it or not, the world regards this country as the blessed nation and our country's leadership doesn't only affect us. You can bet that the rest of the world is watching closely and often follows our lead.

It is my unbiased opinion that leadership is the one true element which will ultimately decide the fate of our nation.

Any compromise in the character of our leaders will leave this country orphaned forever, standing alone facing the realities of a hopeless future.

Those of us who sincerely love this country must look at leadership as an ongoing challenge. We must do our utmost to nurture and develop its continual progress. America can be compared to a small child who needs guidance and direction; but, who will someday evolve into a strong and mature adult. As the parents of this young child, we must nurture its spirit and guide him towards the future with the knowledge and wisdom that we have gained from our past.

My Initial Encounter With Leadership

I was in the second grade, when through a request from my teacher I first took on a leadership role.
One week into the second grade I found myself standing on the corner of Elysian and Ryan Streets in my hometown of Houston,Texas, struggling with a huge orange flag at the end of a long ten foot bamboo pole.

I was only a little over three and a half feet tall, but by carrying this pole I had the power to make cars and trucks stop. Wow! What a feeling that was! Every Monday, Wednesday and Friday afternoons I was (Flag Boy) at my school. Come on now, you know what a Flag Boy is don't you?

I was one of those little kids standing at the crosswalk decorated in bright orange reflective decals. I would get out of school fifteen minutes early and patiently wait for the three o'clock bell to ring. It was my job to make sure that my fellow classmates would get safely across the street.

There were a lot of nice perks about the job. Getting out of school fifteen minutes earlier than everyone else seemed kind of special. My Flag Boy gear was stored at the office. Getting there made me aware of the internal goings on at James D. Ryan Elementary. Walking down those quiet hallways, I would look into each of the classrooms.

Some of the rooms seemed to be buzzing with activity while others seemed to be filled with students anxiously awaiting the close of a long day. I would often look inside one particular classroom.

Half of the students inside were sleep! The one thing that I remember most is the feeling of having control over the older kids at the school. Waiting at my post I could see my peers slowly sprinkle out of the school like little ants. Eventually they would be pouring out like wild, angry bees and all headed in my direction! The kids would gather behind me and wait for my signal, a powerful blow on my super hero whistle. I discovered that I could stop the traffic by just holding out my magic wand.

Once the signal was given, everyone would sprint to the other side. I would go back to my position and wait for the next group of kids.

I was told by Miss Rape, my second grade teacher, that my classmates would listen and follow my directions. She said that I was considered a real leader in the school because of my position as flag boy. Actually, this position did make me very popular.

One day, while walking to my post I thought "it's great to be a leader, everyone likes leaders!" This feeling of authority seemed to give me a little extra confidence.

I decided then that I was going to be a great leader when I grew up and that the world would like me! Little did I know that the events that followed would change the course of history and consequently my naive understanding of leadership.

On November 22, 1963, I noticed that my teacher Miss Rape, had been crying. I was very sensitive to her needs, since I had this gigantic schoolboy crush on her. While the rest of the kids were busy writing, I put my No.2 pencil in my Big Chief tablet and slowly walked up to her. "Miss Rape, are you all right?" I asked. She reached out and grabbed me and held me very tightly. "Yes. I'm Ok, Dexter. Thank you for asking. Now go back to your seat." At the time I couldn't help thinking how great her perfume smelled!

However, I knew in my heart that something was very wrong.

Ten minutes later my suspicions were verified. "May I have your attention! May I have your attention, please!" A familiar voice was calling from the P.A. system. It was Mrs. Anderson, our school principal. I can hear the announcement in my mind to this very day, "Dear faculty and students. Today in Dallas, Texas, our young President, John F. Kennedy was shot." There was a slight cracking in her voice. "Please pause for a moment of silence for our great leader. President Kennedy has been killed."

A rush of silence filled the whole school. Miss Rape broke into tears and quickly got up and ran out of the room. A blanket of sadness hovered in the air. Sorrow permeated into the halls and over the entire building.

Except for a sudden "Oh my God!" from the teachers down the hall, the whole school seemed to be instantly paralyzed.

I felt a knot in my stomach. How could they kill a leader like the president of the United States? Here was a person who was even more popular than I was and he was shot down in front of the whole nation.

It was directly right after the Kennedy assassination that I learned that tragedy brings gifts amid its realities. One gift is often a new awareness.

When I look back on that tragic period surrounding Kennedy's death, I realize that I was learning an important lesson. One aspect of this was that I came to recognize the qualities of leadership. I came to the startling realization that my school was segregated. You are probably wondering what this has to do with anything. James D. Ryan was an all-Black school. The tears and emotions that consumed our little school were of a genuine nature. We all felt the loss of our president who had been a true leader. None of us seemed to be concerned with the fact that the young president was an Anglo-Saxon. Although I didn't fully understand it at that time, subconsciously I came to understand that true leadership is never about color.

One important attribute that John F. Kennedy possessed was the ability to make his followers believe in themselves. He gave them a sense of hope. The tears that were shed that day in 1963, in our small, black school were for the loss of that hope. This hope was destroyed when the bullets riddled J.F.K's body.

Another major lesson that I learned about leadership was that popularity didn't mean that you were liked by everyone. A leader has the responsibility of guiding his people, but he must also show direction to those who would rather see him dead. The Kennedy assassination was a reality check. It created a sense of realism for me.

Things that I had read about, such as the Abraham Lincoln assassination became very real.

As a flag boy I soon discovered just how rebellious my own followers could be. Some started to cross the street without my protection. That year, I recall many arguments with my peers. Once I overheard someone remark, "I'm not waiting for that dumb old Flag Boy to tell me when to cross!" He proceeded to enter the road before it was time and that little meathead was almost killed. What made the incident even worse was that I was reprimanded for allowing him to go without my approval! After the initial embarrassment, I realized that this leadership stuff could be a real strain. Wow! That year I learned more about life being a Flag Boy than from any course that I took in school.

Leadership presents itself to us in many different forms. We learn to judge the quality of leadership in many different ways as well. As a kid, when I thought about Abraham Lincoln, Dr. Martin Luther King Jr., or John and Robert Kennedy, I believed they possessed superhuman qualities. I can still remember the feeling I had on Saturday mornings when I walked out of a Hercules movie. I felt strong and courageous, pure and invincible. That is how I learned to judge the quality of leadership.

I thought that leaders had the inside track that gave them the ability to accomplish things that the average person could not get done. Once I got older I realized that there were both good and bad qualities that characterized the term "leadership."

For the majority of our country's history (at least until the last twenty years or so), white men have served as the principal leaders. The dictionary definition of a leader is a" person that leads." In my search for a better definition, I was relieved that I did not find it written anywhere that God had created the White man for the sole purpose of leading all people to a greater life everlasting!

However, in all fairness, it's easy to see how the White men took on this role.

Let's go back to the period shortly after the American Revolutionary War. During that period it was logical for the populace to select a leader who had military experience. Unlike today, age was a plus; therefore, the older and wiser the better. Since the population was primarily white, it was logical that a white man was chosen to lead the people of a newly formed nation. Let's be fair, there were no other choices. Women didn't have the right to vote, the Negro was not considered to be human and the American Indian didn't speak the language. Anyone can see that the white male was simply the best candidate for the job at that time.

George Washington, the son of a rich Virginian farmer, found himself at the right place at the right time. As a result, he became the first President of the newly formed nation called America. He rode into the White House on his big, white horse and his trump card was his military background. His honesty and faith in people earned him every single vote that was cast by his peers.

In the beginning, truth and representation for all people seemed to be genuine concerns of the political candidate. However, this quickly became an illusion. By the time the third President had been elected, the leader holding the office of the presidency realized that in order to gain the results he wanted he would need the support of Congress.

This was the first step in creating the nation's political party system. When Thomas Jefferson became our third President he fully realized that his office commanded great power and strength. Here is where this gets good! From this position of power, a leader can solicit powerful people to gather around him and create an even greater political machine. It is easy to see that today's political parties still carry some of the ideals of the governmental powers of the past.

If we were to examine the political parties of today, we would find that they are self-creating and their principal purpose is to keep their interests well looked after. For this reason, the political parties primarily address the needs of the people who have money. This money keeps the party alive. Let me make the following comparison regarding the state of our modern day politics. Standing at the forefront of our leadership structure is the male figurehead; however, to win the privilege of representing us in public office he must agree to certain terms.

He must allow a group of political supporters to take from him his most vital organ, his compassionate heart. At this time we have a leader whose internal life-support system is resuscitated by a very large special interest group. The reality is that this leader cannot survive without these people and he has no real power of persuasion without their support.

Most of us fail to understand this simple concept. Unless we come to this realization, we can never expect any real change. It is the financial element of politics that causes our leadership to ignore the needs of the masses, the everyday person at the bottom of the totem pole. Clearly, those who can afford representation are the same people who receive it.

This flaw in our system is reinforced daily by lobbyist and special interest groups.

Those who get what they want and those who don't. Money and power could buy leadership and representation many years ago and it still does today!

Turning back to Washington and Jefferson, I learned through my research that there was a common denominator between them. Apparently neither man truly wanted the job. They took the position of leadership because of a sense of responsibility to their country, A far cry from the powerful political figureheads of the 1990's.

If we can learn a lesson from these two presidents it would be that leaders should have the basic instinct to realize that the welfare of the people should come before anything else. They must take into consideration not only the welfare of the wealthy but the less fortunate as well. This is easier said than done.

This kind of unselfish quality is very sadly lacking in most people today. I believe that our current leaders have helped to separate those who lead from those that are being led. During the last two hundred years the process of governing has evolved into a game of corporate greed and political masturbation.

I also believe that leadership had a greater impact on the people in the early beginnings of our political organization. My reason for feeling this way is very simple. At that time leadership had a real purpose.

That purpose was to create a nation that could stand alone and be independent of other countries. Americans wanted to be free to elect someone to represent them in office.

The past had shown them that having a king or dictator at the head would defeat the purpose of creating this new country. They demanded freedom and having someone at the helm was of utmost importance. Now here's the big question: Which came first, the chicken or the egg? Or in this case, which came first, the leader or those who needed to be lead?

There is a major issue that I want to draw your attention to and by clarifying this issue I hope that you will be able to understand how Americans went astray. The early citizens of this country did not realize that they themselves were leaders. You see, people created the need to change and through that need evolved the desire for leadership. Those who choose to lead are merely the reflection of that need. The sad truth is that man is quick to give his leadership responsibilities to a total stranger.

In this way, he or she cannot be held directly responsible for possible failure.

As long as we can blame someone else for the lack of success in our lives, the easier it is for us to accept our own failure. Ironically, this is what brings about the downfall of many of our leaders. When things are not going the way they should it becomes easy to blame our leaders instead of taking responsibility for our own actions. Our leaders become the target of many unhappy constituents looking for someone to blame. I am intrigued with mankind's need to create leaders on one hand while destroying them with the other. Leadership has been shackled in bondage for the past two hundred years. It is my belief that America's leaders are at least one hundred years behind in their ability to lead with conviction and determination. As this chapter unfolds, I will begin to share with you the many reasons for my opinion.

At this point, I would like to begin to talk about Blacks' role in our country's leadership during America in early years, but unfortunately I can't. When our country elected Thomas Jefferson as the third president, Blacks were called "slaves." For your reference, the American Heritage Dictionary defines a slave as: Slave, n. 1. One bound in servitude as the property of a person or household.

2. One who is abjectly subservient to a person or influence. 3. One who works extremely hard. 4. A machine or component. V. Slaved, slaving, slaves. 5. To work very hard or doggedly; toil.

As much as I would like to speak about the Black man's role in leadership, it would be a little premature at this point. The history of our early American leaders is very simply a story of the White man: his struggles, victories and his defeats.

In the beginning, the Black man could only sit back and watch from a distance as the policies of America were created. Our input was not wanted nor was it accepted, regardless of the fact that the blood, sweat and tears of our people were embedded into every facet of this nation.

We watched as the great white master created his policies and implemented his laws. We watched silently, as he attempted to build a nation by manipulating every race of people that stood in his way.

Lack of Leadership Position & Representation for Blacks

Since I cannot write about the Black man's role in leadership during this period let me at least increase your consciousness regarding its nonexistence!

15

America has had forty-two Anglo Saxon presidents. My heart could easily be hardened by the fact that none of them vaguely resemble a Black man. Regardless of this lack of representation my people have been there every step of the way. This is a truism. After all, this figurehead that we elect as President should represent all the people, correct? Consider the fact that fifteen out of the first sixteen Presidents of the United States owned slaves. And it wasn't until the Lincoln administration that the thirteenth Amendment outlawing slavery was enacted. In addition, not until the thirty-six President was there a Civil Rights Bill introduced to congress which eventually granted equal rights for Blacks.

Now I'm not a great mathematician, but if America has had forty-two presidents and it wasn't until the thirty-sixth President that equality became the law, that means that only six Presidents were elected after the Civil Rights Bill was passed. Stay with me now. With each leader averaging a possible two terms in office, at four years per term, that equals forty-eight years of possible leadership.

> **42 Number of United
> States Presidents
> 36 Number of Presidents
> until Civil Rights Bill**

> **6 Number of Presidents**
> **truly representing**
> **Black Americans**
> **x 4 Number of years per term**
> **24 subtotal**
> **x 2 Term average**
> **48 Number of years**
> **Blacks have been represented**

Now stop and consider this important fact. In 1619 the first Blacks were delivered upon the shores of Jamestown, Virginia. At that time, American leaders allowed our ancestors to land on our shores bound and dressed in iron chains. The one thing that must not be overlooked is this: in 378 years Blacks have had only 48 years of leadership and representation.
To this day history still continues to ignore this fact! I purposely didn't include President Lincoln's term in the above figures. In my opinion he stands alone both as a man and as a leader. I do not include those years of administration as lacking the proper representation for our race of people.

Politics; The Toxic Waste of Leadership

A leader's most misunderstood principle is the difference between leadership and politics.

17

The *American Heritage Dictionary* defines politics as: adj. 1 Using or marked by prudence, expedience and shrewdness. 2. artful, using, displaying or proceeding from policy, judicious. 3. Crafty, cunning.

The adjectives in this definition could become somewhat frightening if the person elected was not for you but against you!

Politics is often the *buy-product* of true leadership; or if I might get a little radical, politics is simply the *toxic waste* of leadership. American politics is the backbone of American history, but its negative effects are deadly. My reason for feeling this way are not to be pessimistic or even anti-American. I am trying to give you a candid view of the American political system.

The comparison between politics and toxic waste is a bold one; however, you will be the one that will ultimately decide if this is an accurate comparison.

The characteristics of politics and political parties have not changed very much over the years. Americans have always had the need to gather together in large masses. One can only assume that this is done to create a sense of power. This power is the tool used to make those who don't believe in the political system become believers. A prime example of this is the political convention.

This political circus comes fully equipped with balloons, banners, music, lights, motivating speeches, excited fans and most noticeable of all-the ring leaders. Their job is to try to convince you at any cost that electing them will change your life for the best. The admission to these events is totally free.

As a matter of fact, political parties have huge budgets to spend just so you can be a part of this main event. Oftentimes, volunteers are willing to donate time and money so that this event can take place. We can sit in the comfort of our homes and watch these well-dressed gladiators or candidates go at one another in their man-made arenas. Although this is somewhat entertaining, it can be also alarming. The candidates resemble immature children, playing in a sandbox fighting to gain control over a favorite toy. The frustration of not getting what they want drives these men to react as irrational and senseless children during a temper tantrum.

The reason for this is very simple. The urgency of time makes it extremely hard for most politicians to deal with the real issues at hand.

Once politicians are in the spotlight they must quickly convince you that they have the answers to all your problems. In order to fix what is broken we must understand why it was broken in the first place.

19

To be able to pinpoint the true source of the problem takes a great deal of concentration. Most importantly, it requires a quality that eludes most human beings, not to mention that group of people we know as politicians. This simple, little quality is called *patience!*

Most of us can see that leadership has gone astray, yet we often overlook the small things that have contributed to its misdirection.

Lack of time causes our political leaders to make many promises they are unable to keep; however, you can bet that you're going to hear exactly what you want to hear. It's very important for you to know that in this political game of chess we are and will always be mere pawns. For us to think that we are more than that is futile. Understanding how the game is played allows us to see the whole picture as it begins to unfold.

Once the pawns have been played you must stay in the game. You do this by increasing your value on the political board and that can only be done by acquiring more capital. Politicians need you to get into the game; however, after the election, out of sight out of mind. After we play our trump card, (our vote) we lose all power until the next election. The vote that we so freely give away is what gives us real power.

When we give up our vote we lose sight of the fact that it is our only bargaining chip. In fact, it is quite priceless!

Most Americans give up the endorsement of the vote entirely too easily. Our vote simply says to the politician, "Yes I want you to represent me!" For most of us, the true substance of this action is never realized. A vote is more than just an endorsement. This four letter word carries with it the power of giving someone else part of our existence.

Once you have helped these ambitious politicians up the next level of play, you can only hope that they will remember those who put them in the game.

Most politicians forget those who helped them get into office. This ultimately contributes to the large turnover in the political field.

During the next voting term they are replaced with new faces by the same citizens that voted them to power. In this game of politics one or two defeats can easily mean the forced beginning of a new career for most politicians. Failure is not considered a process of growth. Abraham Lincoln is the perfect example of someone who failed over and over before being elected into office.

Here is a timetable of Abraham Lincoln's unpromising progress forward.

Failed in business	**1831**
Defeated for legislator	**1832**
Second failure in business	**1833**
Suffers nervous breakdown	**1836**

Defeated for Speaker	**1836**
Defeated for Elector	**1840**
Defeated for Congress	**1843**
Defeated for Congress	**1848**
Defeated for Senate	**1855**
Defeated for Vice President	**1856**
Defeated for Senate	**1858**
Elected sixteenth President	**1860**

Government is the cardiovascular system of America, but it has now developed a cancer that is rapidly eating away every aspect of this country's body. Each year this is made even more apparent by the growing number of non-voting Americans. It is a fact that people today are choosing not to partake in the election process. Elections have basically boiled down to voting for the lesser of two evils instead of voting for the best person for the job. An example of this was the extremely comical California Senate race of 1994.

This election was quite disgusting. The Feistein and Huffington race pretty much drew America a very clear and honest picture of the decay that is polluting our political system. I personally wanted to believe that somewhere underneath all the name-calling, personal mud-slinging and the hilarious attempts to bring out the worst in each other, that these two individuals had the best interests of Californians at heart.

The one element that was overlooked in this situation was the message it gave the people.

If we conducted ourselves as such in our everyday lives, what would our accomplishments be? What level of communication would we have with our neighbors, not to mention our adversaries?

The politics of today have strayed so far off base that we have forgotten this simple fact: our actions are determined by the example set by our leaders! Maybe this is a responsibility that today's leaders do not want to accept.

Somehow I feel that we are all to blame for this cancer that is growing among us.

Americans have been programmed to accept the short-comings of their leaders as a way of life, regardless of how important or meaningless a decision might be. One example of this was the decision made by our government during the Reagan administration to sell military weapons to Iran. Iran had made it perfectly clear to the entire world that it couldn't stand our nation's existence. How did our administration respond? Our government decided to respond by selling Iran military artillery. What did the American people do? We accepted it.

Have you ever stopped to question the repercussions of such a decision? Ask yourself, how many innocent people are killed because of our actions?

Another problem within our political system is that we blame one political party or another for the nation's lack of progress. It's just another way our society deals with this country's failures. By giving us one pill after another, political parties have dulled the pain of our social and economic failures. Democrats blame the failures on the Republicans and the Republicans blame the Democrats for the lack of growth in our nation. American people get eight years of one brand of tranquilizer and then ask for another type of sedative.

Eight years later, when someone else is elected, we go back to the same sedative that we were taking eight years earlier. This is one of many reasons for the lack of growth in this country. Americans are so sedated from all the painkillers they have ingested, that it is easier to ignore the symptoms than take any steps toward true healing.

Leadership Without Heart, Without God

As I try to assess this nation's leadership, I find that there is no delicate or diplomatic way to prepare America for the words that I am about to say. I could try to take a very optimistic approach and say everything is going to be all right. The fact is that the situation at hand is out of control.

What has happened to American government and politics has been self-inflected. In a sense America has cut out her own heart. What has caused a carcinogen to decay our political system is the lack of **GOD!** Yes, my fellow Americans, that's right, **GOD**. The United States was created on the principles of " in **GOD** we trust." It was established with a spiritual foundation, with the belief that a creator greater than ourselves was watching over this nation. As this nation grew in size and strength, the decision was made to remove this spiritual dimension from its core (government.)
How can we remove the spiritual structure from our basic foundation without causing permanent damage?

Leaders cannot lead because they don't have a purpose. They don't have a sense of direction and most of all, American leadership has no heart. The single greatest factor behind this country's early achievements was **GOD,** Himself. Today we profess that we no longer need **GOD.** Now I know that there are those of you who will say I should separate **GOD** from country and that this kind of discussion should be saved for my chapter on religion. My argument to you is that if our foundation has been removed, then everything that we add to the country's growth has very little possibility of surviving. You see **GOD** gave America substance and an infinite foundation to build from.

In today's political discussions the very mention of the name of **God** is followed by the thought, " there goes another religious fanatic!" Being a believer in **God** and His power I can understand why this might be; however, it is still very difficult for me to accept the choices that this country has made, knowing that they will only cause endless struggles.

Medical Leadership Gone Astray!

The questions that needs to be asked are important ones.
How can we begin to turn this situation around and keep it from growing out of control? Is it too late to create a change? I don't think so.

I cannot think of any form of leadership that has not begun to show signs of decay. Whether it is leadership in government, religion, the corporate arena or leadership in the family structure. Something is happening here and we cannot continue to close our eyes to it.
The money element plays a major role in this country's decay. An uncompromising need to feed our greed has caused us to lose sight of the simple things around us. One example of this is in the area of medicine.

This form of leadership should never be compromised for any reason on earth.

26

Recently, a friend of mine, a neurologist in Los Angeles, California, explained to me how the medical industry has been hiding important information of an unprecedented scale. She shared the following information.

"Dexter, you will find what I'm about to tell you difficult to understand." After pausing for a moment, she continued, " The medical institution is aware that we have successfully found cures for both *Cancer* and the *AIDS* epidemic.

However, because of the inability to create a monopoly on these treatments, branches of the government have imposed heavy regulations on research regarding treatment and they have outlawed any potential cure."

I looked at my friend in disbelief, but I could see in her eyes that there was a great deal of substance to what she was telling me. Walking the few blocks home I couldn't help thinking that this couldn't be possible. How could the medical institution selfishly ignore any possible treatment that could cure two of the worlds greatest killers?

I wanted to find out more about these possible solutions. I placed a call to a general practitioner who lives in my neighborhood. He replied " What idiot gave you this dumb-ass information?"

His response was very condescending and some what pessimistic. This led me to search elsewhere for answers regarding such medical breakthroughs.

27

My friend gave me a videotape that explained the outcome of the research and it's validity. *Ozone, the Politics of Medicine*, gave me the ammunition I needed. The information I found on this video was very well presented. The treatment is called *Ozone Therapy* and has been used in Germany for the past thirty years.

The treatment was created on the simple principle of water purification. Human blood is cleansed of its many impurities. Ozone is an energized form of oxygen and is said to inhibit the new growth of cancer cells.

Studies done in Germany have shown that there are very few side effects. This treatment reduced the pain in cancer patients dramatically.

The information on the tape explained that U.S. government requires research to be conducted on large animals before it can be given any credibility whatsoever. The video presentation states that Ozone treatment has been largely ignored in North American. European countries have been doing extensive studies in this area. I could go on and on about what I learned and give you names and dates of the many people involved.

If in fact the medical institution has this kind of knowledge, I sincerely hope that they're not keeping it from the world because of their own selfish interests.

I am appalled to think that thousands and thousands of lives are lost each year because of these actions. Not to mention the fact that Americans continue to pour countless amounts of their hard earned-dollars into research, pain killers, doctors visits and impossible cures.

If you think that the medical institution is beyond such atrocities, then let's go back in history to 1940 when a number of doctors experimented on four hundred Black men. This study took place in Macon County, Alabama, and was called the " Tuskegee Study Bad Blood."

For better than thirty years these American doctors willfully deceived four hundred human beings. They wanted to study the development of syphilis without the intervention of treatment.

These men were given the impression that they were being treated when they were slowly dying from the effects of the disease.

These so-called doctors withheld penicillin from these patients, even though they knew that if syphilis was left untreated it would attack and destroy all the vital organs. This study continued until it was brought to the surface in 1972.

The government paid each deceased family member $35.00 for burial costs in exchange for the right to perform an autopsy on each of the victims. This helped to close the study. The small handful of survivors were each paid $32,500.20.

How did the United States government manage to come up with that monetary figure for a human life? The American government as been in abnegations of its role until 1997, when the Clinton administration officially apologized for this medical misjudgment of character.

The Emergence of Black Leadership

The Tuskegee Study shows just how harsh the realities of life can be. The Black race has had to face many challenges and because of this, leadership for the Black man began with a desperate need to learn just how to stay alive. I believe that it is not an unfair statement to say that what has caused our race to carry such a chip on our shoulders is the White man's tyranny. In the beginning in order to survive, we spent much of our lives trying to understand our white masters. In those days, black leaders had a quiet voice. Our greatest leaders were those who truly knew how to best handle their white master. To pass this understanding on to those that severely needed the guidance was a true work of art!

During that period of time, while White men were creating a new system of government, it was important to keep Blacks uneducated.

On one hand, leadership was to create guidance and direction for the White race; on the other hand, it was meant to eliminate guidance and direction from the Black race. In the mist of this double standard, many forms of Black leadership emerged. The mothers and fathers of that time were the leaders of their community.

Although the house servants were considered to be dumb animals, they learned how to be aware of the ways of the White man. Their knowledge helped the field hands come to a better understanding of their position, which ultimately created a course of action for themselves.

As the plight of the Black man improved, so did the role of their leaders. They sprang forth in the form of self-educators, preachers and anti-slave teachers. Their leadership taught the Black man to survive.

Many Black leaders came from religious circles. Ironically enough, religion was introduced to us by the White man. The reason for acquainting Blacks with religion was not to give us leadership. It was meant to subdue the savage and hostile behavior that was said to exist in every Black man. Instead, it seemed to help lead the Black man towards a broader and a more infinite sense of understanding.

This kind of leadership helped the Black man to deal with his suffering, as well as giving, him patience and hope for a brighter future. This religious form of leadership would ultimately be the cornerstone of the Civil Rights Movement of the sixties.

Throughout American history there have been many faces and names that have represented our race of people. Harriet Tubman led blacks as the underground railroad's chief engineer. Christopher Attaus was the first Black man to die in the American Revolutionary War. Frederick Douglas spoke out against slavery and George Washington Carver was known as an inventor and educator. There were countless others that brought us to the powerful 1960's.

Malcolm X and Martin Luther King Jr.

During the sixties, the American people were forced to stop and take a long look at their leadership. Was it meant to be directed to a selected few or towards the masses? For the Black man, during this period there were two giants which will never be forgotten: Malcolm X and Martin L. King Jr. These two men caused America's eye to focus on the face of the Black man. To this day, their efforts have not been matched by any other leader, Black or White.

The stage was set and because of their dedication, the curtain came up for all the world to see.

As we examine the characters of these two men, it is very easy to see that they both had the same philosophies. The foundation of each of these men was solidified by the element of religion. What is very interesting is the fact that the White man saw fit to accept only one of these two men as a leader, while still denying them both.

Malcolm and Martin wanted to achieve the same goals for the Black race: freedom, equality and opportunity. Though it is often overlooked, the Emancipation Proclamation had much earlier planted the seed of freedom in the minds of the Black man. It took some time for the White man to realize that this seed of freedom had grown into a mighty oak.

By the 1960's, the roots and branches of this mighty tree had spread to every state of the union. There are those who will deny the fact that the Black leaders of the sixties gave the White man an opportunity to admit their wrongdoings and ask for forgiveness.

Both Malcolm and Martin were reading from the same page but Martin's message was easier for the White man to read and accept. Both leaders created fear and uncertainty in the hearts of the White man. Their movement was strong and their popularity grew rapidly.

Their form of leadership was brought about by an impatient need to create change. The kind of change that would resemble fairness and equality for all. Dr. King's nonviolent form of leadership gave the White man the perfect opportunity to see himself in the mirror of life. The reflection that they gazed upon hurt them more than they expected.

There are many elements that create great leadership and timing is one of them. One of the Black man's greatest ally at that time was the television set. Every night on the evening news, the White man was forced to see his own image filled with hatred, anger and destruction. Dr. King's form of leadership attacked the White man's consciousness.

In contrast, Malcolm's approach was " an eye for an eye."

Although it could easily be justified it put the Black man on the same level as the White man.

For our race of people this seemed to do more harm than good and it hampered the overall progress.

Looking back at America's history we can see that the Civil War began in April of 1861, at Fort Sumter; however, in a way this was merely a prelude to war. At this point let me draw a comparison between the civil unrest of the 1960's and the Civil War of the 1800's.

The Civil War of the 1800's like most wars, this country has been involved in, had something to do with the White man and what he had to gain. In contrast, the war of the sixties represented the victory of another race over the white man. For this very reason the civil unrest of the 60's can be considered a war.

The battle field of the sixties claimed the lives of both black and white generals. John and Robert Kennedy, as well as Martin and Malcolm lost their lives in this war. The effect of these casualties are still with us today. Although Americans have tried to maintain some resemblance of leadership, there is no doubt in my mind that we have been shortchanged by the violent deaths of those leaders. I believe that Americans are still asking themselves who will take center stage and create the same kind of leadership that we once had back in the sixties.

Living in an Age of Mediocrity.

If this is truly the case, it is no wonder that mediocrity is the norm in leadership and that we, as a people, have accepted this fact. I've often asked myself, where are the dreamers of greatness? Black or White, who will be the one to show us what is right?

We need leaders who encourage every American to act on their God-given right to dream dreams of greatness. Leaders who will help us to understand that this nation is what we make it. Leaders who will be able to say, "I support the President's decision to help the poor, regardless of his party's affiliation". Can this type of leader be found?

As I watch our leaders pass bills through Congress that will cut benefits for the poor, I am reminded just how far off track that leadership has strayed! If Democrats and Republicans continue to tear away at the fabric of this nation's leadership, then let's get rid of this two-party system and find an alternative system that has this country's best interests at heart.

All the dogfights that take place between the parties distract us from the real purpose and progress that might be achieved. This nation cannot continue to fight against itself if it is sincerely concerned with its growth. After all, what kind of lesson is this for our children?

In many ways, I feel that the destruction of our leaders in the sixties has allowed Americans to simply become detached. Unfortunately, our lackadaisical attitude has made us lose sight of the fact that the world takes its cue from our actions. That's right! The blueprints that produce our leaders are the ones the world will eventually use.

It has always been a big joke to me to learn that every President since I was born has had difficulty trying to balance the nation's budget.
You would think that after forty years someone in that big White House would have figured it out! The leaders of today have managed to put all of society to sleep with their feeble attempt at trying to balance the country's budget and dealing with the national deficit. Have you ever asked yourself the following question: why is it that with this world's most intelligent mathematicians, we cannot manage to find a solution to this dilemma? How can the greatest country in the world, with all its legal minds, professors and astute leaders, fail to find a way to balance the budget?

In every political campaign, each candidate gives his or her plan for attacking this challenge; nevertheless, it is easy to see why these issues never clear themselves up. The fact of the matter is that Americans, rich and poor, are not willing to make the sacrifices necessary to solve this dilemma. The leaders of today are so accustomed of taking from their fellow Americans, that they are simply too afraid to go against the grain and make people aware that the first steps for improvement must come from them.

John F. Kennedy once loudly professed "Ask not what your country can do for you, ask what you can do for your country." His vision inspired Americans to understand that what would make this country better would be for us to better ourselves first. Even though John was said to have had a dark side, Americans cheered him greatly.

This vision gave Americans an awareness and understanding that this country's greatness was determined by the common, everyday people.
However, the fickle leaders of today are simply afraid of disturbing the status quo. Their motto is: let's not bite the hand that has been feeding us, at least not until we have to. Part of the problem with our leaders today is that they are afraid to stand alone and show us the way.

Many leaders take the approach of trying to put themselves on the same level as the constituents. This is supposed to make us feel as if they are one of us. This rarely works. Most Americans are looking for someone who has already gone through the storm, not someone who is going through it for the first time.

A Look at the Followers

It is not just only our leaders who are to blame for the condition that this country is in today.

The followers should also take some of the responsibility. What I find mind-boggling is the simple fact that most people will complain about the lack of leadership in this country, and that is the extent of their efforts. This in itself opens up a new can of worms. It is easy to have a great number of people talking loudly and saying very little. What is it that seems to get people excited enough to talk about an issue, only to the point of doing nothing? To examine this, we first have to go back to the fundamentals and ask ourselves why some people are leaders and others are followers. The inability to follow through with a simple task is one of the things that divides those that lead from those who are being led.

Most Americans are not leaders because they feel that they don't possess the necessary skills to complete assignments. The result of that inertia is the attitude: " let's get someone else to do it."

This gives others the opportunity to go to work with the promise to take their desires and move a little farther along. So to put it bluntly, I am saying that for whatever reason, most Americans would prefer to take the easy way out rather than take on certain responsibilities. I hope that with the use of these simple examples I can make Americans aware of the true problems that exist and will at least help plant the seeds of change.

It is very easy to complain about issues; however, if Americans start complaining with a desire to resolve these issues, then this will increase the quality of the leadership and give more Americans the opportunity to move to the level of leaders.

There are those of you who would say that not everyone can be a leader and that you must have followers. This, in my opinion, is only partly correct. I believe that in order to create better leaders we are going to have to create better followers. Americans can be taught to understand that instead of leaders leading followers, it would be better to have leaders leading leaders. This is one simple antidote will help to create a better quality of American leadership.

I would like to someday watch a national convention where a potential candidate walks up to the podium, amongst the background cheers and music, and starts his or her speech by saying, "My fellow American leaders..."

From that moment in time, it will surely be written that this country, will be at her highest level of progress. To begin to mold and create this type of attitude is going to take a massive storm of pure energy. Like most storms, this process will pick up momentum and develop as it moves along its course.

Unlike the storm caused by natural causes, this one will be directed by mankind.

Its true power will be infinite. It will feed knowledge and understanding to those attracted to its momentum, instead of destroying everything in its path. I feel that if the storm is large enough it will continue to feed itself. If there is one thing Americans are good at, it is the ability to jump on the bandwagon.

I know that by now there is probably someone out there who's asking the question, "If all we have is leaders then who's going to follow?" Look at it this way. Let's say we are watching two Southern Pacific trains on parallel tracks heading North, and each train has the same number of cars. Train A has one engine pulling the cars northbound through the countryside and all the cars on Train B are engines. Each of the train's engines represent leaders. Now both trains are carrying the same amount of cargo. Very simply, which train has the greater possibility of reaching its destination? Suppose they're each traveling a distance of 600 miles. Both trains in time will eventually reach their goal; however train B has the greater opportunity to get there first.

I am sure that some would argue that too many chiefs can ruin anyone's village, but only if these leaders are fighting against each other. Most of the time this of course is the case in American politics.

Infighting, Mud Slinging & Wasted Time

Like me, many Americans wonder why we never seem to accomplish things in government and politics. I feel that it is because we spend at least eighty-five percent of the time fighting amongst ourselves. The time we spend on *infighting* slows down the train of progress in our country. Is this a flaw in our human character and something that mankind simply has to accept?

I believe that the negative energy that this country's political parties carry with them acts as a bacteria. We all know that there is healthy bacteria and bad bacteria. The only thing that seems to matter is, which one is multiplying more rapidly. This last decade has created a very arrogant, negative strand of bacteria.

For the Republicans this type of bacteria takes on the form of a television talk show.
The host is an extremely negative, outspoken journalist. For thirty minutes each evening, this very overweight Anglo-Saxon American tries to single-handily take on the whole Democratic party. He is always supported by an audience of middle-aged White Americans. They remind me of little birds, waiting in their nest, to be fed by their mother. Except in this case the food comes in the form of vaguely humorous information. We are reminded of the misfortunes that have befallen the Democratic party in recent days.

I can see no positive purpose for this show. It is in my opinion a thorn on the side of progress. How sad it is to see this! We are teaching our young Americans that it's okay to pick at one another, by criticizing what others are trying to accomplish. The most uneducated fool can see that this will do nothing to speed up our country's efforts toward progress. Why would intelligent Americans allow themselves to be pawns in a game that is both negative and destructive? This is far beyond my comprehension. I hope that it is not a reflection of the state of affairs of this nation. I think that every voting American should take an oath of allegiance, not to a particular party, but to the United States of America. This oath would be similar to the one taken by foreigners when they assume citizenship.

This oath should say this: "For the welfare of this country I will not tear down the fabric of the United States regardless of my political affiliations. At any time that I disagree, I will replace my grievances with a positive and constructive alternative action." I believe that this will help put back the pride in our political system, only moments before it is set to self-destruct.

I don't believe that we can end the political decay that has taken place because many of these cancerous attitudes and philosophies are far beyond repair.

I strongly believe that we have a difficult challenge ahead. It all starts with this simple thought, "Yes we can create a change!" America is patiently waiting for the opportunity to stand up and be the nation that so many of us want it to be; the America we read about when we were kids.

There is a part of me that feels that this country has turned the corner of no return, often the hope for guidance and direction is a mere spark surrounded by total darkness. I also feel that this nation has approximately twenty years before it becomes a second-rate country. Not in power, but in credibility. My thoughts will become a reality if we don't seek the change that is necessary to break our present course and direction.

American leadership is on a collision course and we will ultimately have to ask the big question, "Live or let die?"

Women and Leadership

On a positive note, there are many new faces in American politics today. Women and many other minorities are taking center stage. The issue of leadership and where it is headed has to be settled right now.

If our new leaders have only the past as a reference for the future, then we will need to pause for a moment of silence, for the death of a once great nation.

To take a closer look at these new leaders in training, let's begin by weighing their chances for survival. Let's start with women in leadership roles. If I haven't raised any eyebrows yet, I'm certain to do so in the next few paragraphs!

During most of America's history we have established the fact that the Anglo-Saxon male has dominated all leadership roles. The Civil Rights' laws generated a rapid movement for change that has opened the doors for many to gain the ultimate challenge of leading.
One group which has stepped up to the forefront are women.

Even though women are considered to be a minority there are over 137 million women in
America alone. After the passage of the Civil Rights Bill in 1964, many women jumped on the bandwagon to advance themselves toward what was considered the future progress and development of this country. In all fairness, women have had a long struggle for their rights in this nation, a struggle that goes back to America's earliest years. So to say that it's about time for women to take center stage is an understatement.

It is easy to assume that the Woman's Voting Act of 1920 was the beginning of women's progress to equal rights. However, real progress was actually accomplished with the Civil Rights Bill of the sixties. Ironically the Civil Rights Bill of the sixties was implemented to pacify the Black minority. The constitutional power of the Bill created a backlash of problems for the white man. Surrounded with the armor of constitutional rights, women began to create a movement that to this day is second to none in American history.

Women have always been the silent voices and the sound of righteousness. It's not until the last twenty-five to thirty years that those voices became the echoes of a dolby, digital sound. With all this tremendous progress, I Dexter Clay, will go on record to say that I don't feel it is a woman's place to lead! At least not in the way they are pursuing leadership today.

Black or White,Yellow or Brown I feel that a woman's purpose is to plant and cultivate the seeds that are vital to making the real changes in this world. I know that at this point, I need to explain myself. Many of today's women are very sensitive to such statements and it doesn't leave much room for uncertainty concerning the degree of their abilities.

I often wonder if true honesty is enough to change the aggressive, liberated attitude of today's women. Just about now I'm sure that most women reading this book think that it is written by a chauvinistic male, a lower life form than an animal! Well, that's okay! I want to generate emotions and feelings to be created and felt by the things that I have to say.

If I were to compromise to any degree with my convictions, then I would be cheating myself and my readers and giving you less than you deserve. My fellow female Americans, before you begin to tear out pages from my book *Black Eye on America!,* I urge you to read on and hear the things that must be told.

First of all, let me say that the progress that women have made has long been overdue.

I must say from my heart that if America is to continue to grow and prosper as a world power, that the advancement of all people, especially women, is imperative. However, to take women out of the role that they have played throughout history, will delay, digress and destroy the course of our existence. In my opinion, it is important that women continue to lead mankind; however, in this modern age, the so-called "external leadership" that females have been asked to embrace is very obtrusive.

I am totally aware that there are times when women are forced to wear the hat of leaders.
Often, when they do, it's more for the reasons of survival than anything else. Regardless, this breaks the balance of the way things should be. For example: I watched my mother raise four of her own kids and five nephews, without a man in the house. The different hats she wore were so varied that I still have difficulty counting all of them. She was a mother, father, preacher, teacher, disciplinarian, counselor, a friend, financial provider, planter of hope, a negotiator, and a dreamer. She had all the qualities and substance of a true leader; however, as a woman, being forced to assume all of the above characteristics (both male and female) creates a dichotomy and goes against the divine nature of the creation of man and woman.

The Civil Rights laws passed back in the sixties were very important to the growth of this country. In many ways; however, the same laws instead of creating fairness and equality have managed to dilute and misconstrue the line of social order. Regarding the divine distinction between man and woman, our generation is caught in a revolving door that I believe continues to rotate furiously out of control.

This next statement will sound a little con-tradictory, but I strongly feel that although all men are created equal, men and women can never be equal. I'm sure that the hair on the back of the head of a lot of my readers is standing straight up by now!

I assure you that I'm making these statements with the utmost love and respect for all women. I would be willing to fight for women's rights and any women's organization that I believed in. Regardless, women will never be equal to men. Although women can never be men's equal, in many cases they can be superior. Wow, now you must be completely confused! And I know the hair on my male readers' necks is starting to stand at attention. That's okay. Unlike most leaders and politicians today I don't have to compromise my feelings. I'm not running for office. Forced into a situation of survival many women deal with the crisis more effectively than their male coun-terparts. This too has its repercussions.

I believe in the basic Christian philosophy that **GOD** created man in His own image. From this image of Himself, woman was created.

If you take only a part of something, how can that part be considered equal to the whole it came from?

This issue is very simplistic, as are many things in life.

Some of you are asking "How does this relate to women's role in leadership?" In order to get the best production from leaders you must start with **GOD** first. **GOD** doesn't choose to stand before us and physically lead us. We must lead ourselves with **GOD's** direction. With woman by man's side the cycle of creation is re-established.

If we look at this any other way, we'll devalue the divine creation of man. It is woman that teaches mankind how to nurture and love itself in order to reach its full potential. Ironically, man is partially to blame for this imbalance. By not giving women their due credit for their accomplishments, man has in many ways cheated himself. By taking women for granted, man has also managed to starve a part of his own existence.

In many ways, men are to blame for the resentment and frustrations that many women feel because of our inability to acknowledge their contributions. In turn this, has created a backlash of negative emotions that manifest themselves in feminist outcries. I stand firmly on the principle that woman's role is an integral part of the leadership process. She cannot assume the role of figurehead.

I realize that there are many who would jump at the opportunity to debate this issue, but for me it's just a fact of life! The reality is that women have been leaders for hundreds of years.

I believe that if **GOD** can't get men to accomplish His will, He won't hesitate to choose women to take on the figurehead role. Whether the choice is **GOD's** or man's, the structure of life will break down and delay the progress for the continual development of the human race.

We must all realize that most men fear the continuing progress of today's women in leadership. I do not. This chauvinistic energy that many men have is increasingly apparent.

For the insecure man, woman's advancement in leadership is not an easy pill to swallow. If we are not able to put into proper perspective women's roles, then the battles of the sexes will get much worse before it gets better. Today's woman is armed with a great deal of pride and backed by a higher level of education. In men's eyes this situation is considered extremely dangerous.

I can clearly recall my first encounter with this situation. I was in the seventh grade in junior high school and found myself running for the office of Student Council President at Charles R. Drew Jr. High School. My toughest opponent was a young lady by the name of Cindi Walker. Her first cousin Dana Walker was the incumbent president. The Walkers were an elite Texas family. They were both intelligent and wealthy, and they carried a great deal of clout in our small community.

What made matters even more interesting was the fact that Cindi's mother and my mom were best of friends. If my mom would had had her way, Cindi probably would have been my future wife. After weeks of campaigning on several crucial issues such as whether the school supply store should open thirty minutes or an hour before school started, the Friday of the big election was upon us. The votes had been tallied and the winner was to be announced right before the three o'clock bell was to ring. That afternoon, during the time the announcements were being made, I found myself walking the halls, caught up in the excitement of that moment. I can still remember the feeling of extreme loneliness that came over me just before they called out my name as the winner. The cheers that I heard quickly erased those emotions. I happened to pass by Cindi's classroom, and caught a glimpse of her with her head down on her desk-crying. A couple of girls stood around her consoling her. I wondered whether or not she might have been the best person for the job.

Suddenly, the three o'clock bell rang and I was inundated with handshakes and congratulations. All my doubts evaporated and I was no longer concerned about who would have been the better person for the job. Later, as I was boarding the school bus, I saw Cindi embracing her mom before she got into their car.

I asked myself the same question again, of whether she should have won. In fact, I kept asking myself that same question the entire summer.

My vice president was a young lady by the name of Cathy Sampson, but I couldn't stop feeling that it would have been an asset to have Cindi as a part of my team. The following school year, the first thing I did as Student Council President was to organize a committee of cabinet members. This had never been accomplished in the history of the school. I realized that it wasn't the fact that Cindi would have made a better president, but that she had great leadership qualities that would have gone to waste if she was not part of the team. Her gender had nothing to do with my decision. My first four officers were all young ladies. Hey, my mother didn't raise no fool! Seriously, I realized at a very young age that in life we all have roles to play and that each of us can reach our fullest potential within that structure.

I firmly believe that women's role in leadership will lose its full potential if women are forced to be leaders. I use the word *forced,* whether meaning it's self-inflicted through desires of their own, or because of the incompetence of the male gender, I still believe that the potential of women is infinite. Honestly, from what I have learned about today's leaders, women (in my opinion) would be better off not to get involved.

53

Most women feel that because they are as educated as their male counterpart, they should be allowed access to the big governmental party.
What somehow eludes the ambitious, aggressive female is that she can accomplish more by being at man's side rather than in the front. Quite simply, there is a great element of grounding that women offer mankind. That same element which was meant to be a blessing can turn out to be a curse if it is not kept in the proper perspective. Today's society has created a woman that's not afraid to stand up and flex her muscles. "I am woman hear me roar" can be the battle cry heard all across the the land. From what I can honestly see, man is partially to blame for this misdirection of false pride that seems to be sweeping the nation.

What I have learned in the forty one years on this planet is that the White man only allows a certain course of action to take place, that which he deems necessary at the time.
Because of the great number of minorities in this country, I believe that the White man senses a turning point and is aware of the inevitable.
He knows that he has to allow a new form of leadership. I also feel that the White man is more willing to relinquish this supreme honor to women than to any other minority. Let me clarify this: especially women of his own race.

I think the attitude is that it's going to happen eventually so let it be someone that can be manipulated. This could not have been more evident than during the presidential election of 1988. The Democratic party chose to go with an unknown vice-presidential candidate by the name of Geraldine Ferraro, rather than the more controversial and well-known Black candidate Rev. Jesse Jackson.

That incident, was an intentional slap to every Black in America. Jackson walked side by side with one of the greatest leaders in the history of this nation, Martin Luther King Jr.; nevertheless, this country continued to turn away from this potential leader. That outrageous blunder set the progress of this nation back thirty years. The sad thing is that many do not even realize it!

Women & Blacks as Tokens

Ironically, women and the Black race share many common problems, when it comes to the progress of minority leaders in America. In politics, Blacks and women are merely tokens, simply to pacify the masses; never to be taken seriously. These delicately placed figureheads help keep up the illusion that political progress is rolling along.

If it happens that they manage to accomplish anything substantial, then that's an added plus.

I am not implying that any minority who has something to offer to the public shouldn't get involved in politics or government.

What I am saying is that they must be aware of the real picture of American leadership. Quite frankly, the blood that runs through the veins of American leaders is white. It was white in this country's beginning and it's still white today. For any minority to think of it in any other way is to see things through rose colored glasses.

The Black leaders of today have an enormous challenge. We have to shed the fact that White America compared us to nothing greater than animals. We must also quickly adjust our thinking to lead people away from the bigoted attitudes that we encounter today. To this day, it is complicated by the fact that the White man has failed to recognize or acknowledge his wrongdoings, nor has he asked for our help in leadership.

I have mixed feelings about whether or not the White man's arrogance is so rampant, that he would rather impede the progress of this country than ask the Black race for help.

Why do I call these minority groups tokens?

If I were to show you a political chart of the history of American leadership and those who stand in the key positions, then you could see for yourselves the way things really are. By writing such truisms I would like to stimulate your thoughts and eventually get you to understand why things really are the way they are! As members of society, we refuse to look at America the way it actually is; therefore, we will never be able to begin the process of change. Just asking yourself, "How important is change?" can be something that will stimulate the process.

Final thoughts on Leadership

One of the things that I often wonder about as an American, is whether anyone truly cares about the status of our leadership and the direction that we are taking. Is it fair to simply turn America's future over to fate? Leadership can be compared to a great sickle that is clearing an open field, preparing for what eventually will result in a successful harvest. The expertise and guidance of each step will somehow help to continue to give this country life. Without it, America has very little chance of maintaining the glorious years that she once boasted of.

I believe that the effort for change must be approached with a positive attitude.

57

One of the things that truly gets my goose are foreigners complaining about how bad things are in America. They speak only of the negative aspects and never offer any positive solutions that would help turn things around.

As a true American, I would like to go on record and say that regardless of how bad the situation of this country stands, it's still my country! Today's leadership has somehow lost its edge. To change this we are going to have to stop dissecting those who are trying to lead us. I believe that this one simple thought will help our leaders from fighting amongst themselves. **God** in heaven knows that there is too much that has to be accomplished by us mortals. We must stop choking the life out of the same people that are trying to direct us!

My fellow Americans, you've probably heard the saying, (I always wanted to say that!) "Lets get back to the basics." If we can't say anything positive then let's not say anything at all. My mother handed this philosophy down to us and this same principle should give our leaders a guideline to follow. To the big kids in the playground of Congress: Stop wasting the tax-payers money with your own private battles against one another! This will send a message to the people that honesty, (even if it's on their income tax returns), is the honorable thing to do.

58

We can feel secure that the government is being managed wisely, with a real concern for the well-being of our great nation.

I don't believe that it's too much to ask the entire membership of the Republican party to work as diligently for a Democrat in office as they would for themselves. This alone would send a strong message of leadership to the American people. It would say to them that we are all for one. To climb to the top you don't have to walk over your fellow countrymen. This nation is at a level of constipation a simple change of diet can correct things. We must begin a vigorous exercise program to work off the obesity that has slowed our progress to a halt.

Our leaders have a number of problems to overcome, but there has never been a better time in history to resolve them. We have the knowledge, the resources and the technology to begin the greatest conditioning program ever! Let's do away with the excuses and poor leadership. Let's begin to lead ourselves. The greater our expectations, the greater the quality of leadership. We *can* force this issue.

Our nation's leaders will have to understand that if they want to lead us, they are going to have to be stronger and wiser in character. To be a leader is no easy task. We can be the very best that we can be!

The question that forms the title of this chapter, "American leadership, live or let die?" can be answered here! and now!

This might sound redundant, but if we continue to put **GOD** aside, the One that granted us favor as a young nation, then chances are slim to none that the outcome will not be very positive. It will be a very slow death for us, as Americans. We have witnessed the continual decline of the American dollar, year after year. Very few of us have linked the elimination of God from country and the devaluation of our currency.

I hope that we are not too naive to understand the tremendous effort it will require to get the budget back to where it can be balanced again. We are going to need all the help that we can get.

One of Abraham Lincoln's greatest accomplishments was to incorporate **IN GOD WE TRUST** on every single piece of United States currency. I believe that President Lincoln knew that this country would go through a period when she would forget the God who created her.

Every federal note that changes hands daily has these words *"IN GOD WE TRUST"* in bold letters imprinted on it.

The question we ask ourselves is, "do we or don't we trust **GOD?"** If the answer is "yes", then let's not support those leaders that will allow **GOD's word** to be extracted from every aspect of America's future.

In closing this chapter, some very strong questions come to mind. We must stop and ask ourselves some direct questions that will in all reality tell us just where this country stands in regards to it's future. Is this great nation of ours beyond the point of no return? Can America recover from the massive surgery that has to take place to save her from heart failure?

I pray that all Americans will envision their country in the same sentimental way that I did as a child. The years of constant decay and erosion have destroyed those gracious thoughts that we held so dear to our hearts as children.

Americans must face the reality of where this country is headed. A lack of credibility in politics, government and leadership has given us a very callous outlook. Our country has lost its healthy blood-flow which is so vital to the heartland of this nation. Finally, I have chosen to share with you the following so that you can be aware of its possible manifestation in the future. This might sound like something out of a science fiction picture, but what if the course of this nation is a result of *unseen forces?*

These forces seem to be normal, and have extensive communicational skills; however, the possibility exists that we are being led by sources created from a negative entity.

Imagine this probability: all the problems that America is having today are simply the buy-products of our past actions.

What if America's current conditions are right on track and our leaders are simply programing us to go with the flow, not realizing that the way we live is being manipulated by undetected forces around us?

Perhaps because of our lackadaisical attitude we have lost contact with our inner voice.

We are simply afraid to face the inevitable. The total loss of all our human rights! Fellow Americans, the time to wake up is right now! If this country continues to sleep we will find ourselves awakening to some very harsh and unrealistic truths. Oh yes, don't forget that what we do or don't do will indirectly affect all of mankind. Our leaders are not only leading us nowhere, they are leading the rest of the world as well!

CRITICISM

The question is not what a man can scorn, or disparage, or find fault with, but what he can love, and value, and appreciate.

John Ruskin
English author, Art critic

CHAPTER TWO

Racism

AMERICA HELD HOSTAGE!

On the very day that I began to write this chapter, a predominately Black jury entered a non-guilty verdict for a famous Black man charged with the murder of two white Americans. Of course, I am referring to the trial of O. J. Simpson.

Racism is a point of view that has the power to raise its ugly head in moments of convenience.

65

In the center of this world's most infamous trial, racism, an icon of negativity stood up to remind the world that it is alive, well and thriving! This chapter isn't going to be an easy one for most readers, simply because when you're talking about racism it forces you to take a stand either for or against it. The fact is that most Americans choose to avoid taking a stand on issues concerning the character of mankind, a character which will ultimately affect the survival of this nation.

I named this Chapter "Racism: America Held Hostage!" because it best describes the results racism has had on our country. This nation's population, or their ancestors, have originated from a minimum of at least seventy-five different countries. It is very easy to see how racism can engulf the spirit of a nation with this much diversity.

**Reflection on Racism &
the O.J. Simpson Criminal Trial**

As I ponder on the O.J. trial, (I was constantly reminded of its existence for 474 days), the first thing that comes to my mind is the great progress that this country has made. Most white Americans feel that a Black man got off scott-free for the killing of two White people.

I choose to see a country that has evolved from ignorance and fear, from a time when it hung thousands of Black men. A time when Black men were not allowed to walk on the same side of the street as a White woman. During the trial I quietly smiled to myself and was often reminded of how far this nation has come! The miles that we have crossed should never lose their importance regardless of how far we have to go!

I would like to share with you the things that I have learned during my last 40 years regarding the past and present. You might agree with some of the things that I have to say and disagree with others, but what you will read will be candid. These thoughts come from the heart of a man who has managed to keep this beast at bay.

One thing that I learned about racism is that its seed can lie dormant in all of us. It simply lies inactive, waiting to be fed, only to eat the fruit of negativity. I have found that this beast can only grow from a diet of negative energies, such as: hatred, anger, jealousy, ignorance, envy, confusion, impatience, intolerance, misconception, deception, disgust, despair, fear, mistrust, prejudice, narrow mindedness and abhorrence. These traits can be found to some degree in all mankind. Racism is not a black-white issue; it is a human issue.

I assure you that racism has nothing to do with color! However, it has everything to do with injustice.

I find that many Americans have a tough time dealing with racism, because they are afraid to attack it head on. I feel that their approach is often a subconscious effort. By this, I mean that most people are taught how to respond to different situations regarding racism. In a day and age when so many scholars are writing books on the (internal workings) of racism, it is difficult for the average American to get a real grasp on it.

On the other hand, there has never before been a time in our history when so many people have had an opportunity to hobble on the crutches of racism. It is as if this country openly allows herself to become handicapped by this six letter word.

While some Americans quickly grab tightly to the word as an excuse for failure, others seem to become annoyed at the simple sound of it. As Americans cry out, some in praise and others in sorrow and disbelief for what has taken place, we must not allow our emotions to be blinded by the power of the masses.

The Simpson trial has awakened many emotions, but the most evident is the awareness that racism is rampant in this country.

The Simpson episode showed us where we stand as a nation. Americans formulated their opinion of whether Simpson was guilty or innocent based on the color of his skin and by the second-hand information that was fed to them. The fact that this country still harbors racist energies is a truism. These energies surface when voices gather together and the true feelings about a particular situation manifests itself.

At this stage of life in America, many Whites feel that they have been greatly wronged by an unjust system. From every part of the country there were cries that justice was not served. To this I say, you are absolutely wrong! Justice was served so perfectly that its hand reached out and slapped itself in the face. The realization of the outcome of the Simpson trial has sent many Whites into shock.

The outcome of the verdict has caused many Americans to question the fairness of the judicial system. Most White Americans have totally over-looked the fact that it was their race of people who were responsible for what we know as justice today. Point of fact, it was White America that formed, created and shaped the illusion of the American justice system. After a hundred years of relying on this system, this new reality must hurt like hell!

Well, hell is exactly what many minorities have been suffering, so welcome to the party!

It will not be easy for White American to take a candid look at the situation, that they have been forced to see. Because of the outcome of the trial, I believe that the content of the White man's character is such, that he will somehow attempt to change the course of where this unfair justice system is headed. After all, realizing that something is broken is the first step in correcting the problem! Ironically, the minorities who have been mistreated by this unjust system must somehow learn to extend a helping hand. This hand should be one of love and forgiveness, not of false pride and arrogance. If Black Americans choose to be arrogant (regarding the results of the Simpson trial) then, the heart of this nation will turn cold and we will miss this perfect opportunity for change.

To the families of the two victims, I ask our Father in heaven to bless you with His grace and divine love. The degree of your loss is evident. With God's guidance you must learn to let your loved ones go! This is not an easy task, many people do not have the knowledge of the spirit of God to help them deal with the reality of death. Each family must see that their loss is not in vain.

The very unfortunate death of these two human beings has allowed this great nation to realize that her justice system has gone full circle and that somehow it has lost a tremendous degree of substance.

The death of Nicole and Ronald forced this nation to shed new light on our justice system. We must understand that one day O. J. Simpson will have to stand before God Almighty and be judged on his own merit. This final judgment will not be wavered by prejudice or wealth, but by that which is pure and righteous!

To all Americans who have given their opinions about this case so freely, we must realize that our perceptions have been totally manipulated by the media. We must question the creditability of this source. Our opinions can be compared to a wild windstorm in the center of a brush fire. If our opinion doesn't change the results for the better, wouldn't it be just as simple to keep it to ourselves? Unless we are willing to use our opinions to initiate change, they don't really carry any positive purpose!

In our society murders happen everyday. However, they fall into the category of just another statistic, unless it happens to someone you know. A few days after my eighteenth birthday my middle brother was shot down in cold blood by one of his peers.

The kid who shot him claimed that the shooting was an accident. The justice system dismissed the case. The police report stated that it was an accident the boy walked into his home, loaded a rifle, went outside, pointed it at my brother's heart and pulled the trigger. When a Black kid shoots another Black kid it is simply an accident!
Two days later this assassin was walking our streets as free as a bird. By the way, not one article ever appeared in the paper about this incident.

Several weeks later, at a predominately White school, a Black kid got into a fight with a White classmate. A knife was pulled and the student was killed. This story was widely covered by all the newspapers and television channels. In the following weeks, crosses burned at the school and in the front yard of the Black kid's home. This child was sentenced to twenty-two years in prison. When I hear White people screaming about the injustice of the Simpson case, their voices are drowned out by the hundreds of years of unheard cries.

I totally understand that two wrong doings do not make a right and that justice shouldn't have color boundaries.

The fact of the matter is that until October 4, 1995, justice was a color issue and it was created by those who founded the justice system. When two white people lost their lives and the only suspect, a Black man was acquitted, the nation was up in arms. I guess in some unfortunate way America should see the outcome of the Simpson trial as the first step in the realization that our criminal justice system needs a major overall.

If the O. J. Simpson trial was the result of racism, then we can assume it was this way because White America appeared to be at the wrong end of the justice system. Nonetheless, Blacks must not be disillusioned. The decision of the twelve members of the jury managed to put this country back some thirty years or so! In fact, not since the Civil Rights Movement have I seen White Americans openly protesting with such hatred and anger as in the days following the great acquittal. Most of these protests were disguised under the painted faces of certain current-day movements, (such as) domestic violence and women's rights. However, the hatred and negative energy manifested at the end of the trial resembled the reflections of the past.

To put this trial back into perspective we must look at this situation from both points of view.

This will diminish the amount of rage and anger that is being felt from the aftermath of this emotionally exalted trial. When Simpson was acquitted, there were no winners. As a matter of fact, this whole nation lost a great deal of credibility as far as I am concerned.

Those who cheered the outcome of the trial didn't have a clue of the overall picture of what was really happening. In the midst of all the 'hurrahs' this nation once again learned that she could divide herself in two.

We have learned from the past that a nation divided cannot stand.

Right now I would like to make you aware of something. The purpose of this chapter on racism is to help Americans someday understand the true nature of this beast. I stated earlier that racism lies dormant in all of us, what I didn't tell you was that there is one element that will always bring this beast to life. The one element that breaths life into racism is the act of selfishness.

Whether it is the need to give our opinions or the need to gather in masses to protest wrong-doings, it all falls under the realm of selfishness. As you continue to read this chapter, keep this thought in your mind. There are many ways that racism can be kept in perspective and we can free this nation's heart from being held hostage!

Forming Our Own Opinions

Louis Farrakhan, the religious leader, recently organized a large group of Black men to proudly march upon our nation's capital. His opposition called him the biggest racist since Hitler. Powerful words coming from a powerful opposition! In a world where everything in life has at least two sides, how does one truly find the understanding to choose? I believe this is a question that many people find themselves constantly asking!

A great number of Americans; however, still allow themselves to be manipulated into a particular position without analyzing the real issues. I must confess that at times I have been just as guilty of this injustice.

Before I heard Farrakhan speak I had very negative feelings toward him. After listening to his speech I felt as if I had misjudged him. I allowed my judgment to become clouded by the opinion of others. Instead of interpreting what we know about an individual, we allow our opinions to be created by others. This also gives the media the power it has in our lives. We oftentimes allow ourselves to make an unfair or wrong assessment of someone or something. There is something in our nature that allows us to overlook our responsibility to truly evaluate those around us.

This is not a human flaw, we simply allow ourselves to be programed by what others say or do! It is easy to see where racism comes from and how it was created. In many ways the answers to these questions are self-incriminating for us as Americans. Yes, racism is an issue that faces every nation and country in the world.

The Origins of Racism in America

To take a closer look at the issue of racism in this country, we're going to go back to the time when the first settlers reached this great continent from Europe. To simplify things, let's say that during this period there were basically two races; the White immigrants and the American Indians.

This nation's early beginnings saw racism as negative manifestations of actions and reactions. Thus, the chain of racist interaction began.

The general view among the public is that one race of people has strong views regarding another race. This general view may be considered the normal way of seeing that person or race. The White man formulated his opinion of the Native American Indian with a very limited under-standing, which was based on the settlers' perceptions of right and wrong.

They saw before them what they considered to be an uncivilized race of people. Because of their inability to communicate, the Indians were labeled as "savages" and conversely became the enemy. This was the true birth of racism, at least in this country.

It's a fact that each race that landed upon our American shores became the enemy of these new settlers. Although each had its own unique agenda, they all seemed to come at odds with the White man who had previously settled there.

I'm trying to make an honest evaluation of the circumstances that existed at the time and found that it was the White man who formulated the guidelines for all to follow. Those who followed the guidelines were accepted by those in control much more readily.

The Issue of Respect

One important factor that is lost in racism is respect! Racism severely pollutes society with its negative energy. Before it becomes an issue of race, it begins as a human issue. Generally speaking, when one race of people has strong views regarding another race, this may be viewed as the normal way of seeing that other person or race.

In this process human nature is such that it allows disagreement to lead to disrespect and this creates an environment of mental, physical, emotional, and verbal abuse.

If Americans would make a conscious effort to maintain respect for one another, then, we would see a dramatic change in the state of racism in this country and ultimately across the world. We can *start* this process by understanding that there may be something truthful in our thoughts and opinions of others. Each culture of people offers different characteristics.

Learning to better understand and accept these differences will help society obtain the fundamentals necessary to combat racism! I can see how it might have run rampant in the beginning because of a lack of communication. In these modern times there isn't any reasonable explanation for the rapid growth of this plague and yet it continues to live, gaining tremendous power and strength as it permeates throughout this nation.

Comments & Reactions

The comments that different races make about one another become a double-edge sword. There can be a degree of truth in a many of the statements, but they can still come off as a slurred racist remarks.

Let me give you and example of this!

A few years ago, I was watching an HBO special called *Comedy Relief Seven.* It was a telethon to raise money for the homeless. The hosts were three very talented comedians: Whoopi Goldberg, Billy Crystal and Robin Williams. At one point during the program, one of the Jewish comedians made a joke regarding whites and blacks. He said, " White men can jump, and we can also keep the books!"

Now, we all know that one of the talents of a good comedians is to make you laugh at things that have a degree of truth in them.

Comedians also get you to laugh at subjects that are taboo! This comedian was taking a dig at the Black race. His comment was that White men can jump. He was referring to the fact that most White basketball players don't jump as high as Black ballplayers. He was also insinuating that Whites or Jews are smarter because they keep the books!

Was it a joke or wasn't it? I was personally offended by his remark and I would like to use this opportunity to show you how one person's actions can create reactions. My first response was not to laugh at his remark and to evaluate his comment. I realized that in making such a reference he had made a few key mistakes.

The first was that of stereotyping. He stated that White men can jump.

We all know that everybody can jump only some people can jump higher than others. Correct? Secondly, he made the mistake of including himself as a part of the White race. I think that like many other races, the Jewish people's ultimate goal is to be considered a part of the White race. His third mistake was to arrogantly suggest that only White men have the intelligence to keep the books. This is ironic considering the fact that during slavery the white man made it a crime for Blacks to read or write.

My second impulse, after hearing his comments, was to make a defensive attack directly towards him. Here was this little Jewish man who, along with his co-host, made constant reference to their oversized sex organs. I felt certain that the whole world realized that this inference was the farthest thing from the truth. What was that all about? I finally realized that his only real talent was his ability to act as an old Jewish man.

This is *something*, by the way, that he reverts to in every single movie. As my anger subsided, I shed my defensive shield and realized that I had not evaluated his remarks for their true value. The truth is that, yes, white men can jump and yes, they can keep the books. What he forgot to say; however, was that they don't keep the books very well! If you need proof, look at the national deficit!

Can you see how one remark or reference about a person can quickly cause certain reactions? Responsibility for what we say and respect for others play such an important role in our lives.

False Pride & Racism

Another *thing* that helps to fuel the growth of racism is the *continual* practice of one race of people to consider themselves smarter or better than the next. Where did this come from and what is it all about?
I have tried very hard to pinpoint the key *ingredients* behind man's desire to think this way; however the only thing that continues to pop into my head is *false pride.* Since pride or the lack there of, exists in all human beings, then it would be safe to say that this is where we must begin to look at the problem.
Is pride an asset or a liability? Why is it that something that we can't physically put our fingers on has power to determine the course and direction of the human race? I think that it is important that we ask ourselves these questions in order to hopefully stumble on the correct response. The *American Heritage Dictionary* defines pride as:
"n. 1. A sense of one's own proper dignity or value; self-respect.

81

2. Pleasure or satisfaction taken in achievement, a possession, or association. 3. Arrogant or disdainful conduct or treatment; haughtiness. 4. a. A cause or source of pleasure or satisfaction; the beat of a group or class. b. The most successful or thriving condition; prime. 5. An excessively high opinion of one's self; conceit. 6. Mettle or spirit in a horse. 7. A company of lions. 8. A flamboyant or impressive group".

This word with eight different definitions plays a key role in the *origin* of racism and it is important that we take a closer look at it.

When pride grows to the point that its sole purpose is to elevate one's own status to greater levels, then I strongly suggest that its true intentions needs to be re-evaluated. As the number of these prideful people increase an element of superiority enters the picture. Since this type of pride is less apparent it can grow to very large proportions. Unfortunately, by that time it has taken on very destructive characteristics!

When these characteristics are surround by other negative energies, the end result is *something* we have seen throughout history. The result is years of hatred and killing. I think that the most destructive element of racism is the physical aspects; therefore, the most distasteful. Here racism crosses the point of no return.

In some ways, this destructive element represents the many negative thoughts that are manifested into physical form.

The Development of American Racism & the Klu Klux Klan

When we think of racism and the destruction it creates, there is no doubt in my mind that the Klu Klux Klan is the ultimate manifestation of the physical manifestation of racism. Many Americans saw the negative power of racism come alive through the birth of the Klan.

Most of us have lost sight of where racism actually comes from. What I'm about to say next will be a very difficult pill for many white Americans to accept. In my personal view, the White man was solely responsible for the introduction of racism into this country.

Let me explain how I arrived at this conclusion. Racism originally began with the White man's animosity against the Indian. The White man's hostility grew stronger against his own people, (the British.) Later the seeds of racism were planted by the wealthy towards the poor. It was the animosity the poor had toward those who had more than they did that planted many of the seeds of racism.

Note that the White man, at one time or another throughout history has manipulated every race of people that landed on the shores of this great nation. This is not a racial statement; it is a fact of life! The White man gained wealth and position through the sweat of others. This created a division between those who had and those who had not and it is an important point in the process.

The accumulation of fame and fortune, (whether it was in the form of wealth, land, natural resources, or human property), created a line of envy and jealousy that continues to grow to this day. On one side, was the prosperous man, usually White whose wealth created financial support for the government and the local agencies. On the other side of the line were those less fortunate.

The poor began to hate their fellow countrymen mostly because the needy felt they could do very little to change their living conditions.

At this time, a division began to rapidly grow between the two regions known as the North and South. Between these two areas hatred grew to the point of war. Both parties were willing to give up their lives in order to show their disapproval of one another! The Civil War was the by-product of many years of pent-up anger, frustration, hatred, envy and jealousy. The Civil War could be said to have been fought for many different reasons.

If Americans were to take a candid look at all the elements that surrounded the war they would see that it was an issue of greed. The root of the problem between the Northern and the Southern whites was greed.

Once the North triumphed victorious, the spirit of racism took on a different face. The outcome of the war allowed racism to become buried deep within the hearts of all Americans. Racism was just waiting for the opportunity to surface. Unfortunately, it did not take very long. After the war, the Southerner's retaliated by taking their frustrations out on those that had less than themselves. I guess after the ass-whipping they had just received from the North, the only way to feel strong again was to beat up on those who were economically weaker than they were!

The South's new punching bag was the black man. The klan had an opportunity to come of age and at the same time send a message to the North that the war had just begun. At this point let me recommend a very valuable book by Leon F. Litwick called *Been in the Storm So Long the Aftermath of Slavery*, which describes the conditions of this nation immediately after the Civil War.

At that time, the Klan hated everyone, including some of their own. As expected the black man became their prime target.

After all, it was the former slaves who gained the most from the Civil War. The feeling of hostility that the White man felt towards his fellow man was directed towards a race of people whose greatest fault was the color of their skin. The white man created the first episodes of racism and throughout the pages of history has shown the world an unforgettable side of his character.

I often wonder how I should look at the many years of racist attitude toward my people. Were these the growing pains of a young nation? After all, the White race had fought and died to initiate the beginning of the black man's freedom, but I quickly remind myself that the white man has never done anything that was not to his benefit.

By writing this book I want to generate challenging thoughts which will formulate a change in the lives of all Americans. Change often begins with reflections on the past. I really feel this in my heart.

It really doesn't matter where racism originated, it only matters that it still lives and breeds today.

The predicament of racism is its elusive quality. Racism is an integral part of the present, and without any serious efforts of change it will persist and thrive in the future. It is our responsibility to see that this venom doesn't poison the future of this country.

It is easy to cast blame on our forefathers; however, I wonder if someday others will find a need to blame our generation for not ridding our society of this illness.

Can the Government End Racism?

Like many other Americans, I, at one time or another, felt that it was the responsibility of the government to stop the spread of this insidious disease. I have come to the realization that the American government has enough challenges without adding one more to the list. I smile when I think of the government trying to solve the problems of racism. It is as humorous as a dog frantically chasing its own tail, running around and around in one big circle only to drop from exhaustion.

What would happen if the dog caught his own tail? He would realize that his tail wasn't going anywhere! The government's futile efforts haven't been very productive. Why is this you might ask?

The *Bible* clearly tells us in Matthew Chapter 6, Verse 24, that " no man can serve two masters". Technically, the government can't do away with something that it helped to create. Past governments have fostered a breeding ground where racism flourished.

It would not be realistic for society to expect today's government to completely wipe out all traces of racism. Of course, the White man's government is making attempts to curb racist attitudes. A question arises: Is the present course of action being determined by a white race of people with the same mentality that shaped the negative directions of the past, or is this a new generation of whites?

It is incomprehensible to think that the white man created the policies and laws that made it a crime for blacks to read or write. That segregation was actually the law in the South, is pathetic! As a black man in America today, I try not to ponder on the white man's past history. I will not allow the negative past to direct my present or future. To dwell on the past would ignite the fuel of animosity, a feeling that many of my people still carry with them to this day.

Right or wrong, one of the principles that I live my life by, is a credo of Dr. Martin Luther King Jr.

His teachings taught us to judge a man by the content of his character and not by the color of his skin. This has helped me to think of the White race as my brothers and sisters not my adversaries.

The Affirmative Action Debate

Often, the White man's actions remind me that in his blood flows the same arrogant and manipulating energies of yester years.

A perfect example of this, is the Conservative's attack on the Affirmative Action Programs. They were originally implemented to give minority Americans potential access to a piece of the American pie! There are those who feel that these action programs are allowing minorities too many opportunities and benefits.

I guess after limiting most of their benefits, allowing them to have one or two could easily be misconstrued as a very generous amount.

It seems that when the white man attempts to change the content of his character, a selfish entity takes over.

As I was growing up, one of the things I always admired about this nation was the way she would extend a helping hand to those countries less fortunate. As a young student, I remember reading about the Japanese war.

I was somewhat amused by our country's generosity towards Japan especially knowing that we had dropped bombs that destroyed their major cities. It was as if America was admitting her error in judgment. However, in helping Japan we gained the country's respect and eventually forced an alliance.

It is very important that we realize that throughout history the white man has never formally apologized for the many bombs dropped on the black race! They were meant to destroy us mentally, physically, spiritually, emotionally and economically. Until a few years ago America was still extending financial aid to those Japanese Americans who were placed in concentration camps after the bombing of Pearl Harbor. This action was to forgive our despicable actions.

Affirmative Action was more than a bureaucrat extending a helping hand to those that were less fortunate. It is about white America doing something that had been overlooked for decades. Affirmative Action benefited the white man more than they could possibly imagine; however, the quick action to abandon Affirmative Action reminds all of us of the fact that there is a double standard.

This is another example of the action and reaction aspect of racism that allow, it to grow. One person with strong convictions causes another person to react with strength of purpose. Unfortunately, this most always help to keep the resources of racism alive and well. This cause and effect element of racism doesn't allow it to die out. The potential abandonment of Affirmative Action will always be a constant reminder of just how little we have come as a nation.

(As I watched America's attack on Affirmative Action, I am reminded of the way politics of the past were created. I envision a group of old white men) sitting in a library surrounded by hundreds of books they themselves had written.

Enter an elderly Black man carrying a tray with a bottle of brandy, drinking glasses and a box of fine cigars.

The conversation between them will no doubt affect the course of American politics. Amongst these pale-skinned men sit the authors of our nation. Their opinions resemble those of the Northerners, who fought to see the Black man freed, but didn't fight to help him achieve equality. Today's libraries have simply replaced the ones of old. The gentlemen have taken down the "For White's Only" sign that once hung outside their door as an act of good faith.

One question that seems to follow racism is whether or not things have really changed. Are the times we live in just a reflection of the past?

Final Thoughts on Racism

I sometimes wonder if it is not our purpose in life to deal with such problems.

It just seems with all of our increased knowledge and technical accomplishments we would be a lot further ahead with our communication skills. That something as simple as racism can continue to be such a monumental challenge is somewhat of an enigma.

How can I stop a white man, who has just witnessed his son being killed by a black man, from hating all black people? The reality is that I can't. Meanwhile I hear that his other son, out of anger, pulls out a gun and shoots the high school's black star athlete. The athlete's cousin, who heard about the incident, decides to force himself on a little, white girl who is sitting alone at the bus stop.

The white girl's father, a police officer, pulls over three black youths who are driving a car with expired tags. In the middle of a struggle his gun discharges, killing the young, black man instantly. Suddenly, a whole community has began to march into city hall in protest. *When is this going to stop?*, is the question we must learn to ask.

There is something I would like to share with you that is extremely important in regards to racism! The fact that it runs rampant and out of control makes it essential that we don't become callous to its presence. Oftentimes, Americans grow hardened to humanity's cries for fairness and justice.

Since it doesn't affect our personal life why should we have to deal with it? Although we have the right to feel this way, we must not lose touch with the needs of others.

This ultimately causes us to become a part of the problem and not a part of the solution.

There is no doubt that the spread of racism is one of America's greatest challenges and that it will continue to be for many centuries to come. Even with the greatest weapon that this country possesses, education, we are still light years away from a possible remedy.

This book is not about what we can't do, it is about what we *can* do! As an American I will not accept the fact that we cannot deal with this challenge! Think of David who stood before Goliath. His purpose was to destroy the challenge that stood before him. The resources that we can use to destroy this mighty giant, racism, are as plentiful as the rocks carried by David. We need not lack the courage to do what we must do, for countless Americans have already paved the way for our victory.

If we are aware that there's a need for change, then we must understand what each and everyone of us can do to create this change. I think this country can learn to channel this power that racism has over us.

First, we must govern our own bodies, realizing racism lies dormant inside us all. Just as David used the rocks within his reach as his ammunition to fight against the giant. We have the understanding, patience, discipline, guidance, communication, knowledge and reason to fight racism. We too can unlock the heavy chains that keep us bound. Taking the responsibility for what we do or say will affect others around us and this is something that is within our reach. Knowing that the mistakes of the past are not the mistakes of the present will ultimately help us to change our future. One of the things that allows racism to continue to breed is that it's not always easily recognized.

Here is a quick example of this. The sport of golf had a history of segregating itself from those which were not wanted or desired. Most of the well-groomed golf courses in this country are hidden behind huge foliage. The average person doesn't have a clue they exist. The equipment that is used to play this game is expensive; therefore, you have to be in a certain tax bracket to afford to play.

Large membership fees are required in order to play on these well-manicured courses. The game itself doesn't create a problem, it simply conjures up a negative connotation.

94

Quite Frankly, it is this type of circumstance that continues the spread of racism. It is important that we learn to uproot this type of institution. We must learn to trim the trees that hide the games and the attitudes that surround them. Believe it or not racism only has the power that we are willing to give it.

Determination

O Lord, Thou givest us everything,
At the price of an effort.

Leonardo da Vinci
Painter, Sculptor, Architect & Engineer

Chapter Three

Sports

They've CREATED AN IDOL

In order to understand the importance of sports in America, one simply has to imagine this country without any sporting events at all. I'm sure that many of you are thinking that this is an impossibility to attempt! Sports is the Goliath of all institutions. It is such an integral part of America's culture that very few people question its character and content. I would like for us to examine one of this country's greatest natural resources: American Sports. These are just a couple of the many questions that we are going to be discussing in this chapter, "Sports, They've Created an Idol." It is my view that this institution affects so many facets of our lives.

American athletics can never be overlooked when evaluating the overall content of this nation's character. The millions and millions of dollars that it generates each year make it one of America's greatest *national resources*. In fact, the top five sports in this country generated more than 5 billion last year. The numerous jobs that American athletics create are vital to the economy. There are also countless contributions that sports offer this society.

If I were to try and pinpoint the one common link in sports, it would be the primitive element of man against man. Most of today's activities derive their excitement from this one powerful component. This struggle ignites a perpetual torch that has continued to burn. Whether men are representing cities, states or countries, there is something about the chemical makeup of a human being that propels him to distinctively compete against his fellow man. There is no greater format for this physical display of competition than through sports. The camaraderie and the physical challenge between men intrigues society.

The Grooming of the Young Athlete

Let me explain how young athletes become involved in sports by creating the following scenario.

One day back in May of 1988, I was strolling through Cheviot-Park in Los Angeles, California. The park faces a golf course to the west, and the Twentieth Century-Fox Studio's lot to the north. A residential area surrounds the south and the east. A two-mile jogging trail runs along the outer perimeter of the park. That afternoon, as I walked my old English sheepdog, Cricket, around the path, my focus was drawn to four baseball diamonds.

On the first field, the Pee Wee players were busy with their game. I passed by each one of them and it was plain to see that this was the game of baseball in its infancy. They were hitting the baseball off a little two-and-a-half-foot stand positioned directly in front of home plate. This was to simulate a strike being pitched over the plate. Most of the kids found hitting the stationary ball off this plastic stand to be a great challenge. One kid finally whacked the ball into play and his family and friends screamed and yelled uncontrollably with tremendous excitement.

The little ball player who hit the ball ran uncertainly to his own dugout and his coach guided him toward the area we know as first base. After reaching first base, the child brushed off the dirt that he had collected during two tumbles.

Sitting in the bleachers the fans of the defensive team were also excited. The coach for their side tried to unsuccessfully direct the three little boys fielding the baseball. As I walked away I could still hear the cheers of joy and excitement coming from the parents.

Soon their cries were drowned out by the yells of excitement coming from the next diamond.

This field was covered with slightly taller ball players who possessed greater physical coordination than the younger players. Still the pitcher was struggling to keep each of his tosses in and around the strike zone. It was easy to tell which team was winning. A glow of pride seemed to radiate from the winning players and fans alike. The amount of understanding for the game was obvious at this level of play just as it had been for the younger group.

The experience level was more apparent among the two teams playing at the next diamond. In this field, a game of Pony League baseball was being played. The shrieks of excitement took on a whole new energy level and the game had a much more serious tone, with competition being more apparent. As each ball was being pitched, the call made by the umpire seemed to trigger the intensity of the response from the stands. The fans appeared to take the calls as personal vendettas. It was clear that at this stage, baseball took on a whole different meaning.

The dialogue between the players took on a more direct purpose. I could hear the defensive players calling, "come on babe, come on babe, put that ball in there." It was as if each ballplayer on the field was mentally supporting the pitcher's every throw. As I walked away from that diamond in the distance I could hear an unhappy father's cries. He confronted the umpire who had called his son out on a strike-three pitch.

As I walked up to the final diamond that day something was beginning to stir inside of me; however, I could not put my finger on its meaning. The fourth diamond was occupied by two high school teams. There was no doubt that the persona projected by the players resembled professional athletes, both in their movements and in their speech. They had a predator-like quality about them. This game had none of the innocence that was definitely apparent on the first three diamonds. These young men had all their attention and concentration focused on mentally and physically dominating their opponent. The directions from the coaches were more explicit and the fans were more demanding. The ultimate purpose was to win at any cost. The energy surrounding the players made all those involved understand the objective of the game. As I walked back to my truck there was an awareness formulating in the back of my mind.

There was something insidious about the games that I still can not put my finger on.

Later that evening, as I was flipping through the channels on the television set I noticed that a major league baseball game was on. At first, the game had my complete attention, however, at the end of the inning, my focus was interrupted by a series of unwanted commercials. I must have seen six or seven products being advertised from cars to toothpaste, in less than two minutes. As I was getting up to extract my TV dinner out of the microwave it suddenly hit me. I realized what had been bothering me earlier in the day. It is the grooming process that initiated to create a professional athlete. What I had witnessed that afternoon was the conditioning process of young kids. Their were grooming the players for a possible career as professional athletes. The question as to whether our process is good or bad, or if we even realize that it exists, is the reason why I have chosen this topic as a part of my book.

Sports, Breaking Down the Race Barriers

It is important for me to remind you that although this book takes a very honest look at America today, it is from a Black perspective.

With that little note, I wish to express to you that one of this country's greatest antidotes for her war on racism is the natural resource I call athletics! Today there are many different types of sport activities which are being played and dominated by black athletes. On the other hand, in the early stages of organized American sports there was a lack of black representation. The nonexistence of Blacks in the early years of American sports was a result of a racist country. I smile to myself when I think that something so simple as a game created a format that would ultimately help to change the course of this nation. The games we play today laid down the foundation for many different races to come together as one. When we see a professional team run across the football field, we forget that this mixture of races didn't always co-exist. Because of my chapter on American racism, I don't want to get too deeply into this topic; however, there are a few vital points which should be made in this chapter.

In the early years American sports were segregated simply because of the mentality of our society at that time. Let's take a look at that period. It's said that the first professional basketball game was played in January of 1892. Pro football made its debut in 1895, and baseball followed in 1897.

The Civil War ended in April of 1865; therefore, it is very easy to see how the segregation of sports initiated. I'm not by any means, excusing or condoning segregation.

It is very important to view things with a sense of progressive development rather than to discredit their beginnings because of a gross injustice of the times.

Examining the mentality of both Blacks and Whites of that time allows one to realize that integration would have been impossible in most walks of life, not to mention in the games that the white man created for his own pleasure and amusement. As Americans, we must learn to see this segment of our history as a building block implemented to construct progress for the future regardless how badly the attitude of the times appeared. It was during a period of dissonance that America created these three major leagues. America was in a period of discord with her own existence. In all fairness to this nation, how does one heal the many wounds of destruction that resulted from the Civil War? It is my opinion that at this time American sports received its biggest calling. Sports embraced the challenge of trying to delete racist attitudes and finally created a format for positive change.

After the initial creation of these games, society began to draw up the blueprint for widespread competition. The large arenas, which were originally segregated, gave blacks an opportunity to come together on a wide scale. Teams were made up of players, coaches and fans. Cities began backing the teams' high hopes for victory.

It was the grand scale of the game that slowly helped to shed the radical armor of segregation. As blacks began to infiltrate American sports, opposition came from white teammates and fans, but slowly it fell to the wayside. The challenge of competition and supremacy pushed the opposition aside.

I often wonder how Jackie Robinson felt about leaving the all Negro Baseball League to play in the all-White league. Jackie knew that the league he was leaving behind was just as talented as the White League. He also knew that to prove his worth. And prove it, he did. The Dodgers won six National League pennants during the ten years Jackie played with them.

We must see more than a black baseball player joining an all-white team. We need to look at the harsh realities that society faced 1947. The integration of that one single ballplayer enabled Americans to realize that color had nothing to do with a person's worth.

Jackie brought an even bigger gift to the game of baseball, he helped to teach this country the ability to have a good attitude and that hard work was not based on color. He showed us that the passion to be the best is a common thread found in all men. When white men cheered a black man on the field of baseball it was a giant step towards erasing unnecessary hatred.

Not everyone agreed, but the people who wanted the best for our nation knew that change was inevitable.

The countless American athletes who paved the way for change were true heroes. It was their accomplishments that helped this country become a grander place. They had the challenge of educating their fellow Americans. Their trails of courage helped make American sports an institution like no other. The union and sportsmanship of today's athlete reflect the hurdles that have been overcome by the substance of true champions.

As I review the history of America's love affair with sports, I can honestly say that the confrontations the sport's world had with racism were merely the result of labor pains from childbirth. It was evident that in the eyes of the world this infant would someday become strong and mighty.

Now take a moment to think about the following example a simpler version of what happens on America's sports field.

Let's take two kids, one black and one white. If we were to put the two of them in a large arena and observe their behavior, we would see that at first they might not like each other very much and they would be at odds with one another. However, with the passing of time, the two would become friendly and begin to enjoy each other's company. Eventually they would unite, becoming one in the spirit of sports.

It really doesn't matter how tough it was at the beginning or which one of the two was right or wrong. What matters is the outcome! As long as the spirit of the sports world continues to soar high and strong, then the growing pains of the past were worthwhile.

Americans both Black and White too often get caught up in the past. The past should be viewed only as a learning experience. The inability to let go is what keeps us from moving forward.

Where Are We Now?
Where are we Headed?

Now that we have discussed this major dilemma, let's take a look at the direction of American sports today.

One of the things that I have learned in life is that we can easily benefit from reviewing the past; however, there are times when we cannot see the present clearly until its impact is felt in the future.

The American athlete has one ultimate goal and that is to become the best of the best. To most athletes to be the best is to compete at the highest professional level of play. Just ask any nine year old male child what he wants to be when he grows up and he will probably answer that he wants to be a professional athlete. He might aspire to play one or more of our many sports.

I think it is important for society to be aware of what is being created in the name of love of sports. America's infatuation with professional sports goes far beyond the innocence of childhood admiration! We have created a growing fascination that has become an addiction.

Most Americans are not aware of this aspect or of the powerful idol worship that follows the path of the professional athlete. Using my own story as an example, allow me to show you how the passion for sports initiates and where it is headed.

My Early Involvement with the Games

I can easily recall what brought my attention to the world of athletics.

My initial involvement came from watching professional sports teams on TV. I grew up in Houston, Texas. There were very limited organized sports activities for children between the fourth and sixth grade. There was one exception: the after school big game. It didn't matter at that time what sport it was, we played whatever was in season.

In my neighborhood, our million dollar sports arena was the empty lot next door. This multi-purpose arena was adaptable for all of the three major sports.

The huge oak tree at the back of the lot was used to hold up the backboard and goal for playing basketball. Except for the large roots that protruded at the base of the tree, it served its purpose very well. Football was fun to play on that big lot, (all we had to do was avoid the tree at the front of the lot!) We enjoyed playing baseball, at least until some big kid would hit a foul ball to the left side of third base. The only thing that would stop the ball was my mother's house, and the side facing the field was mostly made up of windows. Needless to say, my mom hated baseball season.

The great thing about sandlot sports was that you could imagine you were any professional athlete that you wanted to be. All you had to do was call out the name of your favorite athlete before anyone else.

When playing football, I was Roger Staubach or Bullet Bob Hayes, both of the Dallas Cowboys. There was something about their character and ability I wanted to emulate. The seeds of (worshiping professional athletes) were planted early during these years of my life.

When junior high school approached, so did my intensity for playing organized sports. Earlier, in the fourth and fifth grades, I had played four musical instruments: the violin, viola, cello and the bass. Once I got involved in sports those old string instruments were history.

I didn't realize until much later why I gave up playing those instruments so easily.

I remember the summer after my sixth grade year, I approached my stepfather, Otis Clay, about playing football for my school the following year. Although I had only lived with my stepfather for eight years, he had became the father that I never knew. His remarks were always pretty much the same; "it's Ok with me if it's ok with your mom."

Of course, to get my mom to (agree to having eleven other guys run over and knock you to the ground) was not going to be an easy task.

"NO! NO! NO!" was my mother's response." Have you both lost your cotton picking mind? Are you both stupid?" Might have been another one of her reactions.

My stepfather and I both knew that we had a couple of months before football season started to see if she really meant what she had said.

I had a birthday coming up on the twelfth of June, and I had decided that my birthday wish was to ask to play football. However, something unexpected happened. On the tenth of June two days before my birthday, one of my brothers awakened me about four a.m. to inform me that our stepfather had died in his sleep as a result of a fatal heart attack.

I grew up quickly that summer. I learned not to take certain things for granted. As the summer months went by, I rekindled my passion for football. It was not until one week before football season that my mom gave me permission to play.

Of course I had to solicit the support of a friend, (an eight-grade quarterback who happened to be a close friend of the family.) The two of us managed to convince my mom that football was not a dangerous sport. We showed her the complete football uniform so that she would see just how safe playing football was going to be.

Although she agreed I knew that it was my stepfather's death that had swayed her decision. I guess mom felt that the summer had been an emotional one for all of us.

The two weeks of football practice before school started were gruesome.

As the practices continued, so did the development of a special bond between my peers and myself.

One of the many elements sports brings to society is the internal need to be a part of a group. I think that sports teaches us a great deal about ourselves. It teaches us how we handle failures and respond to the aggressive behavior of others, and most importantly, what role we are willing to play in the game of sports.

I chose to play quarterback (I think it was the Roger Staubach in me that made me choose this position). There were many elements of football I was unaware of, including the long practices and the conditioning program.

One aspect that I fell in love with was the pep rallies. The cheerleaders had never hung out at our sandlot games and now they were everywhere. During the rallies the speeches made by our coaches and other players convinced all of us how we were going to beat up on the other team. I didn't realize it at the time but it was a sense of *false pride* that permeated throughout the auditorium. The next day on the football field we realized that the other team was just as hyped. I quickly learned that preparation and hard work won football games, not cheap talk.

Unfortunately I learned this the *hard way.*

As the years went on, the one thing I really enjoyed about the game was its tremendous popularity. This is especially true in high school. Students-teachers-parents, in fact, the whole community, adored the players of the high school teams. Idol worshiping was rampant.

The Young Athlete
and Hero Worship

The small seeds of praise that are planted in a young athletes mind seem harmless, but in time they manifest themselves into self-glorifying characteristics. This is more evident when an athlete reaches the very top or what society considers the professional level. I would like to make you aware of the process that takes place. Let's look at a little leaguer's baseball game.

A batter hits a fly ball into deep center and the center fielder runs and makes a diving catch.
The defensive teams goes wild, and the fans are ecstatic, yelling and screaming. An atmosphere of excitement is created, both towards the team and the young ballplayer who made the catch. He runs towards the dugout he realizes he can recreate that internal rush, (a sort of adrenaline shot made up of pride and praises), anytime he exerts himself and steps into the spotlight. This feeling continues to manifest itself.

113

It is ignited anytime the young athlete hustles, in an effort to be in the spotlight of praises and unquestionable favor. Eventually this feeling becomes a drug that feeds on the uncontrollable addiction.

There are countless other characteristics which create this monster of idol worship, and as this chapter continues, I will make you aware of these different aspects. As our consciousness increases, we will decide whether this element of sports is good or bad for society. At that point we will begin to make the necessary adjustments. Most importantly, we must recognize how the problem originated. I am giving you an outline of the developmental stages of this phenomenon from a young athlete's perspective so that you can clearly understand its origins.

In American sports, there is a supporting cast which has helped to create the image of its importance. Let's examine the weekly preparations that go into a standard high school football game.

The week begins with the varsity team preparing for its next opponent.

The junior varsity and the freshmen teams are playing nearby on the secondary fields. Play after play is being performed, over and over, until the coach feels that each play is being perfected.

In the distance, you can hear the echo of the school's marching band rehearsing its special number for Friday night's big game. The big horn and large drum sections always drown out the other instruments in the band. Around the corner, in the gymnasium, yells from the cheerleading squad can be heard. They are practicing and sounding off a few broken cheers.

"Two bits, four bits, six bits a dollar. All for the Eagles, stand up and holler!"

A few steps down the hall, the booster club is creating banners. The art room is filled with huge rolls of white paper, cans of paint, and hundreds of magic markers. In a parking lot, fifty to seventy-five drill team dancers are rehearsing their routines. Their excitement is accentuated by their screaming and giggling. Later that evening, the parents of the booster club will meet in the school auditorium. Their job is to secure the funds necessary to purchase new uniforms. They have secretly decided to surprise the team with them the night before the homecoming game, which is two weeks away. All this activity usually begins on the Monday before Fridays game.

As the week progresses, the energy and excitement continues to mount.

By the time Friday rolls around, the school is about to erupt with anticipation.

Friday at two o'clock the pep rally is about to begin. Here, the cheerleaders get a dry run of the same cheers that will be used later on that night. The coaches and student athletes convince everyone in the school that their support is essential in order for the team to assure a victory.

In the late afternoon and early evening, the preparations and anticipation continue. Outside at the football stadium, the groundskeeper rolls on the white chalk for the boundary and yardage lines.

At the concessions, workers are unloading the ice which will chill the hundreds of soft drinks for the game. Parents fight the traffic on their way home from work so they can quickly get to the game for their son's performance.

Around six-thirty, the parking attendants begin to receive a steady flow of cars. Most of the fans are happy to pay $5.50 for the privilege of parking close to the stadium. Others are patiently waiting in line ready to purchase a ticket.

Many of the parents are commenting on their sons and how grown-up they look dressed in their uniforms. "Why it was only yesterday that little Jason was playing in little league football."

As the parents walk into the tunnel, toward the bright lights surrounding the field, they can see the team going through the pre-game drills getting ready for the long, awaited game.

The voice of a proud parent can be heard shouting, "Look, there's Justin. He's running his practice route." His father's face glows with satisfaction as Justin, #88, catches a wobbled pass from his quarterback. In the corner of the home team's end zone, the school band is gathering to sound off the National Anthem. At this time, the announcer has begun to read off a number of community announcements.

You can feel the excitement in the stands coming to a peak as the horn section of the band begins to march out onto the field. This signals the fans to stand at attention and the band belts out its rendition of the *Star Spangled Banner.* After all the cheers, the moment everyone has been waiting for finally arrives!

A five inch, thick, white line runs down the center of the fifty yard line separating the two teams. As each team awaits the whistle to blow, the excitement reaches fever pitch. Once the ball is kicked high into the air, the fans scream with enthusiasm. The ensuing anticipation, and the hard work are all captured in this fitting moment.

This scenario will repeat itself, week after week, regardless of the final score, as long as football season is with us. This buildup of excitement is part of the conditioning process that subconsciously initiates America's worship of sports and the athletes that play them. Although everyone's role is very important in the creation of America's sports idol, all the activities have one goal to set the stage for the super star athlete. The countless number of supporting cast members rarely come close to the athlete's splendor. He is the star of the show.

Let's examine the young athlete in these circumstances. First of all, society plays an important role in this drama. It molds the athlete into a mini-God. An immortal raised to the highest altar of society, the altar of professional sports. Most high school kids play sports for this very reason. Popularity is very important to teenagers and this is one way to gain the acceptance and approval of their peers. The human bond that is formed between teammates is invaluable. It helps to shape the child's character and the leadership qualities they acquire stay with them until adulthood.

The athlete who tries to be the best at everything often turns out to be the most talented. His drive and determination puts him in the position of leader.

It is important to recognize the course and direction that takes young kids to the road of stardom.

They have not yet realized that a monster is growing inside them and each day of training an insatiable driving force takes unprecedented power over them.

Ninety-eight percent of all high school athletes have an hunger and desire to become a professional athlete. Make no mistake about it, this desire, no matter how large or small, is constantly growing within. At the beginning his desire has an innocent origin.

Let's take a quick look at the life of a better-than-average high school varsity athlete. We'll call him "Jordan." Jordan has a fairly good chance to gain the starting position of quarterback. He has received most of his popularity from being on the team, although he's the kind of kid you would like even if he didn't play sports. Once he earns the opportunity to start as quarterback, his position on the team elevates him toward a God-like status. As each school day begins, he is met by a group of giggly girls on their way to first period. One of them cries out, "Good luck on the game tonight!" He gives a shy reply and continues to walk by.

He is already aware of the fact that most of the girls are crazy about him.

Suddenly, a teammate walks up from behind and gives him a big bear hug. "Hey man, did you hear the good news?"

"What news?" Jordan responds in excitement, but somewhat surprised. His teammate explains how Melvin, the first-string running back, overheard the coach telling David, the varsity trainer, that Jordan would be starting quarterback for tonight's game. Suddenly, everyone is patting him on the back and congratulations are coming from everywhere. Both the teachers and the students are tossing out words of encouragement. In less than ten minutes, Jordan's popularity has managed to triple. He runs to the nearest pay phone to see if he can catch his father before he leaves for work.

He is too late, but he docs manage to relay the good news to his mom. Suddenly a familiar voice cries out, "Jordan, you better not be late for class!" It's his football coach, he's standing next to him with a big grin on his face. " Mom, I've got to go!" He quickly hangs up the phone.

His coach congratulates him on being picked for the starting quarterback position. He explains to him that his hard work and his "never give up" attitude helped him achieve his goal. "Now hurry and get your butt to class."Jordan rushes down the hall bursting with pride and excitement.

Once inside the classroom, his classmates give him a big round of applause. He is treated as if he was quarter backing the next Super Bowl game. The cheers and applause continue for five minutes until the teacher puts a stop to the commotion. Things begin to settle down, when the class is interrupted by a loud knock at the door. Four varsity cheerleaders walk in with a huge cake, with the words,"Good luck Jordan Lee, you are the greatest!" written on it. The class continues its cheers and encouragement.

This is one of Jordan's greatest moments. He is a very happy camper. And he is only a sophomore! He can expect this kind of special attention for the next three years. The preferential treatment increases as his accomplishments become recorded.

Let's not lose sight of the fact that this same script is happening in communities all over the country. It is important to realize this last scenario occurred in less than twenty minutes. The building and grooming process of young athletes happens to hundreds and thousands of young kids. All over the U.S. the stage is set for American athletes to reach the altar of immortality, every hour of everyday.

The Coach, Making or Breaking the Young Athlete

Different elements will have important impacts on an athlete's walk toward greatness. One of these elements is the personal guidance that a young athlete receives from the men and women who coach sports. Coaches are often responsible for nurturing the young athlete in his quest to turn professional. Like most school teachers, the biggest challenge that coaches must face is the ability to be fair, just, and unbiased. I will cover this issue to a greater extent in the chapter on Education, but at this point I would like to stress the magnitude of influence a coach has on a child.

The coach's role in a child's life is as important as the parent's. Patience, guidance and discipline are of paramount significance as well as giving the child a sense of accomplishment. Wc must never overlook the fact that these dedicated men and women have the skills necessary to give children the opportunity to accomplish many of their dreams. These dreams are materialized by achieving the next level of play in any particular sport.

In many cases, male coaches are present in a boy's life because of the absence of a father figure. In my opinion, they are role models on and off the field. The lessons that I learned from my coaches gave me a glimpse of what it would have been like to have a father. I watched my coaches closely.

I noticed the way they walked, the way they talked, how they dressed and how serious they were about the sport that they coached.

The one important lesson that I learned at a very early age was that eighty-five percent of coaches are merely frustrated athletes. These men were never able to let go of the game they once played. Coaching is a very important aspect of the game and since there's a large number of frustrated athletes coaching, it causes some very interesting dynamics and confrontations. In every professional area, there are good and bad elements.

However, when you consider the tremendous responsibility coaches have on athletes' lives, you can begin to see that there is very little margin for error.

It is the coaches' development, guidance and nurturing that will ultimately decide whether these young athletes will compete on a high school, collegiate and or professional level. At times, its the little bit of information a coach gives a child that will stay with him or her for the rest of their life. I remember two different occasions when a coach's decision changed the course and direction of my life.

My eighth grade football coach was a likable man by the name of Emmett Hill. Large and heavy in stature, Coach Hill was Santa Claus everyday of the year.

He had a way of making you feel good about yourself. His extremely jolly personality was a nice change from the usually stern nature of most coaches.

One afternoon, while we were having lunch he asked me a serious question. He had a way of speaking that made you stop whatever you were doing and listen to what he had to say.

"Dexter," he began, "Would you rather have a very beautiful woman as your wife or a woman that can cook, clean and take care of your family, but is not so attractive?" The other athletes sitting with us were all shouting, "choose the beautiful wife, choose the beautiful one!"

I followed their lead and answered that of course I would choose a beautiful woman as my wife. Coach Hill quickly responded that my answer was the wrong one! He explained that a man should consider as a wife a woman who can cook, clean and take good care of the family, for those qualities truly outweigh the element of beauty. He went on to say that his wife was the best cook in the world and of course we all believed him, since he was as big as a house! Nonetheless, I was puzzled by Coach Hill's advice.

A few weeks later, at a sports' banquet, I finally had an opportunity to meet Mrs. Hill. She was absolutely gorgeous!

I smiled to myself, realizing that you don't have to give up one thing to have another. You simply have to learn to demand the most. That same evening, Coach Hill winked at me for he knew that I had stumbled across one of life's little truisms.

Another piece of advice that has stayed with me to this day came from my sophomore football coach Emmett Smallwood.

Early on a Saturday morning I was walking toward Antoine Boulevard, three miles from school, when a car pulled up next to me. I looked inside and recognized Coach Smallwood. "Hey Dexter," "I'm glad that I ran into you. Hop in and I'll give you a ride." Coach Smallwood was a very stern and serious man, but it was also very easy to tell that he had a great heart.

The first thing he said to me was that last night's game was a tough loss.

He was referring to the loss against the Magnolia Bulldogs. He went on to say that he was sorry that I hadn't played in the previous night's game. He knew that I was a real competitor and recognized that it had been difficult for me to stand by and watch the game. At that point, he shared something that I have never forgotten. "Dexter" he said. "One of the most important teachings in life that you must always remember is this: when you are talking to someone you should always look them straight in the eyes.

This will let you know just what kind of person you are dealing with."

There are many reasons why this piece of knowledge was so profound. At the time, I was only three weeks into my sophomore year in high school, attending an integrated school for the first time. I hadn't experienced being around white people before this. In fact, being from Texas, I thought all white boys wore cowboy boots and carried pocket knifes.

It was something of an enigma that a white man would help a young black man become a better person.

Coach Smallwood proceeded to inform me that the coaching staff had decided to give me the opportunity to start quarter backing the varsity team, The Golden Eagles, the following week. He mentioned that they all knew how hard I had worked, but they had felt obligated to give the two seniors the first try at leading the team. He also told me that I needn't be intimidated by the fact that I was a sophomore. I have to say that particular morning, a five-minute ride seemed to last a few hours!

You can see how lessons learned at a young age can ultimately help build a personal philosophy.

The examples above are positive ones, but I can also recall many negative encounters between coaches and students that redirected the lives of many athletes.

The following example describes a negative personal experience. During my freshmen year in college I looked to my coaches for guidance and direction. I engaged the help of a few black coaches regarding collegiate sports and realized that my options would increase if I attended an All-Black University, Prairie View A&M. The motivating factor in arriving at this decision was the persistent encouragement from my community and friends to give my talents to an all-black school. Although I had thoroughly enjoyed my three years at Dwight D. Eisenhower, an integrated high school, I was convinced that I had a responsibility as a Black man to support an all-Black university.

Originally I was to play *basketball* at Prairie View A&M; however, I was informed that the coach had already made his quota of basketball scholarships. Nonetheless, a *baseball* scholarship was available if I was interested. The coach sensed my disappointment, so we reached a compromise. I would sign on with a baseball scholarship, but I would play quarterback on the football team. In exchange for this commitment, I would be allowed to play basketball. Everyone on the coaching staff was in agreement.

I felt ambivalent, and although the situation was an unusual one, I thought it was a small price to pay in order to fulfill my dreams.

Five weeks into football season I experience a bruised muscle in my stomach.

Since this injury irritated my stepping forward motion, I was told by the team physician that I must not throw a football for several months. Fortunately, football season was almost over and basketball practice had already begun.

I thought that I would tryout for basketball but since I signed on with a baseball scholarship, I had no choice but to play baseball. To my disappointment, the coach informed me that it was baseball that was paying for my schooling not basketball.

Unhappy with my situation, I drafted a letter to a coach in Jacksonville, Texas. He had approached me earlier that year. I explained my situation, and he agreed to offer me a full basketball scholarship for the following season. The only requirement was that I maintain a certain grade point average. Trigonometry was a tough class that semester but I was able to get through it, and the following year, I was headed for Jacksonville. I've always been very optimistic, so I put aside the past and began anxiously waiting for a new beginning.

The first few months in my new environment seemed to be a dream come true!

Most of the guys from the basketball team hung out together and getting to know many individuals from different parts of the country was an education in itself.

I spent most of basketball season trying to make the adjustment from high school center to collegiate guard. This was no easy task, but I took on the challenge with gusto and all the substance I had. In high school to play the position of center at 6'4" is acceptable, on the collegiate level the centers were slightly taller, about six to eight inches taller. The fact is that high school coaches simply take the best they have and build a team around it. In contrast, a college coach recruits players for a particular position. It took a few months, but I finally managed to make the proper adjustments to the guard position.

Each game presented a new challenge. You were always playing against athletes you knew were headed for the big show. I recall playing against a ballplayer who was all-American in his position and yet managed to block his shot some five times that game. This player went on to join the Detroit Pistons and every time an announcer would call out the name "Vinnie Johnson", I would always smile knowing that at one time we had competed on the same level.

One day during the season our coach was late for practice.

We were informed by the trainer that the coach had been accused of beating his wife. All of us knew he had a drinking problem, but we had ignored it.

His personal problems never really seemed to affect his job or our relationship with him. At least not until the last three games of the season. At that time I was called into the coach's office and was informed that I was being suspended for the last three games.

I wasn't given a relevant reason for the decision. His only explanation was that he felt my attitude hurt the team. I tried to reason with him but he remained adamant and ignored my concern and genuine intention to correct the matter. Nonethless, he stood firm in his judgment. He also nonchalantly informed me that I wouldn't lose my scholarship and I could still travel with the team. I never expected this to happen to me. I searched my innermost feelings to examine what I could have done to warrant this kind of brash behavior. I kept coming up with nothing.

Later that evening, I saw the team statistician sitting in his car, I walked over to talk with him. He mentioned he had heard about my situation and he thought what had happened was unfair and unjust. He then informed me that I was ninth in the nation in field goal percentages.

I only needed to play three more quarters of basketball to qualify for national honors. This was all the information he could share with me and on that note he drove away.

This incident, in my sophomore year, closed, the door on my collegiate athletic career. As far as playing basketball on the same team was concerned, I didn't want to deal with this same coach and perhaps encounter another unfair situation. I thought of transferring to play basketball elsewhere but according to collegiate rules I would have to sit out a year.

I will always remember this event. My coach's decision grossly affected my life. The truth is that these kinds of incidents are far too common.

I wondered if the coach might have been taking his personal problems out on me. His eyes always seemed so red, so I couldn't tell if he had been drinking that particular day.

A coach requires tremendous communication skills and the capacity to be understanding. Unlike most teachers, coaches aren't trained in these basic skills. Their expertise is in the actual knowledge of the game. A large percentage of coaches are physical education majors, not psych majors.

As I close this portion of the chapter, (the importance of coaching to the institution of sports,) I want to give those of you who are parents direction in choosing the coaches who will be training and educating your youngsters. To begin, here are a few fundamental words.

Most coaches will tell you that it is easier to teach a child the correct fundamentals of the game right from the start than to try to de-program a child who has been improperly taught. While the basic fundamentals are being internalized, the overall picture of the sport come into play.

For example, a young baseball player first learns how to swing the bat and later how to hit the baseball. Soon the importance of learning to get to, first base comes into play. A step-by-step procedure gives the athlete a broader under standing of the whole game.

For a young athlete who is just learning the game, look for a coach who is patient as well as knowledgeable about the sport, rather than a coach who is overly aggressive with the attitude of "win win" at any cost. The "win win" attitude is important; however, it should come into play later on in a child's athletic development.

It is very important for parents to, nurture a youngster to the next level of play, this is vital to his or her career.

The careful selection of a coach should be of paramount importance. A parent should also discuss with the coach the child's goals and what they would like to accomplish during a particular session or season. Most parents don't realize that they can be their child's biggest enemy! Oftentimes, the coach is trying to accomplish one thing, the parents another, and the child is totally confused.

I know firsthand how important it is for everyone to be synchronized. the last several years, I have coached youth basketball for 7-12 years olds. It is often difficult for parents to understand that the main reason little Johnny is not very aggressive on offense is simply because he hasn't learned to dribble the basketball. This is augmented by the fact that his parents don't always make the effort to get him to practice. When he does make it to a scheduled team practice, Johnny is twenty minutes late and the team has already finished with the dribbling drill for that practice day.

At this critical stage of a child's development, a weak link, whether it be the parents or the coach, can cause a rippling effect that can create havoc in a child's athletic career.

When an athlete begins his high school or collegiate career, the area of coaching becomes more focused, organized and structured.

There is a common standard set up by the athletic administration program. This is to give all students a fair and equal opportunity to excel in the field of athletics.

College Athletics, Scholarships & the Money Game

Earlier I wrote about community involvement that exists in high school sports and how it follows through the college level and beyond!
When young athletes make the transition from high school to collegiate sports, money begins to flex its powerful influence. The Bible refers to wealth as the root of all evil. I'll let you be the judge when it comes as to the almighty dollar and its role in college athletics.

For the young man who is fortunate enough to be accepted to the university of his choice, a scholarship is good as gold. It is a fact that a large number of young Americans would not be able to attend these great institutions of higher learning, without the assistance of the school's athletic scholarship programs. For many high school youngsters their primary incentive for playing sports is the athletic scholarship.

Although the money only pays certain expenses such as tuition, housing, meals and books, it creates a safe and secure environment for the athlete.

The combination of money and sports has put athletics in a category like no other.

It is my opinion that collegiate sports is structured so it completely takes advantage of the athlete. One of the greatest sins of this society is that it allows the money in collegiate athletics to completely engulf the students; however, they do not receive the necessary preparation and understanding of the real world after sports.

The money surrounding collegiate sports is the huge carrot that coaches dangle in the face of most scholarship athletes. Universities recruit athletes with the promise of paying for their schooling and one might think that this is a wonderful thing. Remember the old saying: you don't get something for nothing?

The university receives a better than average athlete, but the schools program is greatly improved. A successful athletic program attracts more students to its institution and this largely increases the university's marketing power, both locally and nationwide. National athletic rankings for universities generate millions of dollars in revenues yearly. Make no mistake about it, college athletics is big business and it always will be. The small amount invested in the athlete's tuition can generate millions of dollars.

By no means should anyone downplay this financial contribution to a young athlete's scholastic career. However, it can in no way compare to the millions of dollars in revenues generated as a result of the students' athletic abilities.

I believe anything that is righteous and stimulates the American economy should be supported. However, you must also be aware of the negative by-product of every situation.

As your awareness increases, you can easily see the correlation between the idolatry of college athletes and the role that money plays in college sports. The *American Heritage Dictionary* defines idolatry with two definitions. The first is "worshiping of idols,' and the second, "blind or excessive devotion to something." The second definition is the one that relates to the beast in American athletics. The blind or excessive devotion that Americans feel toward American sports is our own creation. For me to state that something this monumental exists in an institution this great is simply not enough. It is important for me to show you how, when, where and why this situation developed. The word blind is a very important adjective here! If, America is blind to the existence of this situation in sports, then someone has to take an opportunity to make this country aware of it.

I believe collegiate sports is a great place to shed some more light on this subject of idol worship. It is about this time that Americans begin to lose their perspective and this monster which involves money and sports, raises its gigantic head.

There are many industries that help this huge giant feed itself. You know them, they are the countless companies that make uniforms, footwear, equipment and other merchandise.

These companies serve as an appetizer for the giant's meal. The beverage industry's involvement in sports is a tremendous asset to this institution.

The constant atmosphere of wealth will make it easy for us to see the true potential of America's addiction to athletics.

Collegiate athletes are conditioned to believe in the myth that it's their presence that generates this high energy of money and power. Quite frankly, here is where idol worship accelerates from an embryo stage to adulthood.

I used this analogy to make you aware of how dramatic the changes are.

Collegiate sports is the pivotal point at which an important transformation occurs. The many years of grooming that lead up to this point are merely chapters in a dream.

The collegiate level brings athletes into a new realm of reality and gives them a feeling of optimism and hope at the end of the tunnel.

Though many of the athletes realize that only a handful will make it to the big party, if doesn't stop them from renting a tuxedo just in case they are invited. The big money that surrounds the game has elevated them to a new level and the residue of this high income is a God-like-status. The possibility of being invited, (acquiring a ticket) to the party gives these young men the initiative to overexert themselves physically and mentally, beyond the average human capabilities.

Media exposure increases the college athlete's chances of getting to a God-like-status. As they give the athlete a chance for his performances to stand out above the rest. The media is a catalyst in the creation of an idol. The more these kids are in the news, the greater the opportunity for them to prove themselves as superior icons in the sports arena.

The media brings the team's success to life for every sports' enthusiast in the nation. We must never, ever underestimate the media's power of persuasion. Their views and opinions can literally change the course of this nation's thinking and direction.

Please don't get me wrong. My love for sports is as great, if not greater, than the next guy's; however I believe that one's passion must not be clouded by the lack of reality. The media, like most institutions, has both good and bad elements. Most Americans, either don't care or aren't aware of these elements. They have adopted the philosophy of *so it is written, so it is!*

There is a popular saying that the cream rises to the top. This statement is certainly true when it comes to college athletes. The best of the best do what ever it takes to stand out above the rest. They are the ones who are invited to the big party. In a society where great admiration and pride are the norm, collegiate sports are at the foot of the altar of all American professional sports.

The only difference between the two levels is the players' salary.

In fact, in college athletics, everyone seems to receive a paycheck except for the athletes themselves.

Let's examine this a little closer. Coaches get hundred thousand dollar a year contracts and television stations make exorbitant amounts for their coverage of the games. Everyone involved, in any aspect of the program, from the janitors to the chancellor of the university, all profit from sports.

These higher, learning institutions boast that they're paying for the athlete's education, (an opportunity which should be more than enough compensation). I strongly disagree with this philosophy. Each year universities take in millions of dollars, all because of these talented, young athletes. Why shouldn't the athlete see some of this revenue? After all, ninety-nine percent of the athletes will never make it to the big show.

Often, certain schools are in the news because of recruiting violations. This leads us to believe that athletes are receiving more compensation than the standard rules allow. I believe that the system should permit collegiate athletes monetary benefits or a system should be developed that permits collegiate athletes to openly receive monetary benefits.

Each year society gives adulation and praise to these men for their achievements without taking into consideration the fact that they spend at least six to eight hours a day perfecting the art of their game. Quite frankly, they are supposed to be better than average!

The top one percent who are recognized as the best will move up to compete on a professional level. They will be praised by millions of fans. This is the final step, the dream of thousands of American kids.

Candidly speaking, the only difference between the top one percent of collegiate athletes and professional athletes is the amount of time spent in perfecting their game. That, America, is the only difference! Any other difference beyond this fact is something we have abdicated in our own minds. It is somewhat ironic, but it is those who haven't made it to the big show, that continue to pay for the growth and survival of pro sports.

Every year, the top three major sports initiate a *tribal ceremony* that announces to the rest of the nation the selection of new talent. This gives you, the sports' fan, an opportunity to see who you will be idolizing next. The event is called the draft. This process informs the young athletes which team they will be playing for; however, the professional daft serves a far greater purpose than most fans realize. It is a double-edged sword. On one side, the draft helps to continue the high standard of athletic excellence. On the other side, the athlete knows he has to perform at an optimum level at all times, otherwise he'll be watching Sunday's game from his couch at home, like the rest of us.

The Business Side of Professional Sports

The money spent to attract collegiate athletes to pro sports, comes out of our pockets.

The collegiate player will cost you an arm and a leg once he becomes professional. Let's take a look at how the system of dollars and cents works at this level.

To gain an understanding of this concept, we need to recognize the players off the field. If it were just one city or team, it would be easy for us to give them the responsibility for the debt, the high cost of the first or second round draft picks. Unfortunately, there are many hidden characters in this drama. They also play a huge role in the creation of the sports' idol. Whether or not they choose to take any responsibility for this is something else altogether.

They are the advertisers, the marketing agents, the merchandising companies, and the consumer manufacturers. It's these companies that create the ideal image of what is considered desirable by the general public. How do these organizations accomplish this great illusion? What price are Americans willing to pay for this mirage? First of all, these organizations make licensing deals with professional associations. Once this licensing is in place, they begin to force-feed you with every possible product available. This is suppose to make you feel like you're a part of the action. Professional athletes gain a tremendous amount of exposure (as well as a great portion of your pocketbook!)

You might be asking yourself, "What is the big deal about conducting business in this way?" I will be the first to agree that there is nothing wrong with it. The point I wish you to focus on is how easy it is for companies to create an environment of idolatry. Professional athletics saturate the market with these endorsements and we are exposed to them year round. It becomes virtually impossible for us not to be influenced by their tactics. This is especially true when their endorsements are linked to the individual players! When did it become important for us to be associated with the best? The only thing I can come up with is the element of *false pride.*

Once these large companies begin to latch onto the top marquee players, it becomes very easy for them to brainwash us into buying their products and believing in their jingles and catchy slogans. Society is willing to overlook the quality of these products in an effort to be associated with the person who represents the product.

The top named companies: Nike, Reebok, Fila, Addidas and Converse, have their products manufactured in Taiwan, Korea, China and Indonesia. American businesses consider this practice the normal standard for profit-making. American companies can get their products manufactured in third world countries for pennies on the dollar and then sell them for a huge profits.

Great business sense, right? Well, this might be "smart business",but is it fair and honest? Is it fair that some of these companies endorse poor working conditions and underage, labor sweat-shops in order to manufacture their products? They're not our kids, right? Nonetheless, we are condoning this practice. Whenever we purchase any of these products. You would think that these companies would pass the savings along to the consumer. Wrong! Instead, with the help of America's professional athletes they become even more greedy. Consumers end up paying more than ten times more than the actual cost.

The companies also give away thousands and thousands of dollars worth of free merchandise, much of it in promotional public relations. Unfortunately, this free merchandise doesn't go to the consumers it goes directly to those involved in the sports' organizations. It is the consumer who pays for these free gifts through the high prices placed on the merchandise that they buy.

The quality of these products is usually of a low standard. In fact, some pediatricians believe that most top-brand tennis shoes are harmful to children's feet. We are being duped into buying a product at a higher cost simply because of the brand name. Society has allowed propaganda to succeed in a format of corporate greed.

Those of us less fortunate that cannot afford these outrageous purchases are often made to feel less than adequate.

I'm sure the conglomerates will argue that the cost of acquiring the endorsement contracts with the professional associations is extremely high.

Each year, the scale of professional contracts is increased by the record-breaking numbers in guaranteed salaries for athletes.

This sooner or later has an effect on the everyday consumer. The professional institutions don't mind this at all. They want to saturate the market with endorsements. The hype only increases the magnitude of their universal appeal.

After all, the key to any successful business is mass advertising. Through a subliminal message we are programmed to recognize the product and logo on sight.

Toward the end of this chapter, I will give you a simple, but effective solution which will show you how to regain control of the situation. Again, my purpose is to make sure that you understand the overall picture. It is important that we, the consumer is aware of our role in creating the sports' idols we worship. Taking all of these factors into consideration, it is no wonder that the professional athlete is elevated to a God-like status! American institutions have force-fed society to the extent that we have become gluttonous.

But this is only the appetizer to the main course.

The Media & Its Role in the Creation of the Sports Idol

We have now come to the main course. The Media! The American media is one of the biggest contributors to the idolization of the American athlete.

This sleepless giant creates the drama, excitement and enthusiasm that feeds this colossal industry.

The media's involvement is the nervous system of any sports' event. The media is a powerful entity that has total control of any situation. It can manipulate any circumstance, or create an alliance with anyone it wishes. Day after day, We are reminded by the media, in some form or another, that to have the opportunity to be a part of this American institution is a great privilege.

The information the media presents to us comes in different formats. A story is reported because of its human interest value, or we are given performance statistics on our favorite athlete, updated facts on any of the mini-Gods we worship. A touch of a button and we can get twenty-four hour a day programming, so we can digest the same information over and over until we are inebriated with its redundancy.

Americans have allowed themselves to create and worship these sports' idols who appear in the media. I often wonder if we aren't envious of these God-like gladiators at the same time that we are cheering them on from our living rooms. I believe that our inability to deal with our own lack of accomplishments has manifested itself into the dreams and desires of those whose careers are greater than our own. My point is that perhaps we create these idols as a reminder of what we lack in ourselves; therefore, in some cosmic way we are satisfying a void within ourselves that was never fulfilled.

Athletes & Product Endorsements

How does all of this praise and worship affect an athletes' human spirit? This question has never been more relevant than in the present. Today, superstars have the balls to arrogantly state that they don't have to be society's role models!
I guess these man-made superstars think they have the right to suck every possible dime out of our pockets and then tell us that they are not responsible for their actions. In other words, they become leaches to society. They take, but give very little, if nothing back in return.

147

Athletes who manipulate the public through their many contracts and endorsements have a conscientious responsibility to society. This responsibility cannot be shrugged off because of their status and popularity. It is fair to say that not all professionals have this attitude, but we must not tolerate those few that do.

When an athlete endorses a particular product, he is responsible for this as mush as the manufacturer. For example, Shaquille O'Neal does a commercial for Pepsi Cola in which he infers that when an athlete is thirsty he drinks Pepsi, I'm insulted. Pepsi is not a healthy beverage, especially for an athlete.

I understand that this is a very popular drink nationwide; however, to endorse the image that this product will somehow make an athlete respond and play better is an insult to our intelligence. I would like to make it perfectly clear that Mr. O'Neal is a tremendous asset to his sport. It is obvious, that it is his contribution to life that he will finally be judged!

Another case in point is the very entertaining Mc Donald's commercial in which Michael Jordan and Larry Bird are shooting baskets. The television ad is very amusing, the fact is that Mcdonald's food is very unhealthy. This message is totally lost.

I know that I am not the only American who gets a good dose of heartburn and gas every time I eat a Big Mac. I realize that this is very hard to put into an endorsements contract, but an athlete's responsibility should be to endorse products he believes in. Money should not be the factor.

We must disassociate ourselves from these idols that we have created, if for no other reason, than for the selfish act of doing what is best for ourselves. After all, it is the everyday citizen that pays the bill for the high profile existence of athletes. This action cannot change the problem, but through careful and diligent awareness we can initiate a positive change.

The reality of this situation is that athletes cannot play the big game without us! However, when it comes to the political logistics of the game we, the public are the very last to be considered. How quickly we have forgotten the recent strikes that have plagued this institution in the past few years. The continual greed that surrounds these games lets us know just where we stand. We must not be fooled. The American public is the biggest asset in professional sports. Regardless, whenever there is a problem between the players and management, guess who is asked to patiently sit back and wait for the results? That's right, we are the ones told to shut up and sit patiently while they can work things out.

Greed in the professional sports' world continues to grow out of control. It reflects a drug users' addiction to drugs, the more he gets, the more he needs.

A couple of years ago, a couple of friends of mine and I got together and purchased season tickets to the L.A. Clippers. We were disappointed that we were not able to acquire tickets for the L.A. Lakers. We decided to fork out $11,000 and buy two, third row seats at the Sports' Arena. The same seats, for the Lakers, would have cost us almost $30,000. Our excitement peaked when we received our tickets in the mail.

The letter that we received from the Clippers' organization, along with the tickets, burst our bubble. The letter welcomed us to the Clippers' family and included a registration form for a party with the players on the team. The cost was only $60.00 per person. Although my friends were excited to have the opportunity to meet the players, I was absolutely appalled by this blatant solicitation of funds. Such audacity! They wanted to charge us for the privilege of spending an evening with the team's players. I don't think so!

At that very moment I understood very clearly how this element of greed starts at the head and trickles down through the players, the associates, the marketing and the advertising agencies, and anyone else that can make a buck from it.

Needless to say, the following year we canceled our tickets. Hey, with the Clippers' record they should be paying us to come and see them!

My Personal Journey on the Road to Pro Sports Stardom

The dream of someday becoming a professional athlete is special. For many years I had that dream. From the first day of practice in high school, my goal was to one day make it to the big show. Like so many other young Americans, I saw this as the only way to help my family financially. Through sports I would have been able to offer them the type of luxuries they would have never been able to afford. By my sophomore year in college I had lost all hope! The world seemed a very hard place. Three years later, a little spark of hope gave my life a new direction. My softball coach, who was a member of the Houston Sports Writers Association, invited me to one of their weekly luncheons. This particular luncheon was in honor of King Hill, the wide receiver coach of the Houston Oilers Football Team. My heart trembled as I listened attentively to Mr. Hill's speech.
I realized that in front of me was the person who could help my dream to materialize. This made my body shake with nervous energy.

One of the things that sports' training teaches an athlete is to seize the moment and that is just what I did! After the luncheon, I cornered Mr. Hill in the hallway. I introduced myself and asked him if the Oilers were going to have a free-agent camp that year. He regretfully answer "no", but looked me right dead in the eye, and asked" do you know of someone who wants to try out?" I couldn't believe my ears. The opportunity of a lifetime was presenting itself. In joyous disbelief I stuttered that I was interested in the opportunity.

The luncheon was on a Monday and he told me to go see him the following Wednesday in his office at ten o'clock. I was absolutely beside myself. I rushed home, called my family and friends and shared this important news with all of them. That Tuesday afternoon, I tossed the football around anxiously waiting for the Wednesday tryout.

The day of the appointment, I got to his office twenty-five minutes early, anticipating the meeting with Mr. Hill. He walked in and greeted me with, "I'm glad you could make it." It was strange, but after he said those few words, I felt very relaxed.

At that point he gave me a pass and told me to walk across the street to the practice facility.
He said he would meet me there in ten minutes. I found the person they called MoJo and gave him my pass. He treated me like I was royalty.

He asked me if I needed anything and handed me a new jock strap and a pair of Houston Oiler shorts, (the ones with the oil derrick on them.) He asked what size of shoes I wore and I told him thirteen.

When I walked out to the practice field, my world began to move in slow motion! I slowly jogged around the outer edge of the field to loosen up. As I was running, I began to recognize some of the players who were on the team. My heart began to race with excitement.

I was on the football field with the same guys who I had watched play on national television.

King Hill walked out on the field, while most of the players were on their way toward the field house. He called over to Gifford Nelson and Craig Bradshaw (the younger brother of the Pittsburgh Steelers' Terry Bradshaw) and then called out my name. After making the necessary introductions, the two quarterbacks sprinted off in opposite directions, which I thought was kind of odd. The coach told me to run the forty-yard dash and wrote down my best time at 4.54 seconds. He then asked me to run ten pass routes. I ran in one direction on the field for one quarterback and in the opposite direction for the other, without any rest time. Each quarterback would describe the kind of pass rough they were looking for.

After the sixth pass rough, I was absolutely exhausted. Up until the ninth pass, I had dropped the ball only once.

Finally, Gifford had me run a fly pattern straight down the field. After running approximately fifty yards, the football landed perfectly into my hands. I collapsed on one knee and at that point, I was physically drained! Coach Hill dismissed the two quarterbacks and coming towards me, humorously told me that I had to be in shape to play this game. He smiled, patted me on the back, and congratulated me on a job well done.

He then instructed me to give him a call the following day.

I spent the rest of the day trying to evaluate my performance. That evening, I reiterated my experience to friends and family. The next morning, I couldn't wait until ten o'clock to make the big call. I finally made the call and when I heard it ring, I could hear my heart racing faster and faster.

Finally, Mr. Hill's secretary answered and informed me that Mr. Hill wasn't scheduled to come into the óffice that day. I felt as if someone had rammed my heart with a dagger. I left my name and put down the receiver. I continued to call for the next two weeks only to find that Mr. Hill could not be reached. What seemed to be an incredible dream was slowly turning into a horrible nightmare!

On Monday of the third week, I received a call from the Houston Oilers' office.

I can't begin to describe to you how anxious I was feeling.

Mr. Hill told me that he had twelve messages in front of him and they were all from me. He apologized and explained that he had been on a two week vacation. Then the good news, he announced his team wanted to sign me to a two-year contract. He went on to say that I had a lot of potential and thought that I could be an asset to the team. By this time, my whole body was numb! I was to meet him in his office on Wednesday of that week to sign the contracts.

Once I signed my first NFL contract, I began to join a group of new players. I welcomed each day, I felt as if the Gods were smiling graciously upon my head. I began to associate myself more and more with the other players. Never before was the element of male bonding so dominant. For the moment, I was forced to put my excitement aside, because there was a great deal I had to learn.

Since training camp was less than four weeks away, I had very little time to learn the proper etiquette of a professional athlete. Most of my education was self-taught, it came from watching the players around me. I noticed the way they trained, ran, exerted themselves, and most of all, the confident attitude that surrounded all of them. I could see the difference in the players that had played collegiate football.

The experience and the knowledge gained during those four years is invaluable!

Each and everyday the situation improved. I began to feel a little more comfortable with my stance. My communication skills with the quarterback improved tremendously. I became aware of the importance of precision and although most of us were competing for the same positions, we respected one another. We praised each other's strengths instead of focusing on our weaknesses.

Getting together after the short workouts added to the male bonding between the players. I recall one particular conversation regarding a fellow player. A lawsuit had been filed against him, he was being charged by an ex-girlfriend of a sexual offense. She claimed that he ruptured her internally during the sex act. It seemed unusual that the guys spent the whole lunch laughing and commenting on the size of this guy's penis. It was a standing joke that when big John walked into the shower, everyone else left. After one of our practices I finally had the privilege of walking out on John and realized what all the fuss was about. We knew that this particular young lady was justified in her accusations and was likely to win her case. Let's just say that we nicknamed him "Mule Head" and this descriptive phrase was very mild.

The week before the big, two-session-a-day training camp, more of the veteran players started to attend the practices. Their energy was more aggressive than that of the rookies and free agents. It was easy to see how the level of competition escalated three or four levels. The challenge of making the team became more of a threat as well.

Three days before camp, I was having a great day catching the football.

Towards the end of practice, I attempted to catch a poorly thrown ball from one of the quarterbacks (he was known for throwing the ball too hard) and as I reached down to grab the ball, I heard something pop. I didn't think anything was wrong at the time. I made the catch and my peers were congratulating me. Suddenly, I felt a light stinging in my left index finger. I examined it, noticed that the bone had protruded the skin. Needless to say, this needed instant, medical attention. The physician did a thorough examination of my hand, and I was told that I could not catch the football for the next eight weeks. This was a very interesting start to my NFL career!

I was lucky the injury had occurred in the Oilers' facility. Going into camp, I was feeling very optimistic about making the club. The first morning of the "two-a-day" practice I was surrounded by world-class athletes.

Going through calisthenics with such players as Earl Campbell, Billy (White Shoes) Johnson, Kenny (The Snake) Stabler and Jack Tatum, there were moments, when I felt like a kid in a candy store. I knew that this was not the time to be idolizing these men as super heroes, especially if I was going to be competing for their jobs.

Living among the pros, I learned that regardless of how great they were, they were just as human as I was!I never understood why learning that simple truth was such a surprise!

I remember feeling disappointed when I saw one of these great men trip and fall over a small blade of grass or drop a pass a third grader could have caught. I came to the realization that I could actually compete on their level. I had conditioned myself my entire life for this special opportunity. I was right in the center of professional athletics. The fact that I was there has given me a very candid perspective on the world of professional athletics. Seeing the game without all the media and hoopla, allows one to view the world with a sense of realism.

Although I was a newcomer to the game of professional football, I was instantly treated like a mini-God. Interviews from sportscasters were an everyday occurrence. The following incident is a reminder of how Americans view the world of sports.

One afternoon, I walked into a restaurant in Houston, Texas, for lunch. One of the customers immediately recognized me as the receiver for the Houston Oilers. The manager overheard us talking and joined our conversation. He was hoping the Oilers would have a winning ball club that season. In less than ten minutes a crowd had gathered inside and soon everyone was coming up to me for autographs and handshakes. The manager, although he did not know me from Adam, told me that my meal was complimentary.   In the mist of all this excitement, I was the only one who noticed a homeless man looking inside the restaurant window. Soon, his presence began to annoy the management and customers. The manager boldly drove the transient away. He treated this unfortunate soul as if he had the plague or some kind of contagious disease. The manager was cheered by the patrons of the restaurant and as he walked back to my table, ordered me another free refill on my drink.

I was very excited about the course my life was taking, but I also realized the extent of false security that surrounded this world. When I left the restaurant, I spotted the transient a few yards away, sitting under a huge sign. I called to him and gave him a few dollars for lunch.

I apologized for the manager's insensitive behavior and the unjust treatment he had received. As I walked towards my car, I noticed a couple of the patrons waving anxiously trying to get my attention. At that moment, I came to the conclusion that the world we live in doesn't have the slightest clue about what is important in life.

My first lessons at the Oilers training camp were very informative. This circus was nothing more than a breeding ground for the worship of the "would-be superstar." Inside of me, I heard a little voice cry out. I realized that I had allowed myself to become more than a part of the game. I had been invited to the greatest party of the world, only to find out that I didn't like most of the guests. I experienced a great deal of internal turmoil. Part of me was fighting to stay in the big party, and the other part of me was fighting to stay true to myself and not get caught up in the false worship that surrounded the world of professional athletics. My broken finger kept me from actively catching the football during most of training camp, but I still had a great chance to play the game. I learned that to have a legitimate shot at making the roster you had to get your name on the *special teams roster*. I was happy to see my name listed with four of the teams.

Before I go any further, let me share with you the athlete's frame of mind during this period.

Training camp triggers a roller coaster of emotions. It is a physically exhausting experience for all the athletes. There is a great degree of anxiety that permeates the atmosphere, every session is a do or die situation. Players are often afraid to attend the meal after practice, because it is at that time that the pink slips are handed out. Let's just say these slips are not handed out for a job well done! I have watched grown men break down and sob like newborn babies after receiving one of these rejection slips. Many of the pink slips are handed out in the morning at the breakfast meeting. Every player realizes that if he isn't approached by a member of the organization he will have another practice session to try and prove himself.
Oftentimes, a missed tackle or dropped ball will determine a player's future.
Shortly after I was given the go ahead by the team physician to start catching the football, I was handed my first pink slip.

I walked into Coach Phillips's office and for a moment, time stood still. I don't know if it was due to the mysticism associated with his great character or the simple fact that I had never been able to speak to him one-on-one before, but I felt as if I was face-to-face with a divine presence! Looking over the top of his glasses, he said, "Tough break with the finger." He went on to explain that on Friday of that week the team roster had to be cut down to sixty players.

Because of my broken finger, the coaches hadn't had an opportunity to take a good look at my performance. The bad news was that they needed to cut me from the roster, the good news was that they wanted to invite me back the following year. It appears that a little hope went a long way.
I stood up and said, "Sir, thank you for the opportunity." I walked out the door and stood alone on the sidewalk, many things went through my mind.

I looked over at the group of receivers who had once been my teammates. The count was down to seven. Originally the team had started out with twenty-two and now they were down to seven. With each day of training the numbers had become smaller and smaller. I quickly brushed away a teardrop. I had come a very long way from the playground of my youth on Cliffdale Avenue. I walked back to my room and felt truly isolated. It seemed as if my dream of becoming a professional athlete had died. The last ten years of my life flashed before me and suddenly I felt cheated out of my just reward!

In the background, someone shouted a word of praise to Billy "Whites Shoes" Johnson. I didn't look back, but I heard my ex-teammates laughing and I knew that Billy must have been doing his famous chicken dance.

A year later, I finally signed again with Houston, but this time there was a catch. Because I had been on their roster the previous year, the team had to place me on waiver for a twenty-four hour period. Since I was a relatively unknown, the Houston coaches thought no one would claim me off of waivers. They took a gamble and lost.
I was claimed by three, different teams during that twenty-four hour period.

The New York Jets, the Kansas City Chiefs, and the New Orleans Saints all claimed me while I was on waivers. The Jets had the worst win-loss record of all three teams. They were granted the same contract that I had just signed with the Oilers. I learned of this from an article in the local newspaper. Three days later, I received a call from the New York Jets welcoming me to join them for mini-camp within the next two weeks.

I was aware of the Jets' 12-4 record, I also knew that they had a good crop of receivers. I began to make a realistic assessment of my chances. One important thing I had learned from my experience with the Houston Oilers was that a team will often bring players into their camp just to have extra players during the team's preseason to work out.

At this point, it was very important to assess my situation. My involvement in professional sports had taught me how to present myself.

Athletes are the instruments that make up the orchestra. Each player is an integral part of the whole, but a player can be replaced at a moment's notice. The sooner an athlete understands this, the better his or her chances of survival!
Professional sports provide athletes with the best physical training, conditioning, and health care available. It is also to the owner's advantage to make these facilities available. The athlete who's in top form becomes an even greater asset to the business.

The New York Jets organization was second to none in monies spent to build a winning ball club. In just a one week period during camp, the team spent nearly $ 80,000 to feed the team. Many people wondered why the Jets had such a poor season! I will assure you that it's not because of the lack of food on their training table.

There was one thing that made me weary about their operation. It began with the first speech by the owner of the team. He incorporated the slang "God damn!" some two hundred times in his orientation. This is no exaggeration! It seemed to me as if every member of this organization, from the top-level executives to the coaches, trainers and players, used this negative phrase. Some of you are thinking that this has little to do with the team's losses.

Well, let's just say that if I were God, I don't think I would bless a team with victories if it was constantly using my name in vain! It is no wonder they have not had a winning season in the last fifteen years!

A couple of weeks before camp, I was working on a construction job in Houston Texas.

I was trying to install a skylight, but because of a bad rainstorm, I slipped, fell off the roof, and broke a bone in my left wrist. Despite of this injury, I was ready to begin training in New York. Except for my wrist, I was in the best shape of my life. Unfortunately for me, the damage to my wrist happened outside of camp. I could not report it to the Jet's organization or I would have lost my opportunity to try out for the ball club.

At that time, I justified that a little pain was a small price to endure for the chance of fulfilling a lifelong dream. In that three-month period I felt that I had a good chance of making the ball club, especially after the Jets released a couple of big money, big name, wide receivers. The energy level was more intense with the New York Jets organization.

During a practice session of offensive drill, the squad was lined up ready to run a play, suddenly Bear Bryant and Joe Naimath decided to graciously visit our workout. I was in awe of how these two men caused such a commotion.

Most of the athletes were caught up with the presence of these two men. It was as if God and an Archangel had descended from the heavens. It took forty-five minutes before we could resume our afternoon practice! At that point our concentration was severely broken!

On a Friday morning before the actual season was to start I was all excited because there was only one practice to go and I found myself still on the roster. The season's opener was to be in Denver, the following Sunday. That morning, I called my best friend to see if he and his dad would fly up to watch my first game. Before I could hang up the phone, I received that dreaded knock at my door. It was one of the trainers, telling me that the coach wanted to see me. Ten minutes later, I was in Michael's office. Before I could say anything, he rambled on with his dog and pony show. He said that they were looking for a receiver to replace Wesley Walker and Lamb Jones. He candidly told me that they had hoped it could have been me. Mind you, these two men were both world-class sprinters. In fact, Lamb was clocked at a 4.29 forty-yard dash. That year, he was one of the fastest players in the NFL. Ironically, he didn't catch a pass in any of the first seven ball games of that season! So much for the selection process. Anyway, they let me go.

After the New York incident, I lost my heart for the game of football. I did; however, go try out for a couple of USFL teams over the following years. I think the fact that I got so close to a dream and fell short was a great disappointment.

It seemed as if I had spent most of my life preparing myself for this level of athletics.

Once there, I found it to be less divine than what I was brought up to believe. Like many other athletes, I allowed myself to get caught up in the pageantry of the game. With that understanding, I later came to recognize its true worth. Those who have had the opportunity to achieve stardom will agree that the game has been jaded with corporate greed, nepotism, politics, idol worship and the exaggeration of human talent.

Final Thoughts on Sports

In this chapter, I have shared my views on sports, a world that I know well. I can sum it all up this way: this giant institution has become careless with its creation of what I call *the take, take attitude.* This institution continues to extract from society all that it can, with little effort of giving anything back. Consider the tremendous amount of money that professional sports generate.

I would be surprised if the donations given back to society amount to more than ten percent of their total income. In an age of the multi-million-dollar a year contracts. Let's take a long, close look at this institution, especially since we are ultimately the ones responsible for paying these absurd contracts. Throughout this chapter, I have touched on the many assets that American sports offer society. However, the question that we need to ask ourselves is: *Do these assets outweigh the liabilities created by the sports industry?* Point of fact, this institution has made it perfectly clear that our only right is the right to praise and worship their heroes. That is our only purpose. You can bet your bottom dollar that if these institutions decide to go on strike or relocate their team, they will do it and the public won't have any say-so. We are a society that is easily manipulated, but this is how we can change the situation. All we have to do is say; enough is enough! Let's have the wisdom to put all this into its proper perspective. Athletes with endorsements are just human beings with opinions, nothing more. We have to show enough integrity to analyze the quality of their existence, for ourselves. It's that simple! Let's not continue to fuel their advancement with our resources. And remember, sports simply revolves around a game.

This is not something that will change the quality of our future. The salaries of the players have gotten out of proportion. The next time a professional sports' organization goes on strike for more money, we must refuse to support that institution for two to three years.

This is the only way that we can show them our power.

All we would have to do is to stop patronizing sporting events and I will guarantee you that we will gain their attention. Do you think that such a drastic measure will change the structure of professional sports? You will see that the real power lies in our hands.

Don't buy into their propaganda. Yes, we have created these idols. The big question is, does America care? What has become apparent is that these creations will burden us for a lifetime.

It is important that Americans stop settling for the crumbs that are offered to us by the professional institutions. Once we become aware of this, I think we can personally create a better institution. After all, America, let's not forget that these are simply games people play.

EDUCATION

"I will study and get ready, and perhaps my chance will come"

**Abraham Lincoln
16th President of the United States**

CHAPTER FOUR

Fools of Education!

Education, a word for the wise or a word for the foolish? There was a time when the words *fool* and *education* would hardly ever be found in the same sentence, but today one has to question whether or not these words have managed to take on the same meaning. America's educational system should be considered our greatest resource; however, it is apparent that we have some major challenges in front of us. The title of this chapter should spark some curiosity with my readers and eventually you will understand its meaning.

In reading about this controversial topic, I want to capture your attention and interest. I believe that an exploration of this subject can change what kids learn in the classroom but also how they apply that knowledge to the world in which we live.

The Need for Change, Heeding its Call

There has never been a time in history when the educational system of this country has been so openly challenged, by educators and laymen alike. Ask yourself this question. Twenty-five years ago was it a common occurrence to have kids killing kids or students killing teachers? Was it an everyday occurrence to see security guards roaming the hallways of our cities' schools? Let's not forget the rampant use of drugs which are reaching the elementary school level. The only drug I was aware of, when I was in school, was aspirin and it came from the school nurse.

The student illiteracy rate is at an all-time high, despite America's advancement in communications and technology. The level of education in America has reached an all time low and we find ourselves falling behind many second-world countries. One issue that I would like for you to be aware of is this. America's problem with education are self-inflicted. That's right! It's hard to believe, but this is something we have allowed to happen! Whether consciously or subconsciously, socially or politically, we have allowed ourselves to use poor judgment. In this chapter, I am going to try to explain how this happened as well as its repercussions.

Sometimes we allow ourselves to stroll along in life, dealing with and accepting things as they happen. Many of us never question ourselves. "What does it truly take to change the life in front of me?" These people are often not afraid to ask questions and to boldly demand answers. These individuals partake in shaping the course and direction of this nation.

They are not afraid to go back and correct the mistakes they made and admit to their indiscretions! I hope that you will be moved to join those of us that are in this second category (if you're not there already!)

The Deed Behind Our Misdirection

Throughout our history, many poor decisions have been made by countless leaders which have reflected on the rest of the world. This has forced us to ask ourselves if we are a nation that has been blessed with great wisdom. There are many ghosts in our closet. We would like to sweep under the rug, (or simply forget) the overt confiscation of land from the Native Americans, the widespread use of slavery, the nuclear bombs dropped on Hiroshima, and the assassination of three exceptional leaders. All these issues have changed the direction of our nation.

In this chapter, I am going to bring to your attention another tremendous atrocity.
Before I share my thoughts with you, I want you to evaluate what you are about to read. It is important for you to understand that change can never take place without first initiating a change of heart!
What is this drastic deed that has changed the direction of our educational system?
Although many of you are probably not ready to accept the following statement, I'm hoping that by the end of this chapter you will have a change of heart and a clear understanding as to why I feel the way I do. Hopefully, by now I have created enough anticipation to peak your curiosity.
What, do you ask, has America done to slap herself in the face and ultimately change the course and direction of this nation? In my most humble opinion, America has taken out of her educational system her greatest asset of all, her **GOD!** That's right! The elimination of **God** from the educational system has caused countless repercussions. Those of you who immediately disagree with this statement, I encourage you to read on and understand why I feel this way!
The primary function of education should be the increase of knowledge. This should be followed by guidance, communication and direction.

This world seems to create opportunities in which it can turn itself away from *God.*

Education is simply just another means by which these efforts continue to grow. You can read more about this course of action in my chapter, " Religion, Does Anyone Even Care?" I believe that the chapter on religion will also help you look at the overall picture of the world we live in.

The *Bible* says that, "**GOD** is the increase of *all* things." Education of course falls into the category of all things. Quite frankly, we have foolishly allowed the principal source of our knowledge to be erased from the structure of education. Hello! What was America thinking?

Sometimes I think that the smarter we appear to be, the more foolish we become! Now I don't want this chapter to sound like a Sunday school lesson, but I feel that we must go directly to the core of the matter. Let me share with you a few verses from the *Bible* that will enlighten your views on this issue. In the book of Psalms 19:7, " The law of the Lord is perfect, restoring the testimony of the Lord is sure, making wise the simple." Psalms 111:10, "The fear of the Lord is the beginning of wisdom, a good understanding have all they that do his commandments." Palms 119:130 " The entrance of thy words giveth light; it giveth understanding to the simple."

Proverbs 1:5, "A wise man hear, and will increase learning," Proverbs 1:7, The fear of the Lord is the beginning of knowledge: but the fool despises wisdom and understanding."
It appears as if these verses predicted that America would someday turn her back on God!

It doesn't take a genius to figure out at which point the problems originated regarding our educational system. The removal of **GOD** from the school system started the deterioration of our educational system. This simple act has caused many irreversible repercussions to society.

There are those of you who feel that God has nothing to do with our children's behavior or what they become as adolescents. Many are in abnegations to the fact that when God was taken from the schools, our children's educational environment became one of fear and despair. Is there any correlation between the slow progress in education and the removal of **GOD.** I know that there are those of you who would argue that we have made tremendous advancements. Americans are in denial regarding the lack of advancements in education. There is no doubt that this country has made tremendous progress in the field of technology and communication, but what about the minds of our youth?

In the sixties and seventies, when I was in school, school seemed to have a certain wondrous energy. The day would start with a prayer coming from the overhead P.A. System.
Although many of us weren't aware of it at the time, our days seemed to be filled with peace and tranquility. I felt as if I was being watched and guided by the hand of someone or something very special. As this chapter unfolds, I want you to formulate questions in your mind which are instigated by the reality of my words. If in fact, we are responsible for the state of our educational institution, then let us realize how simple it could be for this nation to turn things around.

I want you to follow closely as you read on. There is a verse in Chapter 23 of Proverbs that says, "Speak not in the ears of the fool: for he will despise the wisdom of thy words." I hope that all of you will gain wisdom from this chapter.

The Blame Game

An issue I want to deal with, (which keeps resurfacing) is the lack of responsibility taken by all of us, concerning the direction of America's educational system.
I often hear parents blaming teachers for the poor quality of education that their children are getting.

Students blaming teachers for their inability to teach them. Teachers blaming the administration for the lack of funding, and the administration blaming the government for its woes.

The one thing that truly saddens me is that with this present attitude there is very little possibility for improvement. Blaming someone else for our mistakes will not resolve the problem. I do not want to sound as if I'm being a pessimist, but I sense that this country simply has reached the point of no return.

At this time, the best that I can offer you is a broad look at the annihilation of the American educational system, as we know it. If you can see the eventual outcome of how we are conducting the business of educating our children, then you will understand how I arrived at the title for this chapter.

The Development of An Educational System

Throughout history, looking back at the institution of education, we can see that it has had tremendous growth potential. For instance, let's review the development of education in Europe, the homeland of many of America's early settlers. History teaches us that education was originally only available to the wealthy.

At first, the books available for study were transcribed by hand and only the rich could afford them. Most children were taught at home by their parents. Eventually, teachers began traveling from town to town setting up schools in rented rooms. Children were taught the 3 R's-reading, writing and arithmetic. Many churches began assuming the responsibility of educating the children of the parish. The ideas and attitudes taught in Europe during this period are still part of our educational development today.

In 1455 a German by the name of Johannes Gutenburg published the first printed bible. This created a great change, and as the process of printing progressed, books became more and more accessible and so did peoples's desire to learn.

In America, it wasn't until educational policies were adopted that the availability of an education began to accelerate in this country. The Massachusetts School Law of 1647 required that every town with fifty families or more have an elementary school teacher. This law marked the birth of the American public school system.

Many of the fathers of the American constitution were also considered the fathers of our educational system. Benjamin Franklin founded a school in the 1750's which he named "An Academy." This eventually became the model for the modern American high school.

Benjamin Franklin believed that every man should be given the right to an education no matter the color of his skin! Thomas Jefferson; however, spoke of education with two voices. He said that those people who have the right to vote should also have access to free education. This education should be separated from the church and be paid by tax dollars.

(In another voice) he stated his position on the issue of education for blacks.

He favored education for Blacks, but pertaining to industrial and agricultural aspect only. Although Jefferson had black blood running through his veins, his actions were to satisfy those who carried his skin color. Many of Jefferson's thoughts and plans were initially opposed by his peers, but they eventually became the groundwork for the establishment of public schools.

However, it was not until the nineteenth century that America focused on creating a prototype for a public school system, giving all children the right to an elementary school education. History offered all-white or so-called white Americans the opportunity to learn regardless of their economic background.

These common schools created a standard of education, providing all who attended with the same curriculum. This helped all children coming from other countries to adapt to this new system.

Because of the steady growth in population, this philosophy was quickly adopted across the land.

Of course, this philosophy did not embrace the black man. We were still considered the white man's property and any form of education was prohibited. Eventually, education would be available to all Americans instead of just the chosen few.

If we ignore the total isolation of the black man from any learning, then the educational development of this nation was created on a solid foundation. The fact of the matter is that as much as I would like to pat the white man on the back for his good intentions, I cannot do so without feeling nauseated. How could they have considered themselves righteous when they totally ignored another race of people from the process of learning? This fact will always be a constant reminder of the white man's arrogance.

Unfortunately, it seems that whatever subject is involved, it always falls back on this same theme. Throughout history, the white man has created episodes that have managed to blemish his character. As an author first and a black author second, I try to be fair and honest with my thoughts and writings.

I hate to constantly ridicule the white man; however, it takes a true magician.

To be able to write about any history involving the white man and not come to the same conclusion.

I have found ways to overcome the hurdles of possible resentment. One is to remind myself of the countless white Americans who helped to change the injustices of the past. Another thing that helps me get past this obstacle is to remember that the white man is still my brother. Anytime I refer to my white brother, you should be aware of my effort to hold the anger and bitterness in check. After all, one might find himself disliking a member of his own family, but that dislike must never turn into hatred, (at least not without hating a part of ourselves). wherever we feel this hatred destroying a brother, consider the story of Cain and Abel and ask yourselves, what is truly behind this kind of hatred?

A great number of my white brothers didn't see it fit to include my race of people in their ultimate plan. Black Americans; however, had a slightly unique beginning in their struggle to achieve literacy.

The Issue of Black Access to Education
Before & After the End of Slavery

Before I start to set the stage for my thoughts on early education for the black man, I feel I must draw you a picture of what it was like for us at that time.

182

The American Black Education Movement came to life in 1865, at the end of the Civil War. To a large degree, this movement became a reality because of the emancipation of blacks which occurred in January of 1863. Education also grew from seeds that had been planted much earlier. The first form of education for blacks began around 1674, when a number of slave owners *elected* to provide a certain amount of schooling for their Black and Indian slaves. A religious leader named John Elliot also made tremendous strides toward the education of slaves, teaching them the scriptures.

Before the Civil War, the northern blacks were more likely to have access to the same education as the white man, but it was a rarity. At this time, only 1.7 percent of black, school aged children were enrolled in a limited number of schools, which were available to them. Because there was no organized educational system for blacks and education was not obtainable for our people in all locales, black schools became known as (scatter) schools.

In the South, before the war, the law prohibited blacks from any form of structured learning. In the southern states, blacks were prohibited from any type of learning and any deviation from the law carried with it tremendous risks.

It is hard to imagine at that time, it was against the law for blacks to have books in their possession with the intention of reading its contents. It was also prohibited for a Black person to read or write. This alone should encourage children, especially Black kids, to cherish the precious opportunity to learn and not to take education for granted.

Whites in the South feared that education might lead to revolt. They knew that education would empower the Black man and he would realize the injustice and mistreatment of his people. The white man was (subconsciously or consciously) aware that by giving the Black man the opportunity to acquire knowledge, a number of events would transpire that would ultimately change the course of events.

If we were to honestly look at the meaning of education, we would see that it resembles a source of light. This light helps us to see clearly those things we are trying to understand. If education becomes a basis for comprehension of the world around us, it is easy to understand why it was so important for the white man to keep this light of learning from us.

Why was it so important to keep this knowledge from our people? Unfortunately, the answer draws a very negative picture regarding the White man's character.

To hold back this precious natural resource from another human being, would only be done if one wanted to keep the residuals of life all to himself. Am I saying that the White man was being selfish? Socrates, a great philosopher of ancient Greece made a point of asking his students questions to stimulate their thought process. I like that philosophy, it seems to exclude the need for being right or wrong.

Was the white man being selfish or was he simply trying to protect his lifestyle? It is very easy to see that the black man was one of the white man's greatest resources at that time. To preserve his access to this resource, the southerner had to remain steadfast regarding education of blacks. Was this right or wrong?

I personally think that the methods by which he chose to accomplish his goals stain the source of his integrity. I use the word *stain* because history teaches us that our white brothers clearly made supreme efforts to create the laws that kept minorities from obtaining many privileges.

If we were to turn the pages of history to the early seventeen hundreds, we would witness the following. In 1703, a law in Boston, Massachusetts, established a 9:00 p.m. curfew for native Americans, blacks and mulattos.

This was to prevent possible uprisings and disturbances which were brought about by their unfair treatment. Rhode Island prohibited householders from entertaining blacks or native American servants in their homes after the nine o'clock hour as well.

In an effort to legally protect themselves from possible retaliation from minorities, the white man passed even more laws along this vein.

One such law created in 1708 in Connecticut, imposed a penalty not to exceed thirty lashes for any black "who disturbed the peace, or who attempted to strike a white person."

The question of how important the slave was to the white man, can be determined by viewing the responsibilities of blacks to the white master. Let me explain our duties to our white landlords. A simple chore such as the feeding of the household, consisted of much more than first meets the eye. The task of feeding the White man began with the raising and caring of his animals: the cattle, chickens, hogs sheep, etc. When the animals were ready to be butchered, the slaves cleaned and made all the necessary preparations. Since animals served many purposes, they made sure that every part of the animal was put to good use. Clothing, garments, utensils, jewelry, were all created from the slaughtered animals.

Of course, if the master wanted vegetables to go with his dinner, slaves had to clear the land, plow the soil. They grew corn, potatoes, rice, cabbage, tomatoes, peas, carrots and greens. (Working in the fields kept them bent over for most of the day.) This psychologically made them very humble and subservient. Our efforts fed the white man as well as, other people who paid him for these goods.

Of course, this meant triple the work. In most cases, very large profits were made from the black man's efforts. Needless to say, since we weren't allowed to keep the books, it was easier for us to be oblivious to the goings-on of the plantation owners.

Our white forefather prescribed a certain philosophy, "what we don't know can't hurt."

The pursuit of knowledge is a force that originates from a source much greater than ourselves.

I say this because of the fact that it does not carry with it any of the negative energies that often surround mankind.

Did our white brothers understand the fact that with the consumption of knowledge the black man's lifestyle would change? You're damn right he did! To be treated as a human being would have created a gigantic adjustment for the Black man. However, by keeping the enslaved man ignorant, the illusion of safety was re-enforced, at least for a time anyway.

Many might think that keeping the black man uneducated was all about creating wealth for the white man. That's not even the tip of the iceberg. One of the few mystical things about knowledge is that it finds its way to any and all who pursue it. The black man was no exception. The introduction of Christianity helped the black man speed up his quest for knowledge. In many cases, the study of religion was the 'light' that helped him to see clearly.

He realized that he was not a worthless entity. A concept that our white brother so diligently tried to make us believe. The White race does not stand alone in this area. All races have been guilty of transgressions at one time or another.

After the emancipation of the black man in the early 1860's, the church was the conduit for the channeling of information. Four million newly-freed blacks created a monumental challenge for America. In the aftermath of the Civil War emerged a free, black man. It also forced the White man to see that because of his treatment to his slaves, he had created an ignorant, black man. Ignorant of knowledge, uninformed, but not stupid. The South was not willing to make any form of education accessible to Blacks. A great migration of mission-aries and teachers began to infiltrate the South, bringing with them the desire to spread both knowledge and the gospel.

They quickly realized they were going to have to change the hearts of both blacks and whites. (The mentality of both races had to first be torn down and then rebuilt by the crusaders coming out of the North.)

I came across a couple of quotes in the book,*"Been in the Storm So Long"* that expressed the sentiments of many blacks and whites during that time in history. The first is a quote from a black driver who explains the situation between the two races. It was April of 1866 and the driver was living on Fish Pond Plantation in Louisiana.
"Wat's de use ob niggers pretending' I am studying. Ober spellin-book, an' makin' b lieve if de could larn. Wat's de use? Wat's de be but niggers wen dey gits through? Nigger good for nothing' but wuck in de fiel' an' make cotton."

After reading this quote, I question how a black man of any era could even fix his lips to say something of that nature. I realize that those words simply expressed the mentality of the times. There were just as many blacks who considered themselves unworthy as whites.
The next quote is from a white woman who is giving advise to a teacher.
" You might as well try to teach your horse or mule to read, as to teach these niggers. They can't learn... Had been aimed at the house servant and urban Blacks."

"Some of these were smart enough for anything. But the country niggers are like monkeys, you can't learn them to come in when it rains."

I have often heard it said that ignorance truly has no color; I guess that this is evident here! What bothers me the most about those two quotes is that a great number of Americans today still have that same kind of mentality.

I don't think that any of us can begin to imagine how the missionaries and teachers of that day must have felt walking into the lives of these southerners. Most of the teachers entering the south were white, with the exception of a small handful of educated black instructors from the North who wanted to do anything to help their race of people. The agenda was enormous!

They faced the task of teaching blacks the basic skills of reading, spelling and the gospel, as well as the intellectual and personal development of such virtues as self-reliance, frugality and sobriety. They also needed to learn about relationships and moral responsibility. And last, but not least, blacks needed to learn how to conduct themselves as free men and free women and how to interact with those who had only recently held them as slaves.

As we look back into history, it is easy to see that teachers have always had their hands full.

Many teachers felt the initial strain of separating blacks from the years of negative behavior as a result of being enslaved and treated as animals. It's a fact that many Blacks, for a great period of time after the emancipation, couldn't wean themselves from their old lifestyle. Many of them continued to fall back on the breast of their former masters. The teachers of that time were faced with numerous negative aspects of fear, driven by deception, such as thievery and a filthy unfit environment. Many of these instructors found these negative elements to be intolerable. They had difficulty of handling the responsibilities of educating those who lacked patience as well as understanding.

It is plain to see that today's challenges in education don't even come close to the ones of the past. Today, it is a lot easier to teach the sentiment of patriotism and love of country. In the past, blacks (had to accept being) taught by the same race of people that had previously burned down their churches and newly built schools. The complexion of American society was a true mixture. There were a large number of whites who were willing to give their lives to stop the advancement of black education; however, the black man must not forget that there were also a great number of white Americans that stood alone in the belief that all Americans should have the right to an education.

In many cases they also put their lives on the line. Whites helped to pass many bills that were eventually turned into law.

One of these laws was the Civil Rights Act of 1866. This law was created to discredit the statutes of the colonial era, which were used by plantation owners to keep their former slaves as hired help.

This act would have given citizenship to blacks and equal rights to all citizens of every race and color. Men of all races would have been able to enter into the following: contracts, sue, testify in court, purchase, hold and dispose of property, and enjoy equal full benefits of the law. At that time, the bill was passed by both houses of Congress, but it was eventually vetoed by President Andrew Johnson; however, the bill gain life with a later administration.

I find it very hard to accept that the President of the United States of America actually allowed his supporters to convince him to make such a poor decision! I guess it is more important to note that the bill eventually got passed, that the obstacles it had to go through to get there!

Although most of the Northerns didn't believe in slavery, they didn't support education for Blacks, they only tolerated it. This was considered to be the liberal approach.

In the South; however, there was strong, open opposition on the education issue. The education of blacks was considered a major factor in the demise of slavery. Talk of education for the black man infuriated the white Southerners. The hostilities of the angry whites increased with every step towards educating blacks. This hostility was present even before the notion of integrating the schools ever entered the nation's mind.

To try to evaluate what the heart of America must have been like during that period in history is something that I'm sure many of us would have a real difficulty doing.

Many of us have read about it, and there might even be a few Americans whose ancestors have passed down unbelievable stories or accounts of their lives. In an era when education was sketching the face of a nation, it provided a unique atmosphere and energy that I don't believe has ever been matched in any other country's history.

If I were to create a scale to measure the level of intensity and emotions that were stirred by this effort, I'm sure that it would register high on the scale and would be on the verge of erupting. To question which side was right or wrong in their opinions would be an easy way to view this period. However, one must consider the realities of the times and remember that the adjustments for the South were enormous.

During this time era, America found herself suffering a tremendous amount of growing pains.

In fact, the South felt strongly enough about slavery to fight and risk its survival. To interpret the conditions of that time, it is apparent that both blacks and whites suffered greatly.

I believe the mentality of both races evolved slowly.

One of the major problems at the time was the lack of funds to keep the school system alive. The Southern blacks didn't have the luxury of sending their kids to private institutions.

Books and supplies were always at a minimum, and the constant destruction of schools and churches by hostile whites made it almost impossible to keep the movement alive. Ironically enough, the challenge of finances has gone full circle. To this day, it remains one of America's greatest obstacles.

We will have an opportunity to look at today's financial woes as related to education a little later in this chapter.

Education's explosion, in the Southern states, had a greater importance beyond blacks learning how to read and write. It ultimately reshaped the way in which Americans would look at one another. You see, although education carries with it the basic fundamentals, of what was being taught and learned at certain levels, it also extended itself beyond those boundaries into a whole new world of enlightenment.

To explain this better, we can simplify it. After the Civil War, education provided the black man with the opportunity of seeing himself in a whole new light. The emergence of education encountered tremendous opposition, but it still went on to accomplish its true purpose. It added truth to the belief that *all men **are** created equal.*

If all men are said to be created equal it would first have to become a fact. Education for all simply gave this credo an opportunity to flourish. As it stood, the structure of education would never have allowed this nation to reach its full potential without making a complete mockery of itself.

There is no doubt that many white men of this era felt Blacks were simply an inferior race of people. Perhaps they did not realize that it was their embedded restrictions that made this a truism. Ok, so maybe I'm being extremely generous. I'm pretty positive that the white man was quite aware of what was happening!

Therefore I have tried to avoid this mockery by toning down the content of the material by my comments and reflections.

I hope this will show the reader how easily we can learn to view the often difficult history of this nation in a different way.

When education for blacks filtered its way to the South, what it ultimately did for this country was lay the groundwork for the kind of nation our visionaries had truly desired. The formula of "equality for all mankind" never had a greater ally than the struggles this nation found herself a part of involving education of the early nineteenth century! Sure the struggles were surrounded by racism and negativity, but it was the overcoming of those struggles which gave us progress.

Future Developments in Black Education

Although the years following the Civil War were considered to be a long, painful period in the history of education in America, the challenges were not over, they continued to develop in the twentieth century. Extending education even further meant meeting plenty of obstacles and traveling miles of rocky terrain. The major issues in the south gradually would change from whether or not blacks should be taught in schools to whether or not two races of people should be obligated to attend school together. This dilemma would continue to test the content of the white man's character for the next few decades.

Most of the support for blacks was still coming from the North in the form of laws and legislation.

I wish I could say that these laws were the result of the North's noble attempt to contribute its efforts to help my people.

However, as you look back into history you find many situations to which you can apply the philosophy that "you don't get something for nothing." For example, take the Fifteenth Amendment of the Constitution. Here's how it reads, "The right of any citizen of United States to vote shall not be denied or abridge by the United States or by any state on account of race, color, or previous condition of servitude." This amendment appears to be a very genuine effort towards making Americans equal; however, the simple fact is that it was drafted by Republicans. They realized that the black vote in the South had won many of them their seats in Congress. This aspect shines a different light on the issue of blacks and their right to vote.

Education for all Americans began to create a contagious energy that seemed to spread like wildfire throughout the nation. It fed the desperate need to communicate with one another and to understand the laws that were the instruments of true freedom. In fact, it was the understanding of these laws that helped blacks and whites in the South struggle throughout the pages of history. These pages ultimately took on the challenges of the Civil Rights Movement.

It was becoming obviously clear that our forefathers had created the blueprint for justice and that all Americans had the right to fight and claim it for themselves.

I often ask myself, if it were not for ignorance, would the need for education exist? Is it not the lack of understanding that creates a need for understanding? If there is any truth in these statements, then the pages of history had to unfold the way they did.

All of the early struggles and challenges encountered by our educational system were simply stumbling blocks placed in our path for us to overcome. I'm by no means excusing or accepting the troubles of the past, to do this is to discredit the tremendous accomplishments of our ancestors. There is no doubt that nothing we can do or say can compare with the struggles they had to overcome to make our country what it is today.

The Challenges of Today

Our current educational system has its own set of stumbling blocks. Whether we created these hurdles or not, will determine the progress that this country will make. It is you and I who will be writing the pages of history which future Americans will be reading.

Will they see confusion, ignorance and a lack of understanding in the current period of our educational system? Or on the other hand, will they see the strength, courage and discipline that it took to overcome the obstacles in our way?

I think that it is important for us to ask ourselves if we are faced with problems that are different from those of the past or do we have the same problems with different faces?

These institutions of higher learning cannot legally segregate, but don't be deluded, wealth has and will always be a method of discrimination and separation! If, in fact, asking questions is the first step towards progress, then the sooner we ask ourselves these questions the sooner we'll be able to create solutions to our problems! I have often said that there is nothing new in this world, everything has been here before.

If this is the case, then we must learn the art of recognizing the past when it appears in the present.

Lack of financial resources have always been a challenge in education. Is it any different today? I don't think so. We simply have new terms to replace the old ones, words such as 'cutbacks' and 'discontinuing of programs.' The wealthy private schools are still with us today. They are the parochial schools, or if I might be so bold, their names are synonymous with Princeton, Harvard and Yale.

If we were to turn our backs on the fact that these great institutions continue to carry with them the " separate but equal" philosophies of old, then we would be fooling ourselves.

Several months ago I was reading a rather in-depth article in the *Los Angeles Times*. The headline of the article was "Some Regents Seek UCLA Admissions Priority for Friends." Those who sought help included several people who had pushed to end affirmative action. State officials also asked for special favors.

This full-page article summed up the old adage that those that have get more versus those who have not get less. Whether these philosophies are right or wrong, still remains to be debated.

Turning Point in American Education

Looking at the commitment the government has made to clean up the residual waste of our educational system, of the late sixties and seventies, we can see that the attempted effort has been futile. Schools have begun to slowly deteriorate. At one point, the concept to integrate this nation felt as if America was honoring the structure of the constitution of the United States. This brief moment of fatuous energy didn't last very long.

In an effort to please a white woman's hard-on for her atheist attitudes, the United States government made what I consider to be the single, most unintelligent maneuver in the history of education in America. Somehow, this woman managed to win a lawsuit which determined that it was unconstitutional to allow morning prayer in schools. Wow! Did she ever put a mojo on the people of this country. This woman managed to overturn almost three hundred years of progress in our educational institution. Many Americans still can't see that this one event has caused many indirect reactions. That's ok.

It is my purpose, in writing this chapter, to bring to your attention certain issues that the general public considers taboo and would prefer to sweep under the rug. I want to point out to you just how and why we have crossed the line of no return when it comes to education in this country!

For those of you who do not recall this monumental event, let me refresh your memories! Madelyn Murry O'hair, a self-proclaimed social activist, declared war on the educational system of the United States of America. It all began after her oldest son, Bill, came home from school and expressed his objection to having to participate in daily prayer.

Although she once proclaimed that she "would never try to change anyone's convictions and that she just didn't want anyone imposing their beliefs on her," she succeeded in changing the course of education in America.

Many considered her just another loud mouth activist; however, on June 17, 1963, eight out of nine supreme court justices ruled in her favor.

Am I being unfair to blame all of America's troubles with education on a decision made back in 1963? I often ask myself this question and stand steadfast in my commitment.

I think that what we lost was the source by which we could create change for all of our challenges with education. We managed in less than one decade to completely cut ourselves off from the present and future progress of our children's education! Troubles and problems have always been with us, but through God we have always had the means by which to create new hope and possibilities. America lost, in my opinion, the option to achieve this power when she decided to take God out of the schools.

If in fact the verses from the *Bible* that I quoted earlier in this chapter have any credibility at all, how could we consider the removal of prayer from our American schools?

If in fact our forefathers built this country on a foundation of God, how could we allow ourselves to discontinue our communication with Him in the schools? How could we send God the message that those of us involved in education have no need for Him any longer?

It's as if we were trying to send God a message saying that although we believe you are an all knowing and an all-seeing God, maybe education is not one of your stronger points! Hello America! Knock, Knock! What in heaven's name were we thinking?

This nation has shifted from the point of dealing with the basic challenges of education to the point of completely losing all purpose and direction!

To add insult to injury, I feel that we are going to continue to lose ground because of our difficulty in recognizing and facing the source of the problem. This nation's educational program is a school bus driving uphill-without tires, the gas gauge moving forward to empty. And where do we find the closest gas station? Oh, we passed it about thirty-four years ago! And to make matters worse the bus driver jumped off when he realized that he wasn't getting justly compensated! With all of this going on, we must remember that the precious cargo on board is *our children*. Yet Americans are still idly standing around waiting for the bus to reach its destination.

203

Is there anyone out there who truly wants to help our kids have a chance, not only to survive this educational trip to nowhere, but to direct them on to a course of real change?

Where do We Go from Here?

Something we need to ask ourselves, is God still around? Or has the Divine One that used to be our driving force decide to take a few steps back to see just how uneducated we can become?

If in fact there is the slightest ounce of truth to this self-inflicted cause of educational woes, then we must begin to calculate this possibility into our assessment, for the possible survival in the future.

If this nation continues to underestimate the full potential in discontinuing our relationship with the Big Teacher upstairs, then we had better prepare ourselves for the worst.

If this country is too stubborn to realize the cause of her troubles, then it is certain we will never admit that we have possibly wronged ourselves. So asking forgiveness and regaining God's divine help is most likely out of the question. In a way we have set in motion our course.

And it's certain that the government will give little support to any remedy.

The fact is that the American government is already taking from Peter to pay Paul. At times, I am not even certain that it is any longer an issue of money. However, with all the constant budget cuts in the area of education, it is becoming difficult for any growth to take place. When there was ample funding we still lacked progress because of excessive waste and a desire to capitalize on an opportunity.

Now that the government has fallen upon hard times, it is easy for Americans to raise the flag of blame and hold the government responsible for not getting the job done. Today, all the taxes in the world will not rectify the problems we have incurred. Needless to say, you don't have to be a graduate from Yale to see that any more taxes will cause more difficulties for minorities. This will only create new manifestations of old problems.

Every facet of this country's makeup is so intertwined that each action that happens at the top eventually causes some kind of reaction at the bottom. Our educational institution isn't any different. For instance, if American officials foolishly allow guns and arms in our streets, then why should we naively think that they won't end up in our schools?

The repercussions are felt by everyone. Whether it's a stray bullet that finds its way into the classroom, or a child carrying a gun to school for protection, we are all victims!

The governmental stand-off that Congress often finds itself involved in, often comes back to haunt our children! The Republicans and the Democrats are constantly arguing and debating over issues that ultimately affect us all. Fellow politicians in an effort to make themselves appear better than they are, bad mouth their opponents. Are we to think that the problems that teachers are having with their students, (in the area of discipline) have nothing to do with the behavioral problems of government officials? Politicians set the example.

If you can recognize any possible merit to what I am saying, then you must admit that there is a strong possibility that the removal (or dismissal) of God from our educational system has had an ultimate effect on our children. Do our schools fail to provide our kids with wisdom, discipline, protection, knowledge *and* understanding? Sadly, in many cases, the answer is a resounding "yes." Yet God has been known to render to his people all of the above.

**Money, God's Blessing
& Our Children as the Bottom Line**

One thing is certain, education will always be big business. In fact, education is the second largest area of government spending, exceeded only by the defense budget. It is estimated that four out of every ten dollars that are spent by state local governments go towards education.

If a country is doing well and there is a chicken in every pot, then the resources of the people can support the expenditures incurred for education. What happens when both the people and the government are both struggling? These resources can be severely limited. In turn, God is said to have an infinite supply of resources. During my research, I found that there are 516 verses in the Bible that speak of God and his blessings.
I will never understand why this nation would ever want to separate themselves from God's blessings.

It might be ok for some of us to turn our back from these possible blessings, but what about the kids who desperately need them? Should they be forced to pay for this nation's unwise decision? Should they simply sit back and watch as this great institution of knowledge passes them by? Don't think that this is not happening.

Meanwhile the cost of education continues to soar. Between 1970 and 1991 alone, our federal expenditures for education went from $162 billion to $248.3 billion. From 1970-1999 our state budget went from $78.7 billion to $153.3 billion.

It is not only money that is keeping us from making progress. The one thing that money hasn't changed in this institution is the teachers' salaries. From 1985 to 1995, the average salary has slowly wavered from $32,999 to $36,096 with a possible projection of $39,030 by the year 2003. The teachers and students are the ones being hurt the most by all of today's ills.

It might be easy for many of you to overlook the fact that in 1993 there was a 9.2 percent school dropout rate in the United States.

It won't be easy for those kids to forget the fact that they were short-changed by an educational system that couldn't live up to their expectations.

Our Nation's Teachers, Miracle Workers in the Chaos

In this huge silo of confusion, the people that I'm most concerned about are the teachers. If you are asking yourself why this concern is so great, the answer is quite simple and very pertinent. The teachers are the bloodline to our kids! I said earlier that it seems that as smart as mankind appears, the dumber we actually are.

Common sense should tell us that if our teachers find themselves in constant turmoil, then our kids will suffer too.

When I think of how teachers and students are being impacted by the bleak state of our educational system, I have to shake my head in disgust. They are truly the victims in this scenario and they will continue to suffer. The undeniable responsibility that America has placed on our teachers can never be analyzed as anything other than monumental! These human beings who have dedicated their lives to teaching find themselves at the lower end of this nation's totem pole. They are the first to feel the repercussions from any government cutbacks.

There was a time when I questioned the character of those who call themselves teachers. I thought that they must have been weak in character for even choosing a profession such as teaching. I am pleased to say that these foolish thoughts didn't last long. If you have the opportunity to see into a young child's eyes when he or she is hanging on to every word, in hope of better understanding, then you know exactly how precious our teachers are to us. As I got older, the more apparent it became to me that these helpers of life are more than just gifts to education; they are gifts to the universe.

When we read an article in the newspaper about how teachers are exasperated with their mistreatment in the present system, many of us still don't recognize the extent of their problems.

We have become callous to their needs and many of us couldn't care less. Teachers often find themselves in a no-win situation, which often results in striking or walking out.

Todays teachers find themselves with the added responsibility of not only trying to teach our kids, but of raising them as well. Today many families have two working parents and the teachers have become part-time parents. The quality time that children used to spend with their parents is now allocated to the teachers. In many cases, this quality time loses its quality and becomes of a jail sentence for many educators.

When you add in the conditions of overcrowded classrooms, the large cutbacks, undisciplined kids and the fact that this educational institution no longer has a solid foundation, teachers have their work cut out for them! In fact, I can't think of another profession that (carries with it such a) variety of roles. Beyond part-time parents, teachers are psychologists, motivators, counselors, disciplinarians, organizers, coaches, babysitters, educators, confidants, role models, instructors and preachers.

Society conditions us to worship and idolize athletes over teachers. What an unrealistic world we live in! An athlete's contributions are extremely limited in comparison.

I have had an opportunity to speak with a number of teachers about the dilemma of our educational system. Amazingly enough, teachers have developed an immune system which enables them to deal with their everyday problems. I am not certain whether this eventually affects their productivity; however, what is very apparent is that this nation is allowing our greatest resource to deteriorate without any real efforts to rescue it. Teachers are conditioning themselves to effectively teach in a declining system. Americans must not think that they can let this happen without being aware of the possible repercussions. When I hear of teachers having to fight to gain raise increases, all I can do is shake my head and think to myself, when will we ever learn?

Final Thoughts on Education

What is it about our society that allows a major resource like education to stumble towards extinction? Is it that we do not realize the magnitude of the situation, or are we simply too naive to understand the degree of the damage that has been done? We can no longer allow our teachers to take the blame, and we can't keep settling for the same answers. Is it the fault of the parents or even the kids? And let's not forget the old practice of assigning guilt to government.

One thing is certain, this nation cannot continue to pass the buck for the problems that we are having!

Although I sometimes feel that this situation will *never* get any better, I still firmly believe that as an American I must strive to improve the situation. This nation is too arrogant to admit that taking God out of the schools is the reason for the backlash of problems. I feel as if I'm in a family of alcoholics and I can't get anyone to recognize that the problem is alcohol. No one wants to give up on a family member, but at what point do you draw the line?

American's situation with education reminds me of a story in the *Bible*. It's about a servant of God named Abraham and his desire to keep God from destroying the righteous along with the wicked. He was having a conversation with the Lord about the destruction of Sodom. Abraham wanted to know if God would destroy the city if fifty righteous people could be found in the city. God in His mercy, answered that He wouldn't destroy the city if there were fifty righteous people. Abraham, then asked the Lord if He would destroy the city if there were only ten righteous people and God answered that He would not destroy the city if there were ten righteous people. Unfortunately, the angels of God, only found Lot and his wife and daughters to be righteous.

Once they were led out of the city, God destroyed both Sodom and Gomorrah by raining brimstone and fire down from the heavens.

I realize many of you reading this are probably thinking that this is quite a dramatic comparison. I feel that I need a powerful comparison to illustrate my point. If God was willing to save a city permeated with sin and destruction, He would certainly be willing to save us from the decay of today's educational system. This is true regardless of the circumstances even if what we find in our school system is a product of what we have brought onto ourselves!

The callousness found in America regarding education is great. Our salvation is in knowing and understanding the cause of this decay. At that time, God will have mercy and will save our educational system from demise. The only thing that will continue to make us *Fools of Education* is knowing what is wrong and understanding that we have the power to create change and choosing to do nothing! Think about it!

Achievement

Success is to be measured not so much by the position that one has reached in life as by the obstacle which he has overcome while trying to succeed.

**Booker T. Washington,
American Educator**

Chapter Five

Blacks in A Corner!

Many people around the world wonder what it's like to be an American. Unfortunately, many Blacks living in this country are also forced to ponder what it would be like to be a vital part of this nation. When you consider the dominant presence of the black man in the United States, for him to be in this position is unacceptable!

The creation of this chapter is to give Americans a look at how a beautiful race of people has allowed themselves to be shoved into a corner of this nation. Although it can be said that the black man was forced to be in this country, it still remains true that this is the position we find ourselves in. Now what are we going to do about it?

Of all the different races living in this world, I cannot think of a greater race to be a part of than the Black race!

I don't make this statement out of false pride or foolish misunderstanding. The statement might seem arrogant; however, I understand that it was not by my power, but a power greater than myself that I came to be a part of such a race!

The Stagnation of Black Progress

If the black man were to fast forward through the pages of history, he would realize that he's at a standstill. This is a truism that has to be faced! Looking at the advancement of this country's communicational resources, I question how any races would allow themselves to come to such a complete halt. We have backed ourselves into a proverbial corner. I said in the beginning of this book that my purpose was to give a very candid and nonprejudicial look at this country. So I must not and will not hold back the truth. It is the truth that will create the beginning of change for the present and the future!

As individuals, we often ask ourselves why we are not moving ahead. Very few people ask this question when it comes to a whole group of people. I believe there are many reasons that this stagnation has set in. I think what adds insult to injury is the realization that the source of the problem is ourselves.

Our reactions and responses will ultimately determine how long we remains in a fragile state of mind.

I don't believe anyone can argue the fact that the road the Black man has taken has been a very long and difficult one. I question whether the Black man has allowed himself to get so caught up with the troubles of the past that he has lost sight of the present and the future!

Letting Go of the Troubles of the Past

One of the greatest assets as Americans is having the ability to learn from the many different races found in this country. There is no doubt that Blacks are the most resilient race. In many ways, for the sake of survival, we were forced to create an armor of hatred. It is extremely important to see our past as the foundation that has built the structure of who we are today! A question often asked is, "How do we forget the troubles of our past?" The answer is really very simple! We must not forget the troubles of our past, but we must learn to be thankful for the lessons learned.

Many might ask, "How can we be thankful of such a negative, destructive and unfair beginning?" My response to you is, "we have no other choice."

217

If we continue to live in the past, we will not be able to love ourselves. Constantly resenting the persecution of our past causes our heart to bleed internally. This bleeding circulates throughout our bodies, reacting to the past, instead of concentrating on the present challenges of today and those of the future.

Learning to accept the above philosophy has not been an easy task for many of my people. Needless to say, the healing process and getting on with our lives has been difficult. An initial step is to simply profess the following words, " Forgive them Father, for they know not what they have done."

What I neglected to tell you is that our internal bleeding is not a physical phenomenon, but a spiritual one! It is the black man's spirit that has been shoved into a corner. The things that bound us are of the spirit. Physically, we have overcome any challenge that life has put before us! As Blacks we had to escape the physical chains of bondage and over the years, it was our prayers that created our freedom. However, the Black race has been carrying around these broken chains as a constant reminder of the condition of his past. Many blacks still use the old excuse of persecution as a reason for avoiding the challenges of today.

It is very clear that the conditions of today are superior to those of the past.

Why should we allow the past to determine the guidelines of the future? The only logical explanation's for this would be that the conditions have not changed. On the other hand, are we still looking for excuses for avoiding to take responsibility for our situation.

One thing that many find themselves doing is trying to remind the white man of the atrocious treatment of the past. With that attitude, we cannot control the outcome of either the present or the future! I am not saying we must forget the road that led us here! The history of our people is like none other! Although I believe that it should never be forgotten, it shouldn't constantly be on our minds. Many might ask, "how do you manage to take this approach?" There is one keyword that will answer this question with great accuracy. This word is *perspective!*

Black Americans must view their history with the proper perspective, however wrong and unfair those beginnings were! By doing this, we learn to see the past as just that, the past. We have the common sense to learn and grow from it. We, should take our accomplishments and learn to derive the knowledge and understanding from the past and apply these principles towards the future. We must learn to extract from history these elements that are positive and filter out the negativity!

When we carry the negativity from the past into the present (whether it is consciously or unconsciously) we bring with it those elements that shaped and formed the hatred and anger that prevailed in our past.

I sense that many blacks feel they have to remind the white man of his past transgressions: however, the white man has his own built-in reminder of these errors. Most importantly, I believe something very crucial takes place when Blacks formulate a positive perspective. It teaches us to put aside the crutch of disability that has burdened us all these years. This crutch has been an unconscious excuse for our lack of success.

Obviously this does not pertain to all blacks, but it is important to recognize this dilemma if it applies to you. We don't need this crutch any longer. We must demand more from our own resources and improve our lives.

Blacks have been led to believe that demanding more from the white man is the key to their future. To create the results we are looking for, we must learn to demand more from ourselves. Examining the history of our people, we find that the extremely tough conditions helped mold us into the very special people that we are today!

I know it is very difficult for many Blacks to understand what I'm about to say, especially considering the extreme conditions of our humble beginnings. I would like to go on record and say that it was a true blessing for us to have been plucked from our homes and brought to America. We were forced to live in an unknown land that was not our own. As masochistic as this might sound, I can easily explain my thoughts by simply asking you to look at the difference between the African-American of today and the African of today.

Let me make it clear that by making this statement, I am not belittling the African, nor am I excusing the unacceptable behavior of the Anglo-Saxon. After all, it was the white man's savage and barbaric behavior that caused our original plight. By becoming a part of America, the blessed nation, the Black race is much farther along as a people than if we had stayed in our homeland.

Now I don't expect for everyone to agree with what I'm saying; however, I would like to stimulate some deep thoughts. What I have discovered is that in life there is a true value in looking at the overall picture and putting things into the proper perspective. This ultimately helps to continue the process of growth. It is our attitude that often holds us back, nothing else! We have every opportunity for success!

If I didn't believe this, I would not be writing this book. In fact, I strongly believe that we have an even better opportunity to succeed than any other race of people! If we look at history as a training camp for the future, it's easy to see that it has prepared us for today's survival. I truly believe that the tremendous character of the black people can be attributed to our precarious beginnings! To truly move forward, the black man is going to have to put aside his antiquated ways of thinking. I'm not asking you to forget your roots, I'm telling you to focus more on the journey ahead. Frankly, I feel that this can never happen until we find the substance within ourselves to forgive our forefathers for their misguided treatment towards us.

I realize that this is easier said than done; however, we have to make a conscious effort to accept this philosophy in order to improve our way of life. Presently, America is a melting pot of many different races. It is important for each race to become strong within. In order for this to happen, each of us must realize what it is that makes us weak in character. If we don't recognize the broken wheel, how can we repair it? Many of you probably believe that what I'm suggesting has some merit. The question is, how easy will it be for our race to perceive the past in this manner?

Today, many blacks find themselves jobless and in some cases, homeless. It will be hard for them to revise their attitude. Yet, I assure you that this way of thinking can be implemented by any and all who read these words!

Unless the black man learns to change his process of thinking, the past will become the present and history will repeat itself. The past shouldn't teach us hatred. It is hatred that has kept this nation separate and apart. I know that many of you are thinking that this viewpoint is very idealistic and has no place in the real world. I strongly disagree. I am fully aware that in many cases the white man has not yet experienced a change of heart that would warrant forgiveness. It is important for the black man to plant the seeds that will allow our hearts to open the way towards forgiveness.

Lessons Learned

I would like to share with you just how we can prepare to move forward. First of all, we must review what we have learned from the past. If the white man had his way, he would deliver us into slavery. The white race beat us, whipped us, and hung us from trees. They treated us as if it would a herd of cattle. We had our limbs and sex organs amputated.

The past taught us a lesson in humility. The white man would call our race of people lazy while forcing us to work long arduous hours. He lived in his big, white plantation reaping the benefits of our labor. The past has shown us that the white man is not prejudicial. When he can no longer manipulate one race he finds others to cheat and abuse. We have learned that he has always created laws to protect himself and disallowed the advancement of others.

History taught us that the white man has attacked other countries with nuclear bombs in order to protect what others built for him. The most important lesson that we have learned from the past is that the white man has been our earthly father, teacher and judge.

I'm sure there are many blacks who are not willing to accept this last statement. The fact still remains that every race of people, living in America has learned from what the white man has taught us both good and bad. In view of this, it is easy to understand why so many blacks today find it difficult to forget the past.

We can turn all this around by learning to dismiss the anger and the hatred generated by the events of history. This will help to keep our other brother in check for the future. We know just what he is capable of and this knowledge is good to have.

The past should have taught us to recognize the warning signs that can infiltrate the present or the future. The *lessons* we have learned must be kept close to our hearts, but not the emotions of anger and hatred.

Another thing I have learned is that the white man still feels that he is a superior being. This image of the bigger-than-life (White) super hero is reinforced through T.V. and film.

Many of today's action packed films, starring such actors as Steven Segal, Sylvester Stallone and Jean-Claude Van Damme, are very successful. We all know that it's certainly not the quality of their acting that packs the theaters.

I often smile to myself when I watch Steven Segal jump from a moving truck onto a speeding train, just in time to kill twenty to thirty bad guys and save the world without so much as wrinkling his suit. With this kind of unwarranted image of superiority comes a great deal of arrogance. Frankly, I feel that a lot of this false pride is fueled by the fact that many races, despite the white man's track record, desire to emulate him. I have to wonder why other races would strive to become part of a race with such a controversial history.

Moving Out of the Corner
& Going Forward with our Lives

The key to the Black man's future success is to learn to break down the old conditioning and create a new format. We must learn to hold ourselves both responsible and accountable for our own lives. Letting go of the past will help us regain control over our own existence. This creates a new attitude that will eventually set us on the right path towards becoming better human beings.

Many of you probably are asking yourselves how I arrived at the title, "Blacks in a Corner!" I decided to use this chapter to make all Americans aware of the position in which Blacks find themselves in. Most importantly, I wish to create a true awareness of the possibilities that remain for us, as a people. For the black American to continue to allow himself to remain in this proverbial corner of society is a great calamity. This will probably be a cause of our country's demise. If we are smart, we will learn to move toward the real direction that is available, and that is to move *forward!*

Should Blacks decide to focus on the latter statement, we must be prepared to encounter opposition from all angles. One very bold step forward was the *Million Man March.* One reason that the Washington march was an important step for all of us.

The march added a new element to the Black man's character.

We begin to take action to *create* changes in our lives. Although it was highly ostracized and surrounded by much controversy, this event made a strong statement. The message was loud and clear: from this day forward we accept responsibility for who we are. To be honest with you, I believe that a lot of the controversy was produced simply out of fear. It's irrelevant whether this fear originated in our own community or from outside sources.

I hope and pray the energies that created this march will continue to manifest themselves into a true change of character awareness.

Healing Ourselves through Forgiveness

I know that my generation will never fully understand the difficult times experienced by our ancestors. This fact in itself is a sign of progress. The healing that accompanies time is one of the world's greatest ointments. In fact, the process of forgiveness is a lot easier when we remember the road that we were forced to travel. Forgetting doesn't speed up the process, it actually slows it down. We must understand that it is forgiveness that helps to speed up the healing, but it can only begin after the removal of the knowledge that has caused the afflictions.

In many cases, it takes a long time to get to this point. A wound heals in layers, slowly over time. If you are a black man and feel strongly that the white man has caused you pain, I must assure you it is futile to think you can erase every violators descendants from the face of this planet! To forgive a man's transgressions spiritually removes the object from the wound.

This is enough of a start to initiate the healing procedure. If the black man chooses to initiate the healing without forgiveness then he can never truly move forward. And if we are not moving forward, we surrender ourselves to stagnation, eventually ceasing to exist. What will follow, will be a regression to the past.

Some of you are thinking that this sounds good, but you're asking yourselves if these ideas have a chance of surviving in the real world.

You are also still wondering how I can even begin to forgive the white man for what he has done to my people. Guidance has come to me from what I have learned through the Christian philosophies. The primary principle is to ask someone greater than yourself to give you the heart of forgiveness! Many people may think you have to be a Christian in order for this to take place. Wrong. All you have to do is ask. Ask God for a change of heart. Let him know that you don't have the power to create this change and are asking Him for his help.

This simply takes the pressure away from yourself and gives it to a Higher Source.

This process will work for anyone, (regardless of race), who still carries the anger and hatred of the past! I realize that there will always be people who will not see the simplicity of this type of change but it doesn't mean that we can't achieve it! I call this process *seeds of change.* Before we can have any change in our society, we must first be aware of the need for change. Americans are conditioned to think that change is created by great politicians and bold, powerful leaders. This is a wrong assessment. It is the average American, like you and me, that initiates the beginning of all change. The attitude of placing one's destiny back into one's own hands is what happens when we learn to change our way of thinking.

Throughout this book, I have emphasized that this is the one, true importance in being an American. Both the Black man and the white man must be made aware of how our future will be compromised if we don't comply to this rule of change.

Forgiveness is the real key for change in a man's heart. A wonderful example of this is the crucifixion of Jesus Christ. He gave up His ghost not in anger or hatred but out of a great love for all of mankind.

His words were, " Father, forgive them; for they know not what they do." (Luke 23:34) His act will marked the beginning of change, in the same way, our act of forgiveness towards our fellow-man. We must, as a people collectively, in order to stimulate the energy necessary to take the first forward step that will eventually lead us out of the corner of America. This simple step seems to have eluded many of our leaders.

Allow me to give you another example. When our nation decided to drop nuclear weapons on Japan and alienate them, the Japanese could have carried with them a revengeful attitude towards all Americans. It was Japan's forgiveness towards us that helped their country regain their health and strength. If you don't think that it is so, simply see to what extent the Japanese dominate much of the world today! They have major control of the real estate market, film and automotive industries, the hotels and computer technology and multi-media. They have accomplished all this in less than fifty years.

The Next Step: Learning to Survive & Thrive.

Ok, now many of you are wondering where we go from there. If we take this first step, what's next? The next step is to make an honest assessment of your personal situation. Let me share a true story with you.

This will give you an example of what I'm trying to get across to you.

I want you to see that however bleak your situation, you can always take control of it.

On April 1, 1986, I drove my Mazda B2000 pickup truck from Texas to Los Angeles, a journey of approximately 1600 miles. My travel companion was my best friend, my Old English sheep dog, Cricket. I had everything I owned in the back of the truck. I arrived in Los Angeles with only $40.00 and a lifetime's worth of hope and ambition. I didn't know a soul in the city, but I had one telephone number for a possible contact. After dialing the number, I got a recording saying that no one was available for the next two weeks."Oh great!" I thought to myself. Disappointed, I walked back to my truck. Suddenly I heard a voice cry out from behind me. "Excuse me, can you help me?" I quickly looked around and saw a white man in his late fifties driving towards me in a 1985 white Riviera. He introduced himself and told me that he was on his way back from Las Vegas and that he had lost all his money gambling. He said he was a doctor and he was going through a divorce. He claimed to be broke, almost out of gas and had three hundred more miles to go to reach his final destination.

He asked me if I could lend him some money. At that point, I laughed out loud, but then apologized for my outburst and explained my situation. I told him that not only was I homeless, but last and not least, I only had forty bucks to my name. He began to tell me a little bit more about himself and explained to me how distraught he felt regarding his divorce. Suddenly he took off his watch and told me, " Take it, perhaps you could pawn it and the money can help you get started." I objected immediately, assuring him that I couldn't take his watch. Suddenly he had tears rolling down his face and pleaded with me to give him my $40.00 He took off his ring and said that he had paid $2,500 for it. He said he would give me the ring because he was desperate for the cash. I'm still confused as to why I took him up on his offer. I don't know if I took the ring out of desperation or if I was truly caught up in his personal dilemma. After giving my last forty dollars to this total stranger, I had many different thoughts racing through my mind. My feelings all seemed to be overshadowed by the urgency of finding a pawn shop.

After driving around for approximately thirty minutes, I finally located a pawn shop. The employee buzzed me into the store and as I entered, my heart began to race. I walked in very proudly, with a professional attitude.

I handed the ring over to the owner. He looked at it closely and asked me how much I wanted for it. I hesitated for a moment. Recalling what the original owner had paid for the ring, I boldly told him $1,500. The two men in the store looked at each other and started to laugh. After about a minute or so, they gave me a serious look and pointed to a glass case that contained about twenty-five identical rings to the one that I had brought in. He went on to say that if he didn't have so many of them in the shop, he would have given me $10 for it. Because of the circumstances, his hands were tied. I began to laugh as I told them my story. However, as I was walking back to my truck, I found myself fighting back the tears. My sheepdog must have sensed that something was wrong because she crawled over to me, in an effort to cheer me up, she put her head on my lap.

Suddenly, I had a feeling that everything was going to be all right. I realized that the situation was not as bleak as it looked. True, I only had an eighth of a tank of gas and no place to live, but somehow my relationship with God was taken to another level. The fear and the questions were replaced with the reality of the situation. I was forced to address my problem one step at a time, and the power of each step would be based totally on me!

The first thing I did was to make a realistic assessment of my situation. This took about ten seconds! I soon found a park and that evening I began to create a game plan for the following day.

Falling asleep, I slowly began to think about the things that had happened to me my first day in L.A. Reflection is very good medicine for the soul, (even if your thoughts are not all positive).

The lessons that I had learned that day were bold reminders of what I already knew.

The episode with the ring reminded me that you rarely get something for nothing and that it is important to be aware of those around you who offer it. I went to sleep thanking God because I realized that the situation could have been a lot worse. I tossed and turned all night long. The Mazda B2000 truck is not known for its wide and roomy cabin space. When morning came, I encountered a little, Jewish lady named Sandy Lewis. At first I was annoyed at her boldness, but as it was she turned out to be an angel in disguise. Sandy had an Australian sheepdog named Sheba that she walked in the park every morning around 7 a.m. Sandy insisted that Cricket and I join her for a walk. I had sleep in my eyes and a cotton mouth (which is Texan terminology for how you feel when you don't get to brush your teeth in the morning). By the end of the walk, Sandy and I had become good friends.

I told her about my hilarious episode with the ring, and it actually felt good to be able to laugh about it. Never underestimate the healing power of laughter!

Sandy and I stopped at a park's bench and here she drew a rough map of the city of L.A.

She explained to me how all the major streets, Sunset, Santa Monica, Wilshire, Olympic and Pico, all ran parallel to each other in a east and west direction. She assured me that by going west on any of these major streets, I would always end up at one of the many beautiful California beaches. She was very knowledgeable and suggested I go to a couple of local churches for possible, immediate help. My second day in the city, I found myself sitting on the steps of a Lutheran Church, located on Olympic Boulevard. I waited there for several hours and kept myself busy by counting the number of Jaguars and Mercedes that drove by. After about two hours, I asked a maintenance man where I could find the pastor. I was told that it was the pastor's day off and that he was playing golf. The maintenance man suggested I come back the following day.

The minister was a heavyset gentlemen with a beard and glasses. After making a formal introduction, he started sorting through all his mail. He soon looked up and asked me what kind of work I did.

I mentioned a number of different trades I was proficient in and also told him that I came to L.A. to study acting and music! He chuckled and said that I "should forget about the last career choice because there were so many other young people with those similar goals." He began to jot down something on a piece of paper and then tossed it to me. He said that his church did occasionally work with an organization called PATH (People Assisting the Homeless). He gave me directions, then pulled out a checkbook and wrote me a check for $13.43. He told me that I could cash it at the supermarket down the street without any ID. He said the money would help with gas and food. I thanked him for not turning me away, and he replied that he had been turned away several times himself at a certain time in his life.

As I got up to leave, he asked me why I choose to come to his church for help. With a tone of confidence, I told him that I had been raised in a church.

PATH was located in a very rundown building in Culver City. The people were kind and friendly, but as I looked around me, I realized just how wealthy I really was. Although we were all in the same boat, it was my positive attitude that gave me an edge over many of the others.

The shelter itself was only available for women and children, but it did give me access to a telephone and an address for incoming mail.

I drove away with a bag of cheese, crackers and bread, all of which I later gave to a woman in the park who was digging in a trash barrel for food. I can still remember the grand smile on her face after she received the the bag of goodies.

After visiting the PATH office, I felt a certain urgency to get myself back on my feet. The following morning, I got up around 5:30 a.m. and drove to UCLA. With a duffel bag over my back, I walked into one of the old gyms, showered and shaved. During the next two days, I filled out twelve applications of employment. In less than ten days, I had two jobs. On my job, at the Old World Restaurant in Beverly Hills, I went from being a waiter to host, to assistant manager, to manager. This happened all in less than two weeks. My second gig was doing fragrance modeling for Saks Fifth Avenue in Beverly Hills.

These jobs weren't a big deal, unless you take into consideration that all this was accomplished while I was living out of a Mazda pickup truck. The first forty-five days in L.A. I lived out of my truck, with few being privy to the situation. Understanding the fact that people perceive you by the way you present yourself, I knew that certain information should be kept to yourself.

No one ever has to know what your situation is unless you choose to tell them! In Los Angeles, the majority of the people don't care about your situation anyway, so why give them an opportunity to think less of you?

For those of you who are asking what this has to do with this chapter, I wanted to share this very real episode in my life to let you know that no matter what your situation, you have the power to gain control of it. First, assess your personal circumstances and then create your own game plan. No matter what's going on, you always have the power to regroup and carry on.

The first forty-five days in Los Angeles were in some way some of the happiest days of my life. It was during this time that I realized this important fact: nothing would ever change unless I put forth the effort! Every phone call that I made in my behalf and every application that I filled out was totally within my discretion. It is important for people to learn that all our actions are manifested by our thoughts.

In any situation our approach will determine our success or failure. While I was living out of my truck, I saw many others who were in the same situation. The difference between those people and myself was simply my attitude toward survival. The black race must learn to utilize these same principles in a collective manner.

The black man can learn to create this by learning to take responsibility for his own future. This is first created by an attitude for accomplishment.

We must make an assessment of our position in society and only then will we be able to take any real steps towards strength. Have you ever asked yourself how the Jewish race, which is less than six percent of the American population, has managed to control, create and manipulate such a great portion of our society? Ask yourselves how has this race been able to influence foreign policy, and create a strong political climate? Many Blacks consider the Jews their enemy; however, this creates negative thinking. I see them as an example, a role model from which other minorities can learn from. Instead of being jealous of our Jewish brother, we should thank them for their examples of accomplishment. I learn from their efforts and presence in this country.

Although it can be difficult to overcome the sometimes arrogant attitude of our Hebrew brothers, we must find a way to learn from their successful ways. I recall the remark of a prominent Jewish plastic surgeon at a children's soccer game. Someone mentioned the lack of talented Jewish athletes on the professional level.
He responded that they didn't have to play the game because they owned the teams.

My first reaction was to approach him in rebuttal, instead I took a deep breath. This allowed me to reconsider his comment. The funny thing about truth is that it sometimes presents itself surrounded by a small layer of arrogance.

We must not let this layer of arrogance devalue the degree of its authenticity!

It is important that we don't allow a person's arrogance to distract you from the substance of what they are trying to say.

Finding Our Voice, Reflections on Rap Music

Much of white society has replaced its deaf ears with ears that are more willing to be heard. My concern is, now that we have a voice that can be heard, what are we going to say? It is very obvious that we have managed to work ourselves toward the great microphone of life. Now that we are in this position, it is important that we truly have something to say that is worth listening to! Finally, now that we have an opportunity to present ourselves, are we prepared to show America how we have evolved? It is very important that the quality of what we have to say is first on our minds, regardless of the amount of time that it took us to voice our opinions.

Let's take a look at rap music and it's tremendous progress during the last few years.

Rap groups have been springing up everywhere and this music has been saturating society with the ideas and beliefs rappers feel must be heard! Although many record companies are fighting to convince us just how priceless their contributions are to society, I believe that many of us who have worked so hard to achieve credibility have been shortchanged by this industry's progress. At a time when so many people are hustling to frantically jump on the bandwagon of success, many of us have lost sight of what we have to give up in return.

The real power of rap music is in its ability to cross the racial barriers and offer an element of communication to the masses. And though this music might be considered popular by many, it is very important that the black man not lose sight of what he is trying to accomplish. This should be integrity, hard work, discipline, courage, understanding and wisdom. Make no mistake about it, rap music has given the white man the opportunity to present our race in a negative way! This type of music portrays today's black man and, in doing so, it has set the progress of our people back twenty-five years. This music carries with it the violence, negative energy, attitude and the jive that depicts blacks as non-educated violent individuals.

One of the things that saddens me is that there are so many of us who are not even aware of what is taking place. I have said this before, it is not in the white man's nature to do anything without a purpose. Many blacks think racism doesn't exist because we see ourselves on television and film. Wrong! Racism is alive and well in America. Just because it is not easily detected doesn't mean that it doesn't exist. Racism has taken on less recognizable characteristics.

As I write this chapter, I know there are many of you who still do not understand. That is why making an assessment of the situation is vital to our growth as a people. What I have been trying to say in these last few pages is this: in the past, the white man would not allow our race to be on TV. The roles that we were allowed to portray were demeaning. Times have changed. Today's white man realizes he must be more sophisticated in accomplishing his goals. What better way to do this, than by giving many blacks the opportunity to be in the forefront. What better way than to give Blacks, many of whom have never had a command of the English language, an opportunity to taste the fruits of a materialistic world?

As our black brothers step up for the whole world to judge, they will become the image that society will see as the representation of today's black man!

Magnify this with the involvement of marketing and advertising agencies. Need I say more about how it will be perceived around the world? Blacks simply do not have the luxury of presenting themselves as hoodlums.

Let me make something clear, I would never criticize someone for taking the opportunity to get a piece of the American pie! It is important; however, that we are aware of just who's baking the pie! I despise rap music "in part' because of these elements. Not only do I have to fight to understand the lyrics, but I am offended by the tribal-like connotation that often accompanies it. The jive-time presentation causes rappers to walk like animals with some sort of spinal-cord disease. It must be very insulting to many talented entertainers to be overshadowed by the hundreds and hundreds of instant rap groups that have flooded the scene.

It is apparent that the rap form of music is here to stay, but I think if we assessed it for its true value, as an art form, we would see an inconsistency of talent. There's no doubt that for every fifty rap groups there are only two or three with real talent. And if you listen closely, you will hear sounds from the past and become aware that much of the music has been plagiarized from tunes of long ago. I think much of this can be attributed to the lack of true creativity.

One of the things that has allowed rap music to survive is the thing that keeps most music alive; the beat of the sound. Most listeners are unaware that it is the beat of the music that causes us to become addicted.

It sends an internal message, a vibration that stimulates our physical mechanisms. I hope that you don't think that I'm tying to destroy the dreams of my fellow black artists. I owe it to my readers to be as candid as I can regarding all issues affecting this nation. I truly want to make you aware of the possible deterioration of our race that accompanies this art form. If the black race was aware that this type of presentation is destructive to its progress, then our objective would be to ourselves. We are a regal and sagacious race of people. To those rappers that have the heart and soul of knowing what is good for the human race, I say, "Keep on Keeping on!"

It is wrong for anyone to say that rap music is all bad? I am the first to realize that a good deal of this music expresses the suppressed feelings of society. Feelings that have been either ignored or forgotten for years. The question isn't whether or not people hear the words or the reaction they cause. I feel most rappers lack purpose! Sure they deluge society with their music, but is that enough?

What would happen if rappers were responsible for creating a huge voter registration drive, backed by the support of their young listeners? Instead of complaining about the system, these kids could be doing something positive to help make it better.

I don't think anyone can deny the fact that many of the things that these rappers are saying carry a great degree of truth. It is what you are willing to do after you have spoken that you will be judged on! Simply screaming the words that the methods the white man are unjust and unfair will fall on dead ears as it did in past generations.

This is a truism especially if the screams are associated with the energies of destruction and decay. Understand this, that you are screaming against white America. A race of people that for the most part already has deaf ears towards our needs. Rappers have a great energy, now they must learn to incorporate purpose and direction.

Redefining Ourselves & Reassessing Our Direction

The substance of any man can in many cases be defined by the opinion of others. But most of the time, we give this philosophy more power than it warrants. History has taught us that our other brothers have never thought very highly of our race.

245

What really counts is how *we* feel about ourselves as individuals first, and then, collectively as a people. One of the questions I often ask myself is "how can my generation change the negative propaganda that has been passed down through the generations?"

In contemplating this answer, I find myself face-to-face with the possible conclusion that we can't (at least not to any degree that will truly make any difference) change what America thinks of us. What I have learned during my stay on this planet is that it truly doesn't matter what others think of us, it only matters what we think of ourselves.

I believe that as we begin to think positively about who we are as individuals, we will create a by-product that will force the world to view our character clearly. When I say we should think positively of ourselves, I don't want you to confuse self-confidence with arrogance, conceit or false pride. I feel that the true essence of how we perceive ourselves is based on our personal relationship with the God that created us.

This relationship with God helps to teach us how to love ourselves, despite what the world thinks of us or even what we may already think of ourselves. It's amazing that even though many of us try to push God aside, He still manages to be an integral part of our lives. In my chapter on religion, I will discuss this topic at length.

What value is there in our advancement as a Black race, if the human race as a whole stands still? If our betterment doesn't create a residual effect on those around us, then have we truly made any progress as a people? I don't think so. The white race seems to have overlooked this concept.

As the black man begins to find the courage to move forward, away from our proverbial corner, it is extremely important that we are aware of where we are headed. There is an old adage that states, "out of the frying pan into the fire."

I simply say this because the important thing about moving forward has a great deal to do with purpose and direction, rather than speed. As we move into the mainstream of the American way of life, it is important that we continue to pursue the values which have been instrumental in getting us to this point.

I am often reminded of how easy it is to lose sight of our goals because of the battles we fight on a daily basis, not only as a people, but more importantly as part of the human race.

Today blacks find themselves in an unusual position. In some ways we feel as if we have *arrived;* however, it is important that we back up two or three steps to see just where we are heading.

I would like for you to consider the following fact. Many of you will not understand what I am trying to say and some of you will agree with my opinion one hundred percent. In the last fifty years, many of you have spent a great deal of time trying to be an equal to the white man. I'm afraid that many of us might be losing sight of the fact that the white man's direction might not be the one which is best for the growth of this nation. In fact, the white man can be made accountable for many of the mistakes that have been made towards the development of this nation. Imagine for one moment, our white brothers on trial for their past transgressions. I believe that although many blacks want to emulate the white man, they find themselves drawn to judge them. So as we continue to rush forward to become the white man's equal, we should be reminded that we have always been his equal, even in the mist of slavery. We must be careful not to try and run his race. We must learn to run a race based on the course and direction that will benefit all mankind.

Let me give you a clear picture. In the past, blacks have found themselves fighting major obstacles in the area of voting rights. The loss of lives and property was so great that to this day it cannot be accurately documented. At one time, the right to vote was essential for our progress.

Let's ask ourselves, were we fighting for the right to emulate the white man or the right to be as destructive? Since the right to vote was so valuable, why is it that so many Americans (both Black and White) stay far away from the voting poles today? I'll tell you why. It is because of the lack of quality in the ideals and principles of this nation! And yet many beautiful people were brutally beaten and murdered just so we could have that right-to vote! I often wonder if they would have fought quite as hard knowing that this country was going to come to a standstill because of the lack of political substance and decay in the system.

Finding New Role Models

Somehow we must learn to understand that our future is not found in our effort to liken ourselves to one people. Instead, we'll increase our chances of a strong and positive existence by emulating other races of people. I do not want to appear abrasive with my opinions; however, sometimes the truth cannot be diluted with delicately placed adjectives. If we were to take a look at other races, we would see that there is a great deal of credibility to this statement.

The Japanese are a race of people who have acquired knowledge as the white man's ally; however, they learned to demand more of themselves. Their concentrated effort has helped them become the strong, world force they are today.

They have never tried to liken themselves to the anyone, instead they have always wanted to be better. Japan has accumulated a tremendous portfolio of wealth based on American real estate, automotive sales, computer technology and the entertainment media. I know there are many who would question the social order of Japan, but no one can question their results.

Again the Jews are another race of people who have managed to overcome tremendous social obstacles. Their sense of family and business has helped to make them a pillar of strength in many levels of our society. When you consider their small numbers, you have to be impressed with their accomplishment. They somehow have managed to have a controlling hand in almost everything of a social value. I feel that one of their strengths is their ability to keep things in their proper perspective. For the Jews, family and religious worship are at the head of their list of priorities!

If Black Americans begin to take a closer look at the behavior of other races, then our advancement will take on a faster momentum that will initiate and instantly move forward.

I believe that this dramatic surge forward will create an understanding that will erase the importance of how we think of ourselves. Learning from others is truly one of the forms of understanding that all men can count on.

Every race of people living in America is an integral ingredient of the melting pot. What qualities does the Black race add to this mixture? It is a simple question, but one that nevertheless should be asked. Blacks, as all other races, should see themselves as a part of a greater picture. The quality of paint that represents the black man is a reflection of what we have learned from the past. The content and texture of the paint should not be diluted because of the many colors that surround it. It cannot be removed because someone or something wishes it not to exist. As part of the big picture, blacks must learn to see the white man only as another shade of paint, a part of the collective array in this huge piece of art. Like us, the history and future of other races will determine just how well the portrait will turn out. Each step forward will increase and enhance the quality of our strokes in this portrait of life.

Remembering God as the Source of Our Strength.

Blacks have accomplished many levels of success in American society; therefore, it is imperative we do not lose sight of the great source of strength that has gotten us to this point.

I say this for the well-being of our race as well as the good of all mankind. It is important that we remember the first commandment of God, "I am the Lord thy God, thou shall not have strange Gods before me."

If any of you are questioning the purpose of my last statement, my response is that if in fact, our successes have caused us to weaken our relationship with God. The One who has given us strength, courage, wisdom, direction and guidance. We have lost contact with our greatest ally. If we have allowed success in our lives and the things success offers to become our God, then we have devalued the increase of our gains. And those of us who have knowledge of God's word know that He is a very jealous God. (See Exodus 20:5 and Ezekiel 39:25).

We must consider the possibility that if Blacks find themselves in this proverbial corner in America, it might have a lot to do with the fact that we have lost contact with the source that has been our creator. This is one of the true enlightenments in life and many of us find that we hold our own key to our destiny. More importantly, this is also true for the status of America.

If in fact God is a jealous God and I am using His words *in the Bible* as a reference, then it's safe to assume that his reaction to our lack of action could cause (Blacks and all other Americans) to remain in a state of stagnation.

When we began to claim the power of our future as a race, then we will find that we don't need to blame others for our lack of movement. It is important to understand that we have to remove these personal crutches we are leaning on, before we can try to slowly move towards progress.

Everything that we have been given has been given to us as a gift from God. All Americans must be aware of the fact that in a sense we are creating mini-Gods of the material things we have been blessed to possess. This places the importance on the increase instead of the source. This is not a very wise decision on our part.

Evaluating Ourselves & Our Role in our Stagnation

I feel I had to insert these spiritual anecdotes in this chapter because it is important that we understand the fact that there are many elements that make up our character. If we find ourselves stagnating in a corner of this nation, we must examine all the possibilities as to why we find ourselves in this predicament.

Blacks, like most of society, tend to forget that mankind is made up of the mental, physical and spiritual energies.

To evaluate someone, we must address the entire structure of their existence.

Blacks, as well as others, have a tendency to forget the importance of nourishing their entire being. We feed our bodies with food and exercise our minds with information and knowledge; however, we forget to consider that our spirits are slowly dying because of the lack of spiritual nourishment. What is so ironic about this is that the spirit of man carries with it the greatest potential and the least restriction! It is our *spirit* that has the ability to conquer the seen and unseen. Unfortunately, we have been programmed to give the spirit the least amount of nourishment. (See the Chapter on religion for more about the spirit.)

In an effort to understand why we are where we are in this nation, it is crucial for the Black man to review his whole being. I believe that by using a process of elimination, we can easily discover the problem and begin correcting the reason for our stagnation. It is very important that we learn that blaming others for what is happening in our lives is a waste of time and energy. And we begin to exhaust ourselves with all that wasted energy. One of the greatest challenges that blacks face is creating a sense of unity as a people.

254

Frankly, I feel we have allowed the conditioning of the past to stain both our present and our future. In our fight to become accepted by our white brother, we have lost the unity of our own race of people. I'll start by first looking at myself. I must ask myself what role I've played as a Black man.

As I force myself to evaluate my response and take a candid look at my life, I realize once again that it is through this process that true change and direction begins. By pointing out my situation and circumstances I hope to give you an opportunity to look at your own situation from a different perspective.

Entering the White Man's World, My Story

In the Fall of 1972, I was headed to a predominantly white school. In Houston, the busing laws at the time gave me a choice as to where I wanted to attend my sophomore year. I had just finished my freshman year at an all black school, George Washington Carver.

I was very excited at the opportunity of choosing schools. Before this occurred, I had seen this country through only a Black perspective. I went to visit the school during the summer and I was so impressed with the fresh new exterior and interior, that I made a conscious decision to attend in the fall.

As I look back on my decision, I see that it was made purely on the basis of new vs. old . George Washington Carver was the oldest school in the Aldine Independent School District.

In the South, the new schools were built in an areas outside of the Black communities. I was fascinated that I was offered an opportunity to pick something new over something old and run down.

It's interesting what black kids think about when they first see the white man's world. When the school bus picked us up on the first day of school, it seemed to me as if my senses were sharper than ever before. I noticed things I had never cared about. First of all, the school bus was clean and bright, as if it was brand new. I noticed that the streets in the white neighborhood weren't covered with potholes like the streets in our neighborhood. There seemed to be more street-lights and I was intrigued with the three-foot wide concrete path which ran parallel to the street.

I soon learned that these paths were called "sidewalks" and they were there to keep the people from having to walk on the street. I thought "what a cool idea!"

Most of all, I was amazed by the fact that the white man's world seemed to be free from trash and the lawns were well-groomed.

When our bus reached its final destination it had its manicured own private area for us to disembark. I thought to myself, "wow, we don't have to get off the bus in the middle of the street like we did at our old school."

As I exited the bus, I knew that there was going to be a major difference between my world and the white man's world.

It might have been at this point in my life that I felt the desire to become a part of the white man's world. I am not sure whether my desire was formed from an innocence found in youth or from the qualities that every human being possess. What I do know is that I felt myself being led by powers greater than myself.

These powers pulled me towards the white man's way of life.

For the next fifteen years of my life, I made a point of finding out just what was behind the mystical nature of this man. Having the opportunity to live amongst white people helped me to understand how they perceived this country as their own. This understanding was fueled by the intention of wanting to have more for myself and my family. To truly understand someone, it is important to spend as much time as possible with them. One has to be able to eat, sleep, work, play, talk, pray, and worship with them.

Initially, I allowed myself to get caught up in their world, but my heart never lost contact with who I was as a Black man and what was truly important to me.

The things I learned from the white man I wanted to share with my own people.

What I found, however; was that in the 70's many Blacks either tolerated the white man or hated him.

Unfortunately, blacks had those same feeling for other blacks who were associated with the white man. I remember being called a " white nigger" many times by those who did not really understand my motives and my ability to communicate with the white man. The one thing that I can say about my black brother is although he didn't see eye-to-eye on such issues as integration, he was not violent with his disapproval as many whites were at that time. I recall on at least four different occasions having shotguns or hand guns pointed at my face.

The first time this happened I was a sophomore in high school. One evening I was hanging out at a local game room where many kids gathered to play fuss ball. Like most other times, I was the only Black person. That evening I was looking around for a friend who was supposed to meet me there, when, I saw a long-haired guy walking towards me.

At the time I didn't notice that he was carrying a nickel-plated 38 in his right hand. As he pointed the gun at my forehead, he certainly got my attention! My heart begin to race wildly and I realized that he was definitely on drugs. He started to give me orders. "Put your hands up. Now put them down." He did this over and and over for a few minutes. Suddenly, I realized that although he was pointing a gun at my face, the activity around me was continuing as if this scenario was not happening. He eventually walked me over to the bar and bought me a beer. I didn't drink beer at that time, but I handled that Bud Light like I was a pro. A few minutes later, a kid in my class walked up to the bar and said, "Dexter, I see you been introduced to my older brother." The gunman put down his 38 and extended his hand in a friendly gesture. He said he wasn't going to shoot, but he wanted me to know he didn't play that shit." I never did fully understand what *shit* he was talking about.

The second time I had a gun pointed at me was the evening of my brother's funeral. After the service, I had driven to the local Burger King to get something to eat. The hamburger joint was in a white neighborhood near my new high school. Out of nowhere, two white guys pulled up and began yelling obscenities, "Hey nigger, go home."

Because of all the pent up emotions I was experiencing, I ran towards their old beat up Chevrolet Impala. Suddenly the guy in the passenger seat pulled out a double-barreled shotgun and pointed it at me.

I continued to run towards the car and as I got closer, he placed the shot-gun back in the car and drove off. Needles to say, I lost my appetite for a whopper. It didn't really hit me until later that I had looked death in the face. My mother could have buried two of her sons within one week's time!

Again, a friend and I found ourselves in the wrong place at the wrong time. Terry Robertson, a black All-District guard on our basketball team and I were driving around on a Saturday evening. Bored, we decided to cruise by the high school and see if anything was going on. In all honesty, I recall Terry mentioning that the girls drill team would be getting back from a competition around that time. As we drove down the street, I could see there were a few parked cars in the far parking lot. Without warning, five, heavily-armed, white guys jumped out in front of our car. They demanded we get out of the vehicle with our hands up. Unbeknownst to us, approximately twenty minutes earlier, a silent alarm had been triggered. The five would-be terrorists turned out to be cops.

They called our coach, Mr. Smallwood who lived a few blocks away and he in turn called my mother and Terry's dad.

Nothing came of it except that our parents were extremely irritated by the inconvenience that we had caused. For some reason, they lost sight of the fact that their teenage kids had been scared shitless. Having five loaded shotguns pointing at us.

Four out of the five times that I had a gun pointed at me, it was being held by a white man. And How many times have I heard it said that it is the black man who is the aggressor?

In the last twenty-five years, strong efforts have been made to break the psychological chains the white man has created through their attitudes of superiority. One thing that I learned about the white man is that there is a reason why he wants the world to think he is superior to others. Almost every time, the reason seems to be his lack of confidence.

Any white man who is secure with himself almost always carries himself, with a degree of honor and integrity. On the other hand, those who are insecure with themselves try to cover up their insecurities with those elements that create a division in communication between the races.

It is easy to see that the white man created laws to protect his dominance over those who were considered to be a threat. This leads me to believe that it was the white man's weakness, not his strength, that created the image of his dominance over other men.

As I reflect on my past, there is no doubt in my mind that the busing laws of the 70's, gave me the opportunity to see the white man's world for what it really was. Good and bad experiences have allowed me to see this world with realistic eyes.

As the black man continues to put his best foot forward, it is very important for many of you who have never taken a step across to the other side of the tracks to take a moment and examine just what is on the other side. Another thing I have learned about the white man is that his only true power, (much like the black man) comes from God. It is good to know that all mankind is truly created equal. One race doesn't have any special power over the other. To truly understand this releases an awareness that enables a person to feel as good as anyone else, anytime and anywhere. This kind of realization helps to make one aware that the keys to success are found in one's own hands. To make the black man aware of this, is an important step in moving forward.

Final Thoughts on Blacks in A Corner!

Now that we have been made aware of this fact, it is mandatory to put aside the old luggage of the past. That part of the black man that feels the white man is responsible for our position in America can be changed and we can begin to take a dramatic step forward. We can make ourselves accountable for our own success. As a result we will discover that our choices are the ones that determine our success or failure!

As long as blacks consider themselves a minority, then they will be! As long as we ask the government's help and support, there will be a limit to what we will get. Those of you who truly wish to see the black man move forward, will never experience this, without the desire to see America move forward. Although the black man finds himself in a corner of American society, America finds herself stagnating in a corner of the world. Only with the understanding that every race must communicate with one another, will we experience a true change throughout this nation! As we look at this melting pot of countless nationalities, in this country called America, there is no doubt the events that happen in this country will affect the rest of the world. The betterment of the black man in America should initiate the betterment of the black man in Africa.

The Jews in this country should create an example for the Jews in Israel. Just like the Hispanics here should be the strength of their mother country, Mexico!

In closing this chapter, I hope that you can hold on to the thoughts that will help you become better human beings. Although this chapter is dedicated to the advancement of the Black race, I sincerely hope that it will be an enlightenment to all others who find the need to move forward in this great country in which we live. Finally, I wish the world to know that to be a Black American in the year 2000 is to be a part of a race of people that, despite humble beginnings keeps getting better with time!

CONFIDENCE

I can see how it might be possible for a man to look down on the Earth and be an atheist, but I cannot conceive how he could look up into the heavens and say there is no God.

Abraham Lincoln,
16th President of the United States

Chapter Six

RELIGION,
Does Anyone Even Care?

This is the one chapter that probably causes me the most heartache. With all the changes that have taken place in this country, religion has somehow managed to be erased from the lives of many Americans. As we look back at this country's beginnings, it is evident that religion was a principal motive for the establishment of the first U.S. colony. The potential growth of religion as a driving force in the modern world is questionable and I often wonder if anyone even cares about its place in society.

Although the history of religion goes back many thousands of years, my concern is the lack of a religious presence in our nation! Religion, like many other facets of life, carries with it a doubled-edged sword.

Depending on our choices and our attitude towards it, religion can either provide protection or provoke an injurious assortment of possibilities. Today, this word happens to be lodged right in the center of the heart of our nation.

At this particular time, religion's value and purpose seems to be a major issue. This topic is one that has been written and talked about by far greater men than I. My focus will be on the two elements of religion: *right* and *wrong!*

What's It All About?

A gradual understanding of this subject has helped me to add this topic to the book. For a general view of the concept of religion, let's look at a few dictionary definitions. The American Heritage Dictionary defines religion as: 1. The belief in and reverence for a supernatural power or powers regarded as the creator and governor of the universe. 2. A person or institutionalize system grounded in such belief and worship... 3. A set of beliefs, values and practices based on the teaching of a spiritual leader.

Although there are many different definitions of the word itself, the most relevant is the one that comes from the feelings in your heart.

For me, religion is simply man's search for God! This search travels many different avenues, some understandings strewn with ceremony, symbolism and earthly traditions. If you stop and really think about it, for centuries the beliefs that encompass God have not changed much. As you read this chapter, you'll see that it is the constant changes that mankind has initiated that have created our insecurity about religion today. God has been the one true element who has set this nation apart from all other countries on this planet!

As we continue to fumble through our search for God, it is apparent that religion has changed its course and direction. In our struggle to maintain contact with Him, mankind has managed to redirect the purpose of his search by simply putting God aside and moving on without Him. Our goal should be to find God. The search for God should be the main issue rather than the process of reaching the ultimate goal.

Religion in America's Early Years.

America's initial settlers decided to strike out on their own and create a country where they could freely worship God. In many ways, this was the ultimate test of their beliefs.

Quite frankly, their quest gave God an opportunity to prove to the rest of the world that He was the God He claimed to be, a benevolent and omnipotent God. In a sense, the pioneers were asking God for His help every step of the way. They started out by praying for a safe trip in reaching their destination. They asked God to create the resources and elements needed for survival, such as: food, shelter, clothing and safety from external forces.

I imagined there must have been a very pure and honest relationship between God and man.

I can almost feel the love that embraced these early pioneers. Their every hope came from this one main source. If we are to envision God as the Father of this country, then imagine the love He must have felt in His heart knowing that He was the source of hope and inspiration. God is the lifeline to anyone who believes in his Divine Providence.

At that time, God was the center of this country's' existence. Our forefathers were almost too conservative in their religious beliefs. This conservatism of ideas and principles has caused us serious problems. At the center of this conservatism were the beliefs that separated those who were true believers in God and those who weren't.

As the first settlers established colonies in this country, the initial form of religion was established by the Puritans and Protestants. The early settlers became accustomed to one form of worship. Any belief which didn't fall in this category was said to deviate from the spirit of the living God.

In many ways I'm surprised religion survived this period. In certain respects, religion was as destructive as it was constructive.

At that time, God and America were truly united as one, as a parent would be to a child. This relationship blossomed into a strong bond which grew despite years of growing pains.

Looking at the many difficult episodes throughout history, it is very easy to understand that there must have been times when these children of God lacked the sense of communication with their everlasting provider.

There has never been a period in history that equals the turmoil of today. The same nation that was created in the name of God has quietly chosen to dissolve this almighty bond. To explore how this happened is one reason for writing this chapter. More important than addressing that issue, I want to make you aware of the repercussions that this act initiated.

Searching for God's Presence & Taking Sides

True belief keeps religion alive. The logic that there is a supreme being and the need to maintain contact with Him has always existed. Most of us know who mankind is and our place on this planet. Our presence here on earth makes it easy for us to study and understand who we are and where we are going.

God's lack of physical presence has left us with no other choice but to look at the written accounts of those men and women who have supposedly had some kind of contact with Him. Very few of us during this lifetime can actually claim to have seen or heard from God. We can only read and learn from the encounters of others. One of the most difficult challenges of today is to get mankind to understand that once we acknowledge God, we must acknowledge God's intentions and our role in this world. I must add this is not an easy task.

Religion makes us aware of God's presence. It also does a very good job of teaching us that there are certain elements and characteristics which please God, as well as those that displease Him. This system draws an imaginary line, which establishes the boundaries of those who are worthy of God and those who are not worthy of Him!

With this division, it is easy for us to understand how sides are drawn and how mankind is forced to walk on one side or the other.

A Keystone of Religion, The Bible as the Word of God

The *Bible* is said to be the written word of God, and it was written by men who were *inspired* by Him. The credibility of the written word of God has always been dubious for many! Ironically, it is the same men who question the bible that choose to discredit God. These men believe that this world of ours was created by a process of evolution rather than by a greater source. They refused to believe that one single power could create a planet with every detail as refined as the planet Earth.

One can not study or worship God without this holy doctrine. It keeps us focused on our direction in life and explains where we came from. If we believe that the *Bible* was written by men who were inspired by the hand of God, then one has to assume that to be true. This thought process includes one important element which is many times overlooked in the study of religion. This is the important element of choice! This choice gives mankind the opportunity to decide whether or not to accept God as the creator. If you stop and think about it, we have been given an incredible option.

272

There is a negative side to this and we'll discuss it as well.

Those who study the doctrines created for Christians know that the *Bible* tolerates very few possibilities of choice! The *Bible* teaches us that if we chose to follow God, we must follow a set of rules in order to maintain a sense of order and discipline. Failing to do this creates a road full of ups and downs. It is this concept that isolates those who diligently seek a better understanding of God, from those that question His possible presence.

Without accepting God's existence, how can we explain the fact that the teachings of the **Bible** are the foundation of so many religions? Who else but God has the authority to determine what is right and wrong regarding the ideas and principles behind these religions? Is it by accident that God has allowed us to pursue so many different areas of study?

Some Personal Observations Along My Road to God

How can the love of one God create so many different types of worship? In my personal religious journey, many fundamental questions have come to mind.

How does one manage to believe in a supreme presence, especially at a time when man's technology and scientific studies seem to be far superior than those of the past? How does mankind believe that an ancient God still cares about the future of this world? As I grew older, these questions began to answer themselves.
Studying the many aspects of different religions enabled me to see how strongly mankind feels about worshiping God. I learned that there are many different degrees of communication by which man develops his relationship with God. Religion carries with it as many liabilities as it does assets. In America's early years, religion became a very arrogant search for God. The pioneers were in many ways reckless in how they carried the torch of light in America's road towards the Almighty. Escape from religious persecution was one reason for immigrating to the New World. However, it seems that the early settlers were generally unwilling to grant religious liberties for different beliefs. If the men and women of that time did not closely follow the examples set forth by those in charge, discipline became the leaders' ultimate responsibility.
Why did man feel the need to protect God, an all-powerful being and creator of all things, from those who were said to be weak and unworthy?

America's early religion carried with it a need to reprimand "sinners" and this caused great divisions.

It appears that human beings have a built-in self-destructive mechanism.

This causes us to not only to subconsciously destroy ourselves, but to destroy those around us as well. In fact, our behavior is a real test of God's love for us. The reason why God has not given up on his people has to do with His infinite love for us.

God's infinite love has always been a mystery to me. Religion teaches us that although God truly loves us, we are unworthy to receive Him. I have learned that in order to compensate for this fact, I must accept deliverance from the son of God. This philosophy is part of the Christian doctrine and it teaches us how to live our lives in such a way as to please God. The King James version of the *Bible* gives us a history lesson that not only helps us to understand the past, but also the present and the future.

In my forty years of life, I have witnessed the fact that many people, at one time or another, have had a love/hate relationship with God. Many others fall into the belief that He doesn't exist. There is even a small sector that believes God exists, but as a woman.

In my opinion, no matter what your belief is, it all falls under the category of religion. I am a true believer of God's infinite greatness; therefore, I believe that man's search for God must be equally as great. One reason so many religions exist is man's attempt to find the one, true God.

**American Minorities
& the Introduction of Religion**

At this point I'd like to give you an overall synopsis of God's relationship with the Black race. I mentioned earlier in this book that Christianity was introduced to Black Americans for very selfish reasons. This is also true of the American Indian.

White Americans felt an insatiable urge to indoctrinate all those around them with their sectarian principles. This impulse; however, did not originate from an overwhelming love for mankind. Actually it stemmed from other important needs that had to be met! To assume that the introduction of religion to the American Indians and Blacks was an act of kindness, is purely hypothetical. Religion was meant to tame the savage and restless spirit of the Indian and the black man. Religion was to ease the anger and hostile energy that was prevalent among these two races of people.

The behavior was widespread because of the white man's selfish character and actions.

This plan would ultimately backfire. Religion became a source of understanding, wisdom and inspiration for our people. Frankly, to put this bluntly, God would never allow Himself to be manipulated by anyone, not even the white man. The power of God's written word could not be held to the realm in which it was planned. No one could manipulate the word of God not even the white man.

The Word of God, seemed to spread to higher levels of manifestation. This was beneficial for all involved. It gave the white man a feeling of false security against the underlying rebellion that was brewing in the black community. We cannot deny the fact that the white man forced himself into the black man's existence. The white man also took land and everything else that he wanted from native Americans. This instigated many negative feelings and resulted in a multitude of vindictive actions and reactions.

As the white man strived to build a civilized nation, amongst those whom he had taken so much from, the indoctrination of religion eased the guilt he subconsciously felt. Meanwhile, religion helped the Black man to better understand the white man's mentality.

This understanding would eventually set the groundwork for communication. It also helped to dilute much of the anger and frustration that the Black man felt towards his captor. Most of all, by understanding the principles of God, they learned to free their spirit and release their physical bodies from the hand of the white man.

The American Indian had his own spiritual beliefs prior to his introduction to the white man's religion. For him, religion became a poison that the white man used to capture his soul. The Indians knew first hand that the white man did not follow the words that he preached. The white man spoke with a forked tongue and religion was the snake in the grass.

An element of diversification kept religion strong in the early years of colonization. As America grew in size and population, religion was truly the center for the foundation of our country. Many different aspects of religious doctrines were being practiced, but it was the understanding that there was one and only one God that made it survive.

Answers for the Body & Soul

At that time in history separation of church and state created the guidelines for religion; therefore, I believe that there are more principles involved than first met the eye.

The study of religion carries with it a desire to learn the reason for why things are the way they are and how the past and the present relate to the possibilities of the future. Many religions don't actually teach the word of God. They use the Word as a point of reference rather than the substance by which to live by. When government institutions overlook the power of the word of God, it causes many Americans to become clueless to the realities of life. Many religions address the same fundamental questions.
If I were to select the most common of these, they would include the following:

Who we are?
Where we are?
Why we are?
Where did we come from?
Where are we going?
Who created us?

If we are not alone, then who is it or what is it that quietly watches over our existence? Because of what is considered the standard teachings, I feel as if I need to stray from those teaching in the hopes of creating guidelines that will get you back on track to the main course of what we call religion.

In our attempt to; answer some of these questions, we have lost sight of the fact that mankind is a spiritual being as well as a physical one. Many religions offer only one response to each of these questions; however, there are two responses that should be given to each question. One gives light to the physical being and the other the spiritual being. Most religions don't understand that these two elements will always be one! Ironically, it's these two aspects that cause so much confusion in the teaching of religion.

The Forces of Good & Evil

I often ask myself if in fact the whole purpose for our existence on this planet is to make a choice in relation to what is right and wrong! What can be learned from this is the probability that there are at least two powerful forces behind our choices, one good and the other bad. If we find ourselves denying the existence of these two powers, then we have already underestimated religion's true content. Understanding the presence of these powers should teach us, if nothing else, that we are not alone.

Knowing that there are two great powers which influence our existence one way or another, then it is to our advantage to learn as much as possible about what we are dealing with. This is where the true study of religion comes into play. Universally, I believe religion is a book filled with countless chapters each of which teach us that many worlds comprise this universe. Hence, by reading only one chapter we limit the extent of our knowledge. On the other hand, by reading the entire book many times over, we increase our possibilities for enrichment would increase and our ability for understanding would be endless.

Good and evil have been at the core of all religious teachings. The positive and loving things are God-like; where as, the negative and evil things are associated with the Devil or Satan. Throughout history, society has acknowledged the existence of these two powerful entities. History also teaches us that great battles have been fought in the struggle between good and evil. I believe that even the greatest mathematician hasn't figured out the billions of lives that have been lost as a result of this great effort. Most of the people in the world see life only in one dimension; therefore, it is very difficult for many of us to perceive the tremendous spiritual battles that go on around us every day .

If in fact there are two conflicting forces working against each other, it is safe to assume that a constant battle is taking place.

Many of us cannot see how these adversaries came to be. How did we become the pawns of their physical battles? In this case, I have to go to the source, the Bible and explore the possible likelihood of how this came to happen. Hebrews, Chapter 1, verse 2 says, "Hath in these last days spoken unto us by his Son, whom he hath appointed heir of all things, by whom also he made the *worlds;*" And chapter 11, verse 3 says, "Through faith we understand that the *worlds* were framed by the word of God, so that things which are seen were not made of things which do appear." I italicized the word *worlds* in both verses I wanted to bring to your attention the fact that in both verses the word is plural, meaning more than one world. We must conclude from this that God created many worlds not just the one we are aware of!

If this is the case, then we can assume there are many unsolved mysteries! If we consider the existence of a positive energy or entity in the universe: conversely a negative being must also co-exist. Yes, the possibility of a powerful negative entity is out there as well.

I said earlier that I consider religion to be man's search for God; however, you can bet those energies that oppose Him have a tremendous understanding of His divine purpose.

Religion's & The *Bibles* Status in America

Let's turn to the earliest known blueprint, the original source, the *Bible.* Most Americans have very limited religious knowledge. As a matter of fact, if we eliminated God's preachers, the instruments of God's word, then most of us would be oblivious to the wonders that encompass the spiritual world. For those who seek God, there is an abundance of positive rewards. In our country many find themselves feeling disappointed, defeated and destroyed by life. They find that even religion can't offer them a solution to the woes of everyday life.

Though there are many who choose to worship God as a part of their quest for survival, there are countless others who question whether or not religion has any purpose at all in America. Is it the pursuit of religion which helps to keep the moral fabric of our country strong and steady, or is the lack of it which causes us to grow weak? There are many different aspects of religion. Where do we begin?

The only logical place to start is at the beginning.

In the *Bible* lies the Word of God, written by those who have been inspired by God himself! Many people refuse to accept the Bible as the word of God. They believe that mankind, with all his imperfections, couldn't have been capable of transcribing God's works. How could man, with all his imperfections, be capable of accomplishing this feat? Mankind is the most intelligent creature on the face of the earth; therefore it would only stand to reason that God would have chosen one of us to carry on his message, in the hope that it would help guide us in the future.

Most Americans' desire to learn the *Bible* has never been strong. However, to those that use the *Bible* as a guideline by which to grow spiritually stronger and wiser, it takes on a whole different meaning. If we were to take a survey, I am sure we would find that nine out of ten people in this country have very limited knowledge of the contents of this great work. The average American, will possibly recall the birth of Christ, the death of Christ and of course, the story of Moses and the Ten Commandments! Many people recognize these stories because they have been told and retold in books, television and movies.

But very few people have read the Bible from cover to cover, not to mention taking the time to read an occasional verse or two! The reason for this is that we simply don't care! Most Americans feel there are many other books to learn from.

Throughout this chapter, you will find many references from the *Bible*, for those of you who shy away from the word of God, it is important that you have an opportunity to hear His words. Proverbs: chapter 1, verse 7, " The fear of the Lord is the beginning of knowledge: but fools despise wisdom and instruction."

The above verse is important for us to understand. The Bible explains to us the necessary requirements for the beginning of one's understanding. Whether you agree or disagree is strictly up to you! It is important for to you realize that in order to open your eyes to the possibility of other worlds it helps to understand the conditions of this one.

The *Bible* on the Powers of Good & Evil

We are made aware of the evil prince of this world throughout the Bible. This awareness will give you the understanding of how and where these powers, both good and evil, come from.

These forces of good and evil have been around long before you and I ever began our walk on this planet! The *Bible* teaches us that these forces know each other's existence and understand the power of their perimeters.

An example of this can be found in Matthew, Chapter 4, Verse 1, "Then Jesus was led up of the spirit into the wilderness to be tempted of the Devil." Verse 5, "Then the Devil taketh him up into the holy city and setteth him on a pinnacle of the temple." Verse 6, "And saith unto him, If thou be the son of God, cast thyself down: for it is written, He shall give his angels charge concerning thee: and in their hand they shall bear thee up, least at any time thou dash thy foot against a stone. Stay with me closely, there's a reason that I am leading you towards this direction. Verse 8, "Again, the Devil taketh him up into an exceeding high mountain, and shewth unto him all the Kingdoms of the worlds, and the glory of them;" Verse 9, "And saith unto him, all these things will I give thee, if thou fall down and worship me." Stay with me now, "Verse 10, "Then saith Jesus unto him, get thee hence, Satan: for it is written, Thou shalt worship the Lord thy God, and Him only shalt thou serve." Verse 11, "Then the Devil leaveth him and, behold, angels came and ministered unto him."

Ok, I'm sure that many of you are trying to figure out where the above paragraph is leading. Well, here's a Sunday school lesson, after all, how many of you find the time to go to church on Sundays? Actually, the reason for my preaching is to help make you aware of the powers at hand and to point out once again that they are aware of each other's existence.

In fact, these adversaries even know one another by name. "Get thee hence, Satan," God said. And the Devil left. This is a very important acknowledgement! One power tells the other to leave! It gives a direct command which means that one power has authority over the other. The point I am making is that the power of one source is greater than the other.

Once this information is absorbed, no one can take this knowledge away from you!

I hope you perceived that the encounter between good and evil took place in two alternate worlds, the spirit world and the physical world. As you read the Word, it is important that you grasp every single word. Many of us see and understand the physical world, but now we have just read for ourselves that in fact there is at least one other world, the spirit of man.

An Untapped Power

I would like to take you from the norm as far as religion is concerned. I'm not really sure that you are ready for what I am about to share with you. The fact is that within man's search for God lies a very potent power.

Many religions, stumble over the word without getting close to tapping the core of these infinite resources. I have studied a number of religions and the common ground between them in most of them is that they hold back an internal power that comes with man's search for God. Often, many religious teachings are afraid to dig down into the well of knowledge and unleash the true potential of the word. Perhaps, society is too simple-minded to handle the utmost power that accompanies the word of the Most High! Many who study religion often put too many limitations on its content, rather than gaining a full understanding of its meaning. Granted, I am aware that with an increase of knowledge comes the slow process of evaluation. What is evident to me is that although society has been built on a solid foundation of reasonable understanding, it is very naive when it comes to any kind of relationship with God. Of course, Jesus said that we should go to Him as a child, so who am I to argue? By following America's traditional approach to religion, we are missing the big picture.

There are infinite possibilities that exist in the many worlds that surround us!

My Walk Towards Enlightenment

My family, like many other minorities, was educated in the Catholic faith.

Catholicism is regimented and oftentimes methodical. I can still remember the program we had to study in order to become Catholics. It is called *Catechism*, the study of certain religious doctrines and a prerequisite to joining the church. Catechism teaches us the Commandments or the rules by which to live by, and the basic rituals of Catholicism. In a way, the teachings are a form of programming and deprogramming. This instruction gives us the basic rituals and the understanding of their importance. The Catholic religion taught me how to be a good Christian. The Pope, who is at the head of the Catholic pyramid, is the next best thing to God. He is followed by the cardinals, the bishops, archbishops and finally the parish priests. They remind us that we are at the bottom of the totem pole of this righteous order.

As a small child, it was comforting to know that God truly loved me and that His love stood next to nothing else in the world.

In fact, the early years in a child's life are the most important years for religious instruction are the early years of a child's life. During those years our hearts are open, they are not yet hardened by the disappointments of life.

When the government prohibited prayer in our schools, it cut off an important communication process for our kids. However, when I grew up, the acknowledgement that God was watching over me was a truly wonderful experience. We were taught that in order to truly become one with God, we had to follow the ways of our elders.

In the Catholic religion there are many symbols that must be revered in the worship of God! I am still mystified by the power of that strange looking necklace, the rosary. This necklace of strategically placed beads is used in prayer. To this day, I am still not sure if the beads were a reminder of how many times I had to repeat the same prayer or if they were there for some divine reason! In addition to the rosary, there are also statues of saints, that demand respect as well. We were taught to bow or genuflect in the presence of these saintly statues.

In the Catholic church, there are many things that are considered sacred. To become a good Catholic, one must understand the importance of each symbol.

An important aspect of the Catholic religion is that there's a superstar and a tremendous supporting cast! On our altar stood the direct family of Christ, His mother and His cousin, John the Baptist. Many times a statue of one or more of the apostles, such as Peter and Paul, would be present. The church windows symbolized the story of the death of Jesus on the cross were made up of glass pictures that told a story of the last moments before Jesus died on the cross.

At the time, I didn't mind learning the many aspects of the Catholic religion. There wasn't anything I would not have done for the love and acceptance of God or the church that worshiped Him. I even went through the training of becoming an altar boy. During one of the services I attended, I remember thinking, this is as close to God as is humanly possible.

I didn't recognize it at that time, but there was something stirring inside of me. This feeling surfaced after my stepfather's funeral. During the service, I was the lead altar boy, although I was only twelve years old. I remembered looking out over the congregation and thinking to myself, "Is this all there is to God and the people who worship Him?" There had to be more to church than what I was aware of! My mother had the same ambiguous feelings about her faith.

Since then, the pursuit of religion has become a hunger. Unlike the hunger we feel for food, this hunger nourishes the spirit inside of us which is often neglected.

This nourishment is often overlooked, and as a Catholic, I saw that the church lacked a sense of spiritual growth. The Catholic religion seems to take great measures to educate its members with the knowledge and understanding of the ways of the church; however, in the process, it seems to ignore the fulfillment of a man's spirit. I can see how this has happened. One of the main reasons is a lack of time spent teaching the Word of God. During mass, there is only a short verse from the *Bible*. Most of the service is made up of ceremonies and rituals.

If I were to give you a comparison between the Catholic church and food for the human body, I would compare the members of the Catholic church to infants, breast-fed by their mother! A mothers' milk is good for an infant, but it doesn't offer any real food for the spiritual body. It is not meat and potatoes! Now don't get me wrong, I don't want to appear negative towards the Catholic church. What I am saying is that there is a limit to one's spiritual growth with this religion. Although the members of the Catholic congregation increase in numbers, the person's spirit remains stagnant.

During mass, which lasts approximately one hour, there is only a few minutes devoted to the word of God. Let me take a moment and make something perfectly clear. I am not discrediting and will not discredit any religion that offers any degree of spiritual guidance for mankind. My purpose is not to put any religion down, so please don't even go there! What I am trying to do is to give you my point of view from a very candid perspective.

The reason we have so many different religions is so that we can offer society the opportunity to find a personal relationship with God. For the record, I want to say that I truly cherished my time with the Catholic church. I am glad it had its place in my spiritual foundation! However, like many things in life, there comes a time to move on.

At one point, as my family searched for a more fulfilling spiritual path, I made a quick stop at the door of the Baptist church. One of the many things that I appreciated about my mom was that after the age of twelve, she gave us the opportunity of free worship. The only criteria was that we had to worship somewhere! I recall my family going to three different churches on Sunday mornings. (I also remember not wanting to go to church!) Let me say that if the wrath of God, was anything like the wrath of my mom, then it was better to go to church than to stay home!

The Baptist religion was a good change of pace from the excessive ceremonies of the Catholic church. Its structure seemed to contain more of what was needed to stay in tune with God. It was at this point that the Word of God seemed to ignite a spark. The Word of God came alive for me and existed for the first time in my world as a life source. These present-day disciples of God take the *Bible* and bring it to life. It is important that we understand the following from the Book of Romans, Chapter 10, Verse 17, "So then faith cometh by hearing, and hearing by the word of God." I realized that if this statement was true, then the Catholic church lacked faith, because they lack the hearing of the word in their services!

Preachers offer many the opportunity to hear the word of God. In a sense they plant the seeds for those who hear it, to grow spiritually. In Catholicism, there's a lack of preaching the "word" of God. This missing link causes the spirit to become weak. I discovered many eye-opening revelations in the Baptist religion. One of the biggest things that I noticed was the personal change that happened in my life. It was at this point and time that I experienced a difference towards my perspective of the world around me. Life's good and bad elements seem to take of a whole new meaning.

I learned how *not to love* this world, to observe this world without the entanglement of materialism. The understanding of a better world awaiting me found its place. Sounds like a little bit of a contradiction, right? That was my thought at the time. The Baptist church taught me that although we live in this world, we are not to love the things of this world. Understanding this simple concept has taken me many years. I don't expect you to grasp this general idea by reading this chapter.

My purpose is to plant a seed that will begin your journey towards a better understanding towards this philosophy! The Bible says this about the matter: John, Chapter 15, Verses 17-19, : "These things I command you, that ye love one another. If the world hate you, ye know that it hated me before it hated you. If ye were of the world, the world would love his own: But because ye are not of the world, but I have chosen you out of the world, therefore the world hateth you."

Religious institutions should teach the Word of God because of its power to strengthen the spirit. If you find yourself in a church that does not teach the written word of God, then you must run! My walk through life has taught me that religion should bring the word of God to life.

Regardless of your choice of religion, if you are not studying the principles of the actual word of God, simply gather up your things and haul ass!

There were tremendous rewards in studying the Baptist religion. Eventually I felt that its concepts carried a degree of conservatism that kept *my* hungry spirit from emerging totally fulfilled. Friends introduced me to the Pentecostal religion and it was here that I found an opening into the spirit world unlike anything that I had encountered.

My initial feeling was that the members might have been nipping at the holy water a little too much. I soon realized that they were high all right, high from the spirit and the Word of God! These teachings not only brought the Word of God alive, but they bought the spirit of God alive as well.

Earlier in this chapter, I mentioned that we are made up of the three different properties: the mental, physical and the spiritual, Most of us address only the mental and physical parts of our being. We leave the spirit to fend for itself. The Pentecostal religion devoted itself to man's study or search for God from a spiritual perspective. This enlightenment brought with it a whole new world of possibilities.

The Power of the Spirit

The Baptist religion brings the Word of God to life and the Pentecostal religion gives that life power. Unlike any other power, this spirituality generates a power that needs to be kept within its proper perspective. Let's not forget the harm and destruction caused by an unleashed power. Am I comparing mankind's spiritual power to his physical powers? Yes, I am. In fact, I will even go a step further and say that any physical power is a mere one sixth of the spiritual power offered to us through the spirits!

This is quite a bold statement, but it's the truth. It is this simple truth that brings the power of the word of God into reality. This philosophy is elementary to when you accept the fact that mankind was created by a source much greater than ourselves. If we could go back throughout history and assemble the most highly evolved human beings, those with the greatest strength, courage, intelligence, wisdom, wealth and love, we wouldn't come close to creating a supreme being as perfect as God. I often question man's wisdom and his lack of effort towards communicating with the spirit.

Often many of the miracles found in the *Bible* seem out of the ordinary, and although they could be considered great phenomenons, the truth is that these are small examples of the power of the spirit of God. Once we begin to understand these things we consider extraordinary, it will become a lot easier to bring these spiritual powers closer to human reality. The Pentecostal church has managed to tap into these spiritual gifts and unleash many of its powers. Unlike many other religions, this religion has given man the possibility of communicating with the spirit of God. Other forms of religion limit the study of God because of the methods by which they worship Him. It is important to understand that there aren't any physical limitations in the spirit realm.

If you were to ask me if I thought religion has the ability to teach us everything regarding the word of God, my answer would be yes and no. Yes, I think most religious institutions have the ability to guide us in many aspects of life. No, I don't think most religious leaders understand the extent of that responsibility!

Those whose spiritual hunger has lead them toward a particular religious study are in most cases ready for spiritual growth.

Whether or not they achieve their goal will be determined by the spiritual foundation of that particular church.

Here's a little food for thought. The human body is comprised of the mental, physical and spiritual elements. It's also a fact that we use less than ten percent of our mental capabilities, then how has mankind been able to accomplish what he has with less than ten percent of his brain's power?

Just think what our world would be like if we learned to use twenty-five percent of our brain's ability. Better yet, imagine the same scenario using our spiritual instead of the physical power. What if man's greatest assets were of the spiritual world and we had the ability to tap into twenty-five percent of them? I am trying to enlighten you to the fact that unless we enter the door of our spiritual resources we are cheating ourselves of our own existence! This simply means that we can spend our whole lives without reaching our full potential! What does all this have to do with religion, you might ask? I say everything. In order to increase our awareness of the powers of the spirit, we need religion. Religion helps us to learn how to be aware of our surroundings, as well as to understand how to harness these powers. Religion also gives us the proper perspective in order to utilize as an asset to our existence, not a liability.

Could you imagine if America made a spiritual bomb to replace the one that it dropped on Japan? Think what we could do for this world. One thing is certain. Because it is of the spirit, it is not limited to the conditions of the physical world. I can understand why mankind has been allowed only limited access to these mental, physical and spiritual powers. God knew that man during his lifetime could not achieve the discipline and wisdom to truly handle these higher powers. If this is the case, it is very easy to determine just what our future really holds for us!

Our Limited Knowledge of the World of the Spirit

Many Americans who acknowledge the possibility of the spiritual world realize that this world carries with it both positive and negative resources. However, most Americans are not aware that there are constant daily spiritual battles going on around us. While many religions teach us about these powers of the spirit world, they often fail to uncover the realities which accompany them.

The *Bible* states in bold print in different verses "acknowledge the term *Principalities*". This word carries three definitions in the dictionary.

The first definition is: "A territory ruled by a prince or from which a prince is titled. The second states: " The position, authority, or jurisdiction of a prince; sovereignty." Lastly: "Theology. The seventh of nine orders of angels." The dictionary gives us prime examples of this lack of acceptance of a world we cannot see! I find the dictionary's definition to be evasive and incomplete.

The dictionary's first definition, a territory ruled by a prince, is incomplete. What it doesn't mention is that this territory is ruled by the prince, of Darkness, a term used to describe Satan or the Devil. When it comes to the topic of God and the Devil, it is plain to see that our knowledge is quite limited. The powers and energies of both worlds would have to be manifested into physical form before any real awareness can be recognized. Society deals with the physical nature of the universe and often refuses to see any other realm of life.

The film industry capitalizes on our fears of the unknown via the movies. However, Hollywood's deliverance of this realm of life falls short of anything other than the superficial. In most cases, Hollywood gives us a very vague and uneducated presentation of this subject matter. We often allow ourselves to see the negative elements of the spirit world and lose sight of the positive.

It didn't take the movie industry very long to figure out they could exploit our fears. Movies like *The Exorcist* and *Poltergeist* helped to stretch our imagination regarding the dark side of the spirit world. Cute movies like *Ghost* and *Heart and Soul* explored the positive aspect of this world. These portrayals do very little to awaken our internal need to have our internal spirit nurtured and fed.

Our healthy desire to feed man's spirit has always come from the study of religion. Granted, man has been given many different avenues in an effort to increase his spiritual understanding. Astrology, Tarot Cards, Yoga, Meditation, Horoscopes and Physic Readings are just a few of the many ways we delve into this realm. Organized religion has been the one that has managed to make the masses feel safe with its pursuit of spiritual food. I don't think it is by accident that mankind has created so many different religions, in the pursuit of spiritual guidance.

Society forgets the powers that are unleashed with its involvement in the spiritual world. Spiritual powers for the most part go undetected by the human eye. Many Americans celebrate Halloween, this once a year event is growing in popularity and manifesting very powerful repercussions.

Christ teaches us that if two or more are gathered in His name that His spirit will be there. Guess what America? The same principle when it comes to negative spirits as well. You can bet that this innocent, little celebration of Halloween doesn't go unnoticed to the spirit world. Most of us think that because small children are involved that Halloween is a safe holiday. Yet, year after year Americans put more effort in celebrating Halloween than they do for Easter Sunday. Quite frankly, I believe this can be attributed to the signs of the time.

The innocent ritual of dressing in ghost and goblin costumes really seems insignificant.
Very few understand that this is a form of evil worship, This is worshiping gods of a different realm; a realm that encompasses darkness and not light.

Reflections on God

A frequently asked question is, "Whose God is the real God?" This question pits religions against religion in terms of their principles and philosophies. A number of religions even offer the world a choice of Gods to pick from. Being of the Christian faith, there is no other God like the One I have grown to love.

And I know of only one God throughout history who has had the complete power over death and that is the Son of my God, Jesus Christ!

I often ask myself the question, is there more than one God? I ask this being humble in spirit and yet open to the possibility that if my God had a son, then wouldn't it stand to reason that the son would have a grandfather or a great grandfather? Religions are limited in this form of study, so questions like these are usually never addressed. Perhaps in our effort to understand this world, it just doesn't matter what we think or feel about the origin of God. Our knowledge is limited because of our inability to deal with this understanding. Many of the Christian philosophies have two principles which seem to have a common thread in both. These principles are, what God thinks of us and how we should relate to Him! Many religions lose sight of the fact that those two threads link man to his God.

As our society struggles to mature, our aspiration to clarify our feelings regarding our relationship with the Almighty is often lost.

It seems the more we think we have learned, the less we feel the need to associate ourselves with God. In our never-ending journey to evolve, many of us have found the confidence to grow, but many others have tried to erase the traditional concepts learned in the past.

A man's heart needs spiritual guidance to survive and in many cases, religion has not been able to keep mankind on the path of true righteousness! What does this mean to the state of religion in our world today? It simply implies that man must somehow find his own path on the road of life. Religion can begin by guiding us towards the right path. Without establishing a one-on-one relationship with God, we will never come close to truly finding our way. This fact becomes very important when you consider that there are many who live an entire lifetime without becoming aware of the need to embrace God.

God's Adversaries & Their Attacks

We must not overlook the thousands who dismiss God altogether. Most people would rather blame God for the lack of substance in their lives, rather than taking the first step towards communicating with Him. In an effort to separate themselves from God, their hearts have become hardened by the unmeasurable distance between them. Many of these same people take pleasure in criticizing religion. They describe it as a deteriorating institution and accuse it of lacking the credibility to set their spirits free.

In the past, many people did not take the challenge of declaring war against religion, the church, and all those involved with such institutions. They boast that many religious institutions lack the ability to lead the people towards a greater knowledge of God.

I ask myself if the battles against those representing God are not meant to be a direct attack on Him. The forces that oppose God's word don't have the power to directly attack God; therefore, their only alternative is to attack those who teach the Word of God. Quite frankly, since mankind is unaware of his adversary, (the devil), he doesn't possess the power to overcome this negative power. We often hear of the troubled times experienced by the teachers of God's word. These servants of God find themselves vulnerable to the powers that be!

At one time, I heard from someone who didn't know God. He asked, "If God is so great why does he need man to speak for Him?" That question has always stayed with me, even though I have always known the answer. It is mankind that needs salvation; therefore, it is man that should make us aware of that salvation and where it comes from. After all, *if a horse walked up to us and said Jesus Christ died for all our sins,* I think we would have a tough time dealing with that!

Those who choose to represent God also take on the responsibility of His adversaries as well. Society quickly gets on the bandwagon and persecutes any preacher that doesn't follow the straight and narrow road of preaching.

In discrediting God's conduit, they think that they are damaging God's credibility. An example of this is the Jim and Tammy Faye Baker episode.

I felt that this public persecution was a manifestation of the fight against God. Those who understand the battles that Christians must fight also understand that the Bakers simply became greedy, a characteristic that we all possess. Although there are many verses in the *Bible* that prepare us against this type of negative behavior, many still chose to view the Baker incident as a public hanging of all Christians.

This also brings to mind this verse from the *Bible:* "Many would come in my name." This refers to the encounters of false prophets. Many times the Bible refers to such episodes, but man chooses to continue to persecute God and not himself. There seems to be an element in mankind that enjoys to discredit God.

Throughout my lifetime, I have heard the following question being asked, " If God is so powerful, why are things the way they are in this world?" In many ways, God seems to get a bad rap from the human race that He created.

I believe that it is man's nature to be manipulated and controlled by the forces which dominate this planet; therefore, it is easy to see why there are constant attacks on God.

Throughout our history, religion has kept mankind on life's straight and narrow.

Religion has also been responsible for hundreds of wars and thousands of lost lives. Somehow its presence, or lack thereof, has been felt since the history of man began.

Unfortunately, most things in life have a good and bad side to them. We will quickly learn that this general idea is true when it comes to religion. I realize that this doesn't require any real wisdom; however, it does help me to keep things in the proper perspective. The people who patiently awaited the arrival of the Son of God are the same people that stood idly by while He was crucified on the cross!

In many ways, these various principles have helped me to understand mankind. Knowing it is not religion that has lost its course and direction, but mankind. Realizing this fact, we must realize is that it is not God who has lost the ability to communicate with his children!

God's Judgment of Us

My feeling is that religion matters little to God.

Many still don't understand the fact that it is God who created us to His likeness and not the other way around. The realization that there will be a chosen number that will be a part of God's glorious rapture is very rewarding! There are many different types of religions and churches; however, many aren't aware of the final rapture. It is a moment in time when God will descend from the heavens in a blink of an eye and take those who acknowledge Him.

I have read that God judges the heart of man. If, in fact this is true, then this should be the principal priority of religious teaching. To prepare our hearts and souls for God's acceptance and to guide us in establishing a personal, relationship with Him. Considering this principle, how has religion managed to encompass such political undertones? Has it lost the innocence of guiding us along the path that leads at Heaven's door? I believe that in the final days of redemption, there will be some men of God who will not be able to stand in His house. Men that we call preachers, pastors, priest and popes. Also, since God is said to judge the heart of man, I believe that, on this day of judgment, we will find the less desirable entering the gates of heaven! God sees situations differently from the rest of us.

Somehow religion and the church have lost sight of this possibility.

Religion should set the standards pertaining to God and His expectation of us. However, the many inconsistencies in the religious philosophies of today have caused a rupture in our religious fabric. Can this be blamed on a particular system of faith or should we take some of the responsibility? Considering the fact that our souls are at stake, I don't think there is much room for error!

A Controversial Issue: Homosexuality

Religion has the ongoing responsibility of keeping certain issues in check concerning the moral development of the world. I would like to talk about one such issue. It is a problem that is growing rapidly out of control. Many Americans are standing idly by without realizing the major repercussions that will follow.

The issue that I am speaking of is the manifestation of homosexuality. Will this issue result in the loss of countless souls, or is it just a weakness in man's character?

Homosexuality has been around from the earliest recorded history of man. Presently homosexuality has reached epidemic proportions. America seems to be a breeding ground for this particular lifestyle.

In a period of time when many of us seek shelter under the umbrella of civil rights, the torches of homosexuality are growing ever brighter. Many religions and churches speak out against such an abomination, but many present-day institutions have created an accommodating attitude toward this type of lifestyle.

As a group, the closet gays of the past no longer exist. Today's gays are new and improved. Their numbers are increasing every day and they are getting stronger. Their chant is "Say it loud, we are gay and we are proud."

The Christian philosophy teaches us that God does not condone homosexual behavior.
He destroyed the cities of Sodom and Gomorrah because they allowed this type of conduct to exist! In a world that has little or no respect for God or religion, homosexuality continues to grow.

I realize that this is a topic that many would love to debate but I'm not writing it for that purpose. I'm writing this book to express my opinion about a country which I happen to be apart of! Besides, this is a subject that has been around long before I arrived on this planet and will most definitely be around long after I am gone. So my assessment of this situation can only be based on the time that I am on this Earth.

Today, people find it trendy to be associated with homosexuals, especially in the major cities which are often much more liberal-minded than the smaller rural towns. Most people are aware that homosexuals exist, and so they have adopted the attitude "if you don't bother me, I won't bother you!" At the same time, they have lost sight of what is uncontrollably permeating throughout our land.

Some of you might ask what does this have to do with religion ? My response to you is that it has everything to do with it! Religion has the responsibility of guiding mankind both morally and spiritually.

In my opinion, homosexuality is a personal attack on the spirit of man. This results in the physical manifestation of the act. I have had the opportunity of observing some of the actions and behavior of many homosexuals. My observation has been fair and compassionate, not one of condemnation. What I have learned is that there is absolutely nothing natural about their way of life. They will insist that their lifestyle is completely normal; however, it is obvious there is something that is just not right about the life they lead.

I have also learned to understand this issue through the teachings of the Word of God.

312

Whenever I truly want to evaluate an issue with a real sense of fairness and honesty, I go to God's word for the correct knowledge. If my assessment of homosexuality is wrong, then I am not to blame.

In the book of Roman Chapter 1, Verse 21, "Because that, when they knew God, they glorified him not as God, neither were thankful; but became vain in their imaginations and their foolish heart was darken." Verse 22, " Professing themselves to be wise, they became fools."
Verse 23, "And changed the glory of the incorruptible God into an image made like to corruptible man, and to the birds, and four footed beast, and creeping things." Verse 24, "Wherefore God also gave them up to uncleanness through the lust of their own, to dishonor their own bodies between themselves;" Verse 25, " Who changed the truth of God into a lie, and worshiped and served the creature more than the Creator, who is blessed for ever. Amen. Verse 26, "For this cause God gave them vile affections: for even their women did change the natural use into that which is against nature; " Verse 27, "And likewise also the men, leaving the natural use of the woman, burned in their lust one towards another; men with men working that which is unseemly, and receiving in themselves that recompense of the error which was met."

As I understand it, the above quote states that homosexuality is the direct result of God's curse on his people. If, in fact this is true, then this lifestyle that many Americans have been asked to accept cannot be be considered normal, needless to say acceptable! We need to ask ourselves this question, "At what point is enough, enough?"

A few years ago I was managing an apartment complex on the outskirts of Korea town, in Los Angeles. Sixty percent of the occupants were homosexuals. When I applied for the job, the owner never discussed this issue with me. As I observed them from a distance, I could see that they shared the same problems and challenges as the rest of us.

What I learned as a youth, concerning my fellow man, helped me to keep the situation in its proper perspective. Something that Dr. Martin Luther King Jr. said touched my heart.

In one of his speeches, he said, and I quote, "Judge man by the content of his character and not by the color of his skin." These simple words taught me to judge a man solely on his character, disregarding anything else that might obscure the vision. I have met gays that are arrogant and flamboyant and others that are kind and considerate.

I tried not to explode in laughter when one gay man walked out of his apartment dressed in woman's clothes. I forced myself to see through all the external behavior and presentation. I acknowledged the fact that we are all God's children. I realized that as an individual I needed to accept the existence of these men and women. But I don't have to accept their lifestyle, especially if I truly believe that it causes some serious effects on society. It is a thin line, but one that most definitely must be drawn.

I recall a conversation that I had with one of the tenants. David asked me if I was going to march in the Gay Rights' Parade that weekend.
He said, "After all, I marched for your people back in the sixties on many civil rights' issues." I remember becoming very agitated with him. I questioned how he could begin to make such a comparison between the two.

At that moment I realized that his question was one of genuine concern. I think that one of the elements that feeds the growth of the gay community is that many Americans don't want to feel like they are being discriminating against them. Today's masses have learned to show genuine concern for those who are struggling for their rights.

Since most Americans have at one time or another fought for the right to freedom, we sympathize with the underdog and tend to give our unconscious support to them.

Most religions speak out against homosexuality. There are; however, those who are not affiliated with God and find it easier to support the struggles of the gay and lesbian movement. Those who do disagree with the gay and lesbians lifestyle must ask themselves if God feels any differently today about these people than He did long ago. If in fact God has not changed His mind, then the only way the gay community can continue to believe in its lifestyle is to hope for a society that has no need for God. Guess what? They have found such a society, they call it America!

If homosexuality has been around for so long, why is it reaching such a peak? Americans' lack of concern or pure ignorance of the subject has helped the growth of this situation. Let's stop for a moment and simply evaluate the state of affairs. Our gay brothers and sisters want us to approve of their lifestyles. They want us to believe and accept that it is perfectly normal to go against the natural course of life. Before I go on, let me make it clear that I truly have no need to argue this case. Everything that I have written in this book has been written from the heart, just one Black eye on America.

Many gays argue that their lifestyle is totally natural. They preach that it is natural for two men or two women to partake in sexual acts.
The fact is that anyone can justify almost anything if they truly believe it. If this is the case, then what is right and what is wrong? There is a part of me that wishes to sympathize with the homosexual's struggle. One thing that I feel strongly about is that this country has lost her way. Are we naive enough to allow the gay community to indoctrinate us with their beliefs?
Of course, when the President of the United States of America can stand up during his re-election campaign and tell the world that it doesn't matter if you are gay or straight, then this country had better stop and read the writing on the wall.
When the president is willing to sacrifice the soul of a country for the gay endorsement, then it is time to take a stand.
For those of you who think this is not a religious matter, you are dead wrong. Homosexuality is a curse resulting from a physical act that effects the spiritual being of man. It is religion's responsibility to give mankind understanding and knowledge. Let's take a closer look at the teachings of the Christian philosophy. I often hear people claim that gays can't help what they are.

One thing is for certain, if they do not acknowedge that there is something wrong then there will never be a need for change. Science has given gays an excuse. The scientific explanation is that homosexuality is genetic. In reality science has given homosexuals a reason to justify their lifestyle. Very few people are aware of the first recorded act of homosexuality. If you go to the book of Genesis, chapter nine, you will be able to read about it and the repercussions that followed.

God created man in his own image, and from man he created woman. The gay community would like for us to believe that it is ok for man to lay with man and that this is as natural as a man and a woman being together. The reality of the matter is that man and man, or woman and woman, can never create the balance between God, man and woman! Frankly there is nothing in the world that can change this fact, not even a sympathetic society.

I strongly believe that we were created by a source much greater than ourselves. At the time of creation, we were given certain guidelines to follow. These guidelines cannot be altered or changed by those who have chosen to ignore them.

Many gays are proud of the fact they have come out of the closet. We must ask ourselves why was this community hiding in the closet in the first place?

This proverbial closet of society illustrates someone who has something to hide. The reality is that
homosexuals have always been in the closet
because that is where this type of behavior
belongs. Those of us who are struggling to follow
the path toward truth should not have to be forced
to stumble over their way of life! I believe it is
wrong for their community to arrogantly impose
their way of life on the rest of us. The gays claim
they want to simply be treated equally, that they
wish to be left alone. This is not true! This type of
sickness cannot be cured if it is left alone. In fact,
silence is the homosexual's greatest ally.

Let's suppose for a moment that gays are the
product of a generational curse imposed by God. It
must follow then, that they have worked their way
out of the closet because of a weak element in
society that has enabled us to keep the closet door
locked. Now that they are out of the closet, they
have the power to contaminate the rest of the
house. Let's not loose sight of the fact that we are
dealing with a curse. Eventually, this contami-
nation runs freely into the streets and neighborhoods. This entity then moves to the city and
ultimately to the whole state. Is our society so
gullible as to think that the gay community will
stop here? As a strong society, we must all do
what is best for the whole!

In all fairness, let's suppose that this same closet is filled with something positive, and it finds its way into the house and outside into the streets of the city. Ultimately, the state and the nation are encompassed by this wonderful, positive entity and the whole world begins to sing songs of praise and thanksgiving. Could this be possible? The homosexual lifestyle (which we have been asked to accept) is a hard one to digest. Unfortunately, the fact that it has infiltrated our society tells me it is powered by a strong force of its own. We should demand to know the source of this power. Does it derive from God or from the Devil? The Bible teaches us that one person cannot serve two masters. Homosexuality is either of God or against Him!

Homosexuals have created their own churches in an effort to feel spiritually free and secure. They have made a mockery of religious doctrine. It is as if they were trying to establish an alternative religion which would circumvent the laws that are created for mankind. Recently, I overheard a sixteen year old girl complain about how much she hated her religion class. She attends an all-girl, parochial school. During her conversation, she mentioned that her religion teacher was gay. What's wrong with this scenario?

I thought to myself, "How can a gay instructor teach girls to understand the truth about their search for God?" It is difficult for oil and water to mix. The combination of God and homosexuality do not mix well. It is totally understandable why this young child is having a hard time comprehending the Word of God.

Many of today's gays are trying hard to convince us that their lifestyle will not have an effect on our own. This is not true!

Much of our confusion originates from the film capitol of Hollywood, California. This city is one of the biggest breeding grounds for the homosexual lifestyle. Hollywood can be considered the closet that belongs to the house of America. This small city has managed to slowly and methodically feed us with all sorts of propaganda.

Films and TV shows present us with this lifestyle. There are many who aren't aware of the fact that we are slowly being programed to consider this kind of lifestyle as acceptable. Gays and Lesbians continue to gain pride and strength in their beliefs. It is apparent that they have lost sight of the fact that Hollywood lacks the substance of spiritual resources that are needed to keep this mental/spiritual virus of homosexuality under control. Not all Americans have been oblivious to the fact that Hollywood has become a source for the infiltration of homosexuality.

The negative sources behind the gay community have chosen Hollywood as a base from which to stage their attack. There is a reason for this. Let's look for a moment at how this has taken place. Gays have been known to be a strong force in the infrastructure of Hollywood. Since its early beginning, they have been a behind-the-scene support group. Hollywood has helped to encourage the growth of homosexuality with its representation of it via the big screen. In the past, the gay lifestyle was scorned and easier to tolerate. Today, America's liberated views have opened up the door for the gay community. They are now walking out and shouting, "Guess who's coming to dinner?" The entertainment industry is controlled largely by the Jewish community. It is easy to see how this has happened.

The Jewish community doesn't recognize the teaching of the Christian religion, nor do they adhere to the Christian philosophies. A great number of Jews simply accept homosexuals because of their liberal attitude regarding this issue.

The Christian philosophies do not condone or accept homosexuality, but many in the Jewish community endorse and, in a lot of ways, advocate this way of life. How else do we account for the strong, thriving existence of the Hollywood gay community?

For those of you who still don't understand what this subject has to do with the topic of religion, let me simply state that homosexuality is a by-product of the Devil, religion's greatest adversary. Many of us are oblivious to the fact that the great manifestation of homosexuality is a part of the course of action that this nation is suppose to take. I believe that the mentality of this nation to sets the stage for the Anti-Christ. Even if you aren't aware of this fact, you can bet that the Devil is fully aware of it. It's this ambivalence that enables this lifestyle to be so widespread. There are those of you who approve and think it is cute for men to assume female roles and consider it acceptable for women to undertake male roles. You may think that this behavior has no repercussions on our society; but, again you are dead wrong. The more you see this type of behavior on T.V. and in the movies the easier it is to become accustomed to it. Believe me America, it is no accident that homosexuality is infiltrating the medium of television and film.

The media presentation of homosexuality causes you to lose sight of the fact that its growth is the result of a curse. This is the same God that despite many peoples' opinion, is still alive and well today in this country.

You must realize that there is a lot more than meets the eye to a movie such as *Mrs. Doubtfire.*

This is not a touching story about a devoted father who will do just about anything to spend more time with his kids.

The fact is that the more this issue of cross-dressing is shoved into your face, the easier it is to accept. That portion of society that lacks the understanding of the spirit allows this propaganda to infiltrate their minds. Although society truly understands that this type of action is wrong, it ignores its gut feeling and closes its eyes to it.

I have written these pages to give you a brief look at an issue that many religions, have swept under the rug.

In the last few years religion, as a great spiritual institution, has deteriorated and weakened her stronghold on society, The moral fabric of this nation is now in a struggle for its survival.

Many of you will not understand what you are about to read. I feel that one of the key elements that keeps homosexuality alive in America is our nonchalant attitude towards its increasing presence. In Los Angeles, California, for instance, the gay and lesbian lifestyle is condoned. Many communities accept its presence as a normal way of life. It has been extremely difficult for me to express my views on this issue.

I don't want to attack the gay community per se; however, I find it difficult to write anything constructive about this lifestyle.

They are our brothers and sisters, but if a family member is being destructive, is it not because of your love for them that you try to guide them and help them reconstruct their lives towards a positive path? What can you do when their hearts harden? Does one bow his head and pretend that everything is ok! I don't think so!

Nor should one allow homosexuals to shove their lifestyle into your face. And this is exactly what America is allowing to happen. In a way, I compare the gay community to cigarette smokers. You know that eventually their way of life is going to catch up with them. And when they are sitting right next to you and they start to blow their smoke right into your face, then it's time to say enough is enough, whether they like it or not! Although I won't apologize for my feelings, I want to make an earnest effort to fully understand the extent of the their plight and the burden that they have been forced to carry. To do this, we must have the resources to uncover the fundamental truth about the existence of this community. I will leave you with this: somehow, all of us have managed to fall short in the eyes of Almighty God. What we do after this realization is what we will someday be judged on!

Final Thoughts on Religion

As I close this chapter and my evaluation of religion, I wonder how many Americans are prepared for life because of it. There are elements such as tragedies and death which arouse the spirit of man. Religion should prepare us to be informed. It should teach us how to be mentally, spiritually and emotionally ready for not only the best, but the worst that life has to offer! I think this fact is worth caring about!

For those who believe in the presence of the Almighty, keep the faith. The world has changed tremendously; however, I don't feel that God has. It is important we understand that our life is not even a drop in the bucket compare to eternity! Religion's biggest challenge is to prepare us for the next phase of life, which will someday become a reality!

Religion will always be the element of balance, for a society that is constantly developing. Not everyone will be able to understand its purpose for mankind. One thing for sure, if we lose the format by which mankind seeks to have a greater spiritual understanding then we can count on a society that will not be moving forward.

I wish I could tell you that I have seen God and that He has a message to share with you which will help you to understand Him.

But, like many of you, I am someone who as never seen Him, but in my heart I know that He exists. Because I feel that God's presence lives with us, I have a reason to believe in my fellow man. It doesn't matter how many challenges there are in this world, we must believe that the victories have somehow been worked out for us. We must understand that through our religious studies we can prepare ourselves for being better servants. With the knowledge of what is right and what is wrong, we all should have an opportunity to make solid choices that will be helpful in our everyday walk throughout life.

If America finds herself not caring about religion, she must realize that one day she will have to answer to a much higher source.

The fact is, we are all the children of God. The fact is not all of us are in God's favor.

I believe the time we spend here on this earth is to find the path by which we acknowledge something greater than ourselves. Because of life's many challenges we all have at one time or another lost our way. I also feel that no matter who you are, or what you have done, a great element of forgiveness constantly walks by your side. When we learn to reach out and touch this love, then and only then, will we understand that it is not where we have been that is important, but where we are headed that counts.

327

Each day of my life, I see America move further away from God.

The paths we have chosen are countless.

What I have learned more than anything else in my life is that no matter how far we run away from God, we only have to turn around to be one step closer to Him. I realize that there are many of you who are straddling the fence in regards to your belief in God and religion. To believe that it is ok to live your daily lives without ever finding the answers that are needed to move forward is foolish. Let me leave you with this thought.

If there is a possibility that we have been given the means by which we can come to some understanding about this world that we live in then we must search diligently and pursue all possible avenues.

In our search for understanding, the one thing that we must not lose sight of is the possibility we have been given a gift, a special gift that we have ignored. There is only one thing that I can say about the prophets and religious leaders of the world, with great conviction. That is I know of only one man with the power over life and death, and that is Jesus Christ. If Christ is truly the Son of the living God, then It would be a terrible error for the world to deny His existence. In fact, it would be a **damn shame.**

Chapter Seven

Whoops, There It Is!

101 Facts about the Black Race that Managed to Slip by You.

It's fun to learn things about our people that for whatever reason have managed to slip by us throughout the years. This chapter, "Whoops, There it Is!", will bring to your attention interesting events and facts that I came across during my research for this book.

The following fact is of particular importance and it was recorded in 1517 by a member of the early Catholic Church. In an effort to encourage Spanish immigration to America, Bishop Bartolomes Des las Casa persuaded his crown to award each of their American settlers with twelve enslaved Africans.

In 1566, around the time of his death, Des las Casa expressed his regret in his book, *History of the Indies*, regarding his decision to enslave Africans. The book remained unpublished for over 300 years. Regretfully, this was the formal beginning of the Atlantic slave trade. By 1830, Bishop des las Casa's decision allowed more than two million slaves to pass through a door which changed the course of time.

Have you ever given much thought to the origin of the first twenty Africans that arrived in Jamestown, Virginia in 1619? How many of you knew that these Africans were not considered slaves but were thought of as indentured servants? Better yet, did you know how many were women? Seventeen men and three women arrived at Jamestown that year. Most of the Blacks that were brought to America as slaves come from an area known as Western Sudan, in the continent of Africa. This area extended from the Atlantic Ocean in the west to Lake Chad in the east and from the Sahara Desert in the north to the Gulf of Guinea in the south. It would have been fascinating to hear their life stories. Just think, these slaves were the first seeds that created the 200,000 blacks that eventually fought in the Civil War. Speaking of the Civil War, 40,000 Black Americans died in that fight for freedom.

Who was the first black born in this country? William Tucker, of Jamestown, Virginia, was the first Black child whose birth was recorded in the English colonies. He was born in 1623. During this period many of the white population did not consider blacks to be human. In fact, a Virginian by the name of Hugh Davis was sentenced to be whipped "before an assembly of Negroes and others for abusing himself to the dishonor of God and shame of the Christians, by defiling is body in lying with a Negro woman." It is hard to consider the white man's mentality of that time. One thing is for certain, there was a definite need for change.

Now if you could transport yourself back to that time period, you would see that because of America's rapid growth, laborers were needed to help in the expansion. To increase immigration to this new country, the government offered incentive programs for new settlers. For instance, an award of twenty acres was granted to settlers for each black male slave they brought into the Carolina Colony. And for each Black female slave that a colonist owned, ten acres were allotted.

The white man of the late 1600's was very superstitious. Any variance from the standard was considered unacceptable. Many of you have heard of the great witch hunts of that time and the paranoia caused.

What you probably didn't know is that Sarah Good, Sarah Osborne and Tituba (a slave) were the first women accused of witchcraft in Salem, Massachusetts. Their trials provided a premise for the infamous witchcraft trials that followed.

In many ways, it is obvious that this nation has made enormous strides. In the past, if you looked at a person the wrong way you could be hung for witchcraft. Now you can openly serve and worship Satan without any repercussions at all!

Here's a fact most of you have probably heard. Crispus Attucks was the first American killed by the British soldiers in the Boston Massacre on March 5, 1770. Even though this event (regarding the death of black men) was recorded, many other occurrences involving our people have been left out of the pages of history books. Have you ever wondered why so much information concerning the Black man is missing? Let me tell you how this happened. It's really quite simple. The history of America was written by the white man. Many events involving the black man were purposefully left out so that the White man could save face. Because of the black man's negative beginnings, the less written, the better. Pretty simple, huh!

Well, before this gets to sound too negative, here's a couple of facts to change the tempo.

In 1705, a trumpeter gave a customary New Year's Day salute to Judge Samuel Sewall in Boston, Massachusetts. This incident was recorded in Sewall's diary, and his notations are the earliest references to black musicians in America. Back in 1799, a black man named Demart Vesey opened his very own carpentry shop in Charleston, South Carolina, after winning a lottery worth $1,500.

Waiting to Exhale, a movie with a predominately Black cast, got mixed reviews. Do you have any idea how long the Black woman has been waiting to exhale? Well, it would appear that it goes all the way back to 1831. That's when the first Colored Female Society was organized in Philadelphia, Pennsylvania.

Do you remember going to the icebox as a youngster and seeing that big box of pancake mix? I do, because my mother's idea of making a big breakfast was to make sure that we had a large box off pancake mix in the refrigerator. When Mom decided to bless us with her pancakes, they were the biggest and tastiest pancakes around! Have you ever wondered who the big, Black woman on the box was? Well, it seems that in 1893, Chris L. Rutt hired a woman by the name of Nancy Green to flip pancakes to help him promote his pancake mix. She arrived in a costume consisting of a simple dress and head kerchief.

Five years later, Rutt decided to mass-market Green's character and named her Aunt Jemima. She has become one of the most recognizable trademarks of American culture.

Every day around noon I look outside my office window and watch the postman jump out of his truck and walk up to my mailbox. I always think to myself, "this guy looks a lot like the basketball player, Charles Barkley. Human nature is strange, we take so many things for granted. When I see this black man walking up to my door all I see is a postman. Like most Americans, I rarely take into consideration the years it took to get a black man into a postman's uniform. Yet in Lake City, South Carolina, back in 1898, a riot broke out after the appointment of a black postmaster. The postmaster and his family were murdered, and their home was burned to the ground. Ever since I read about this incident, I make a point of asking my postman, David, how his day is going!

Time allows us to take many things for granted, out of sight, out of mind. This concept helps the black man heal the pain from the many atrocities of the past. Today, we often forget the wrongs of the past. The U. S. Army advertisement states, "Be all that you can be in the Army." It wasn't that way in the beginning. During the Spanish American War in 1899, the Twenty-Fifth Infantry attacked the Spanish garrison in Santiago, Cuba.

334

Private Thomas C. Bulter and Private J. H. Jones were the first Americans to enter the fort and capture the Spanish flag. However, they were forced to surrender the flag to a white man who was masquerading as an officer. The man who took the flag was given the official credit for the capture of the fort. Today both black and white marvel at the fact that America had a Black General, Colin Powel. It is good to see that time has brought about a positive change.

The one thing I consider great about our history is that it gives us the opportunity to recognize the many changes that have taken place. Hopefully those changes will always be for the best. Unfortunately sometimes history reminds us of just how little change has occurred! For instance, in 1877, in response to claims that it was the "Nigger Party" the Republican Party establish the Black and Tan Republican Party. When I watched the 1996 Republican Presidential Convention on television, I saw a predominately white audience. I could not help feeling that in many ways the audience represented the same old philosophies that America had once embraced as a way of life. When you take in consideration the fact that it is the Republican Party that is fighting so adamantly against today's Affirmative Action Programs, then it makes you wonder if the Republicans of today are not yesterday's republicans with different white faces!

Let's get back to army trivia. In 1877, Henry O. Flipper, who was born a slave in Georgia, later became the first black to graduate from the U. S. Military Academy at West Point. Also, I discovered that 300,000 Blacks served as soldiers during World War 1 and 1,400 Blacks were commissioned as officers. Don't forget these numbers, because you'll be tested at the end of this chapter! Just kidding! Didn't you hate it when your teachers told you that in high school? Here's a fact about a group of men who were not kidding. In 1919, the black soldiers who returned from World War 1 service refused to march at the back of a victory parade. They felt that the segregated parade seemed contradictory to the principles they supposedly had fought for.

How many of you have ever been evicted from your house or apartment? Well, I recall a couple of notes taped on my front door that said, "Pay up or get out!" In the 1920's to avoid this embarrassing problem, blacks formed *rent parties*. These rent parties became a common feature of Black community life. To help pay their rent, many families would hold parties where they would raise money by charging patrons twenty-five cents, for admission, selling food and playing music. Wow! This gives a whole new meaning to having a few friends over for dinner!

During the 1920's Americans began to witness the emergence of the black athlete. If someone was to offer you a million dollars to tell them the name of the current heavyweight champion of the world, how many of us would become instant million-aires? However, what if you were asked to name of the first black heavyweight champion? Huh! Huh! Don't panic! His name was Harry Wills. In 1922, Harry became the first black heavyweight champ-ion when he defeated Bill Tate. Here's a related fact. Sugar Ray Robinson's real name was Walker Smith, Jr. He was born in Detroit, Michigan.

The following fact will probably shock many of you. Throughout history, this information has never been recorded in any of the school's history books. Some may even question the authenticity of this data. Let me assure you that the following facts are documented. It is quite interesting how historians have managed to keep these facts hidden so they appear not to have existed.

What did these four ex-presidents, George Washington, Thomas Jefferson, Andrew Jackson, and Abraham Lincoln, have in common? All carried within them the blood of African ancestry! Whoops, there it is! Doesn't this suppressed information say a lot about our American history books? This is a fact that you would never find in the America history of today.

When Abraham Lincoln signed the Emancipation Proclamation, he was helping to deliver his own people from bondage. This was a moment in time to be truly cherished.

I wonder what other important facts have lost their way or been kept hidden, deep in the back of America's closet? Here's a little bit of California history that goes all the way back to President Thomas Jefferson. Jefferson was known to have had mulatto daughters. Jefferson was the son of a half-breed Indian squaw sired by a Virginia mulatto. In 1918, Frederick Madison Roberts, alleged descendant of former U.S. President Thomas Jefferson, and slave Sally Hemmings, was elected to the California state assembly. He served as statesman until 1934.

In 1996, the minimum wage went up to $5.65. However, in 1934 in the South the average annual wage for Blacks was only $ 278.00 per year. The average annual wage for whites at that time was $452. If we translate this into present day terms, it means that in 1934 if you were black and working for $278.00 a year, you would have to work four years to pay one months rent on a large one bedroom apartment in L.A. today.

All of a sudden, the minimum wage doesn't look all that bad!

Here's a good question for all you basketball fans out there.

What team in the NBA was the first to draft a black ballplayer. Ding, Ding Time's up! In 1949, the franchise now known as the Boston Celtics selected Charles "Chuck Cooper ", making him the first Black ever drafted by an NBA team. Also in 1949, the Los Angeles Rams signed Paul "Tank" Younger of Louisiana's Grambling State University. He was the NFL's first player from a black college. Today Black athletes come from all over the country.

At the beginning of this decade if someone had asked you which state had the largest number of blacks, what would have been your answer? California, Texas, Illinois or New York? If you answered New York, you would have been absolutely correct. New York had a population of 2,859,055 blacks at the beginning of the decade. By the beginning of the 1990's the census figure for the nation's total black population was 29,986,060. The fact the Black race has not accomplished greater achievements is not easy to accept considering our large numbers. Our heritage is so beautiful, it would appear that this alone would catapult us into future decades with great swiftness and much momentum!

I guess the fact that each generation has to carry its own load is the reason we have not reached greater heights.

In many facets of life, we all have a tendency of taking things for granted. Our lack of knowledge in Black history has stifled our growth and awareness. Hundreds and thousands of people move into the Los Angeles area annually. I would be willing to bet that very few people are aware that our black brothers helped found this city of lost angels. Twenty-six out of the forty-four people who helped establish the city of Los Angeles were black.

Here's a piece of trivia for you, what was the first movie that actor Sidney Poitier starred in? It was "No Way Out". Like many of you, my family and I grew up watching Mr. Poitier. He carried himself in such an elegant fashion that many of our people wanted to emulate his demeanor. Recently, I had the opportunity of meeting Sidney and I can say that his character was just as real off screen as it was on screen.

It was February 19th. I remember the day very well because it was my Mom's birthday. I was driving towards the car wash on Pico when I noticed a tall, sophisticated black man waiting for his car. I recognized him right away. I drove around the block and into the car wash. Suddenly I had a bright idea! I drove up to Mr. Poitier and introduced myself.

I told him that it was my mom's birthday and I asked him if he wouldn't mind speaking to her on the phone. I dialed her number from the truck phone and once she got on the line, I told her that someone wanted to wish her a "Happy Birthday".
Mr. Poitier got on the phone, and when he introduced himself, I could hear my mother screaming with delight.
He actually spoke with her for about fifteen minutes, and needless to say, it was one of my mother's greatest birthdays ever! Thanks again, Mr. Poitier!

Over a hundred years ago in 1856 in Franklin County, Virginia. another very special person was born. This young man had the distinction of being chosen at the age of twenty-six to head an all Black school in Alabama called the Tuskegee Institute. His name was Booker T. Washington. He began his school in an abandoned church with only thirty students. Washington believed in the value of blacks learning different trades to help improve their conditions. Washington's philosophies were accepted a by White educator. His program which some black leaders were beginning to teach led many blacks from violence. In 1940, he was the first Black to be represented on a ten-cent postage stamp.

Speaking about education, let's look at education and racism.

Today, when a black high-school graduate registers at a state university, we take for granted the fact that he won't be denied acceptance because of the color of his skin. But this wasn't true for Air Force Veteran James Meredith. He applied for admission at the University of Mississippi and although his application was accompanied by a letter from Robert Kennedy, the Attorney General, Meredith was refused admittance. The fact is, the governor of Mississippi had personally blocked Meredith's entrance to the university. This caused many riots throughout the country. Eventually Meredith, accompanied by the Chief United States Marshall, was finally allowed to register for classes. This is something to think about the next time your child tells you that he doesn't feel like going to school!

I once heard a black comedian deliver a joke regarding Black History month. He made the comment that black people have the shortest month of the year to celebrate their history. Well, did you know that originally Black history was celebrated for only one week? Cater G. Woodson, father of Black History Week, created the original, seven-day celebration of our culture when he realized that Blacks had very little knowledge about their own people. In 1926, the first annual weekly celebration for Black history was established.

In 1976, it was extended to the entire month of February.

The next time you sit down to have a good breakfast think about this fact.

The first African-American company to be publicly owned and traded on the stock market was called Parks Sausage. It became available on the market back in 1969. Just the sound of the company's name makes you yearn for a large serving of scrambled eggs!

What is the worst thing that has happen to you while doing your laundry? Well, what ever it was, it was only a drop in the bucket compared to what happened to a black man named Dorie Miller.

On December 7, 1941 while collecting laundry on a U.S. battleship, this mess attendant heard Japanese planes attacking Pearl Harbor. As the planes roared overhead, Miller rushed on deck, manned a machine gun, and shot down four enemy aircraft. In a sense, he was the first American hero of World War ll. Later he was awarded the Navy Cross for extraordinary courage. What made his feat really remarkable was the fact that he was serving as a noncombatant in a segregated navy and he had no training in the operation of guns.

After receiving the Navy Cross, Miller was sent to black communities around the country to promote the sale of war bonds.

343

When this tour of duty ended, he was returned to the war in the Pacific as a mess attendant. In 1943, Miller was aboard the aircraft carrier, *Licombe Bay* when it was torpedoed by a Japanese submarine. All hands on board sank with the ship, including the young twenty-four year old hero. After the war, legislation was considered to award Miller the Congressional Medal of Honor. It was defeated both times.

Have you ever wondered who was the first Black American to publish a novel? It was William Brown who wrote *"The President's Daughter"*, a narrative about a slave's life in the United States. The main character was a daughter born to the President Thomas Jefferson's black housekeeper. The book was first published in London in 1853 but it wasn't until 1864 that it was finally published in the United States. It appeared in the U.S. under a different title, *"Clotella, A Tale of the Southern States."*
This version made no reference to president Jefferson. I wonder if the American editor was Black or White?

The first writer to document the lynching of blacks in America was Ida B. Wells. She was born in Mississippi in 1862 and orphaned at sixteen when her parents both died during the yellow fever epidemic. Wells began writing articles for a local church paper under the pseudonym, "Lola."

She started contributing to several Baptist Weekly in Memphis called *"Free Speech and Headlight."*
In March of 1892, three black grocery store owners were lynched. Wells wrote a series of editorials urging that the murderers be punished and encouraged black residents to leave the city. After the newspaper printed a particularly vehement editorial attacking the motives of Southern white men, The *Free Speech* office was vandalized and equipment was destroyed. Wells, who was in New York at the time, was warned not to return to Memphis. She settled in New York City and became a writer for *New York Age*. She continued to publish articles exposing the horrifying crimes of lynch mobs.

"I would like to thank the academy for the award," are words that very few Blacks have had an opportunity to express. But in 1939, one woman was the first black to have a chance to say that very phrase. Hattie McDaniel received the best supporting actress award for her performance as the mammy in the 1939 hit movie, "Gone with the Wind." Born in Wichita, Kansas in 1898, McDaniel became part of the vaundereville circuit and even starred in a radio show called *Hi-Hat-Hattie*. This actress had worked as a maid before she started getting movie roles. She once wrote it was better to play a maid than to be one.

Ten years later in 1949, another black performer was honored. Singer Juanita Hill's performance as Blood Mary in the Broadway production of South Pacific brought her a Tony award.

Another talented entertainer was Josephine Baker. She was born in St. Louis, Missouri, in 1906. An international sensation while she was appearing in the Follies Bergere, she is said to have received 40,000 love letters and 2,000 offers of marriage. I guess that could be where the saying " just say no" originated! Well, here's a little fact about Josephine Baker that I was told ten years ago. Apparently Baker was a distant cousin of my grandmother, Mattie Dawson. Who am I to doubt Grandma!

While watching the 1996 Democrat Presidential Convention, I was anxiously awaiting the words of the Rev. Jesse Jackson. Mrs. Clinton was the keynote speaker that night, and I recall a reporter asking Rev. Jackson if he was upset that he was not going to be on during prime time. The very eloquent Jackson replied, "It's prime time whenever I speak." I thought to myself, what a great reply.

The first Black to give a keynote speech before a Democratic National Convention was a Houstonian, Barbara Jordan.

In 1972 when she was elected as a U.S. Representative, Jordan became the first Black woman from the South to win a seat in Congress.
I actually heard one of her campaign speeches at a local community park about three blocks from where I grew up. Although I was just a kid, I was touched by the enthusiasm in her voice.
She really made me believe in this country we all call America.

It is unfortunate that American history has been so deliberate in her attempt to discredit the thousands of accomplishments of the Black race. I say this because so many of us are unaware of the black man's great contributions to American Heritage. Let's look at something many of us take for granted. In fact, the next time that you look at a clock to find the time, remember this name, Benjamin Banneker, a Black American born on a small tobacco farm near Baltimore, Maryland. He received an eighth grade education as the only black child enrolled in a Quaker school near his home. At the age of twenty-three, assisted only by a picture of a clock, English journal, and a geometry book, he is said to have designed and built the first clock in the colonies. Completed in 1754, the clock was entirely hand-carved of wood. It reportedly ran forty years.

At the age of fifty, Benjamin Banneker began to pursue the study of astronomy, spending many nights outside wrapped in blankets, observing the stars. Scientists, including Thomas Jefferson, took notice of him when he accurately predicted the solar eclipse of 1789. Three years later, he published an almanac for farmers containing helpful seasonal information as well as weather predications and tides tables.

About this time, President George Washington hired a Frenchman, Pierre L'Enfort, to provide a grand plan for the nation's new capitol and Benneker was chosen as the surveyor. He and his Quaker friend, George Elliott, chose the site for the Capitol and the White House and laid out malls, avenues, circles and parks. In 1792, L'enfort suddenly left for France taking the plans with him. Banneker and Elliott put their heads together, and working only from memory, reconstructed the entire grand design. In 1976, a stone marking the original Southwestern boundary of Washington D. C. was made a National Historic Landmark. In 1980 the postal service issued a commemorative stamp in Banneker's honor. If you are like me, you are probably asking yourself how this bit of knowledge never found itself in our history books. One thing I have realized is how many facts about the Black man are missing from our history books.

We owe it to ourselves to diligently pursue the history of the Black man for ourselves!

It is still possible to find a Crosby rerun on television. In the show, Bill played the role of a doctor. In real life, the first Black American to earn a medical degree was James Smith, the son of a wealthy merchant. He earned a medical degree from the University of Glasgow in Scotland and returned to New York City, where he opened a practice.

David J. Peck was the first Black to earn a Medical Degree in the United States. He graduated from Rush Medical College in Chicago in 1847.

You say that you need to drop your clothes off at the cleaners. Well, the next time you do, keep this in mind, Thomas L. Jerring was the first Black American to be granted a United States patent. In 1821, he was issued a patent for the dry-cleaning process known as *dry scouring*. He owned a dry cleaning and tailoring business in New York City and was said to have used much of his profits to support the abolitionist cause. An activist for the rights of his people, Jennings served as the assistant secretary of the first Annual Convention of the People of Color in June 1831 in Philadelphia.

Have you ever wondered who was the first black baseball player to play in the American league?

Most of us know the great Jackie Robinson was the first to play in the majors, however, Jackie played for the Dodgers which happened to be in the National League. In July, 1947, Larry Doby signed a contract with the Cleveland Indians and became the first Black ballplayer in the American League. He was also the first Black American to score a home run in the World Series.

In 1948, in Cleveland, during the third inning, he hit a 425-foot drive into right field. Cleveland defeated the Boston Braves 4-2. Doby played in the majors for thirteen years and was named to the American League All Star team six times. In 1978, he was appointed manager of the Chicago White Soxs.

In 1989, Andre Ware of the University of Houston was the first Black quarterback to win the Heisman Trophy. The first Black coach in Major league baseball was John "Buck" O'Neal. He was a star hitter and manager for the Kansas City Monards, a leading team in the early Negro League. O'Neal was named coach of the Chicago Bulls', (just kidding) I wanted to see if you were a wake! O'Neal was named coach of the Chicago Cubs in 1962. In 1991, at the age of seventy-nine, he became the Chairman of the Board of the Negro League Baseball Museum in Kansas City. This building was located on the same street as the Negro National League that was started by Andrew "Rube" Foster.

In 1966, Emmett Ashford became the first Black major league umpire when he was named to the American League.

Many slaves were delivered to this country by the Dutch and it appears that these blacks inherited the Dutch custom to celebrating *Pinkster Day*. This became a popular African-American holiday in New York's Hudson River Valley and was observed annually from the first half of the eighteenth century through the early nineteenth century. The celebrations had roots in an ancient spring festival and the holiday was also honored by the Dutch who settled in this region. The celebration was officially opened with the arrival of an African "King" and his entourage to the carnival grounds. These Pinkster Day celebrations lasted up to one week.

People paraded in colorful fabrics and animal skins, competing in athletic events, sold African foods, and danced and drummed into the night. The festivities were by no means just for black people, neighboring native Americans regularly attended the lively event. Apparently fearing the subversive potential of the crowds, since war with England loomed in 1811, towns in the valley began writing ordinances outlawing festivities. By 1820, the festival had lost much of its former vitality. Their was no doubt the large numbers of blacks paranoid made the white man!

Ben Branch became the president of the nation's first black-owned soft drink company. Dr. Branch Products was established in Chicago, Illinois, in 1983.

For some Blacks, the first place in America, they considered home was on the plantation. Here is a fact that you may not be aware of. A tract of land was not considered to be a plantation unless it had more than twenty slaves on it. About eighty-seven percent of the slave masters in the southern United States owned farms with fewer than twenty slaves.

Since the plantation economy revolved around slavery, the term "plantation" eventually took on a range of derogatory meanings derived from the slave culture and came to optimize the inhumane machinery and economic institution of slavery. Small estates worked by their owners with few black field hands were regarded as farms.

Plantations with many slaves were owned by white minority who, because they produced the bulk of the stable crops, had enormous political influence and power. In the United States and the Caribbean, these plantations were sometimes owned by absentee landlords and run by local overseers.

One fact you probably are unaware is the name of the first United States colony to abolish slavery. It was Vermont, and the year was 1777.

Although the impact of the decision on surrounding colonies was gradual, by 1804, all states North of Delaware had taken action to abolish slavery.

Today we watch our government try and do away with most Affirmative Action Programs. The fact is that our government has had a history of turning its head away from true justice.

On January 30, 1797, the first recorded antislavery petition was presented to Congress, but it was rejected. The petition by North Carolina blacks sought "redress" against a North Carolina law which required that slaves, although freed by their Quaker masters, be returned to the states and their former conditions. Black Americans were granted citizenship and equal protection under the law for the time with passage of the Fourteenth Amendment on July 28, 1868.

In 1889, William Owen Bush was the first Black elected to the Washington legislature.

Today, as more and more blacks accumulate their share of the American dream, we often forget there was a time when such dreams were beyond our reach. For instance let's consider owning property, something that is very common for our generation. However, back in the 1800's this was not such a common occurrence for blacks. A black woman by the name of Biddy Mason was known to be the first Black property owner in Los Angeles, California.

353

Born into slavery in Georgia, she and her master went to the Utah territory and then to California. When Mason legally gained her freedom on January 21, 1856, she began working as a nurse and midwife. Her savings and careful investments became the foundation that later enabled her grandson, Robert Mason, to become the richest black in Los Angeles during his time.

"Good morning, this is your captain speaking and today we will be flying at an altitude 25,000 feet." The next time you hear these words, think of this fact; Jill Brown was the first Black American woman to fly a commercial airline. She began flying single engine planes in Maryland at the age of seventeen. In 1978, when she was twenty-eighty, she was hired by Texas Airlines.

When I think of the challenges that Black Americans have had to go through to accomplish their goals, not even my imagination can bring me close to the reality of what they actually endured. In 1966, the citizens of Macon County, Alabama, elected a Tuskegee resident named Anderson Emerson to be their sheriff. Emerson became the first black sheriff in United States history and he served for twenty years.

"And now they're coming into the home stretch. It's For the Money on the inside, with Happy Friend closing in fast. It's For the Money running second and Happy Friend out front by a neck.

At the wire, it's <u>Happy Friend</u> by a nose..." The sound of an announcer detailing a horse race adds to the excitement, whether the race is at your local track or the Kentucky Derby. Did you know that a Black American rode the winning horse in the first Kentucky Derby? From the early days of horse racing, most of the handlers, trainers, groomers and jockeys were Black. In the first Kentucky Derby, run in 1875, fourteen out of fifteen jockeys were Black. In that race, Oliver Lewis rode the winning horse, Austides, across the finish line.

Imagine that you are a child sitting down at the dinner table waiting for a nice, quiet dinner. This is something that probably never happened for professional golfer, Calvin Peete. You see, Calvin was one of nineteen children, so chances are they never ever had a quiet supper. Despite a number of obstacles, including a left arm that he could not straighten as a result of a fall from a tree when he was a boy, he learned to play golf at twenty-three and turned pro in 1971. Peete consistently ranked among the top ten golfers in four PGA statistical categories: driving accuracy, greens in regulations, scoring and putting. He was the first black to earn more than $1 million in golf.

The 1990's have given hundreds of black actors the opportunity to see their work on film and television.

All-Black shows can be found on most television channels. In 1929, the first two full length films an with all-black cast were *Heart in Dixie*, starring Daniel Haynes, Nina Mae Kinney and Victoria Spivey; and *Hallelujah*, starring Clarence Muse and Stepin Fetchit.

Many movies in Hollywood have been reproduced over an over. Basically it's the same story, with different actors.

This next black has the distinction of being the first Uncle Tom. In 1914, Sam Lucas was the first black to play the title role in *Uncle Tom's Cabin* on film. He had been the first black to play the role on stage in 1878.

Today we can take a look at any popular magazine and find photographs taken by many talented photographers, did you know that many of these photographers are Black? The black man's presence in this country goes way back to the 1800's. In 1884, James Coway Farley of Richmond, Virginia, became the first black American to gain recognition as a photographer, he took first prize at the Colored Industrial Fair in Richmond.

" When I fall in love, it will be forever, or I'll never fall in love." When I sing those words, they don't come out as beautifully as when the very talented Nathaniel Cole once sang them!

Better known as Nat King Cole, he lead the first black jazz group to have its own sponsored program on radio in 1948. Nat soon began to concentrate his attention on his singing, and by 1952, he was one of the most successful singers of popular music.

In 1956 and 1957, Cole was the second Black to host a nationwide network television show.

Countless black groups, male and female record albums today; however, many of us never ask ourselves, "who was the first black woman to record a song?" The answer is Mamie Smith.

She recorded "You Can't Keep a Good Man Down" and "This Thing Called Love." These songs were written by her Black manager, Perry Bradford, who also wrote the next two songs, "It's Right Here for You" and "Crazy Blues." The first blues song ever recorded, "Crazy Blues" sold 790,000 copies in the first year.

I am really glad that I had a chance to add this chapter to my book. It has given me a new attitude towards the worthiness of the Black man's heritage. Before we go on to next fact, remember this the next time you pull a dime out of your pocket. Not many people are aware the portrait of the president, Franklin Roosevelt, that appears on the dime was created by a black sculptor, Selma Hortense Burke. She was the first black sculptress to design a United States coin.

She won a competition to design the portrait of Franklin D. Roosevelt.

There are many funny people in the world who have made their way to Hollywood to seek their fame and fortune. Unlike the comedians of the 1960's and 70's, today's comedian has more marketability because of the television medium.

Back in the sixties and seventies, comedians had three basic formats, either live on stage, on the radio, or through records. In 1960, Mom's Jackie Mabley became the first black comedienne to have a best-selling record. In fact, for years she was the only black woman comedienne in this country and was the first to become highly recognized.

In show business today, the term *prime-time* refers to the time when most people are watching television. Some people even give this title to athletes because they are so popular. However, the real "prime time" was a comedian named Flip Wilson, the first Black man to have a weekly prime-time comedy television show that went by his own name. His most famous character is undoubtedly, "Geraldine," a Black woman.

In 1972, the first Black television show sponsored by a Black business was *Soul Train*. Johnson Products, Inc., supported the show, which began locally in Chicago and then spread nationwide.

The Jefferson's was the first Black show to run eleven seasons. It made its debut in 1975 and starred Isabell Sanford, Sherman Hemsley and Marla Gibbs. The show became the longest-running Black series.

Alex Haley in 1977 became the first black to win a Pulitzer Prize. He received the prize for his best selling book *Roots*. Let me give you some background on the man. When he was six years old, Haley and his mother moved to Herring, Tennessee, where they lived in her family's home. In 1939, after two years of college, he volunteered for the United States Coast Guard. He devoted most of his free time to reading, writing letters, and writing adventure books. In 1949, the coast guard created the position of chief journalist, and he returned to civilian life ten years later to become a full-time writer. In 1962, *Playboy* magazine retained Haley to write a series of interviews including one with *Malcolm X*, which became a best seller that outsold his previous work, *Roots*. Haley launched upon a twelve-year venture to track the ancestry of his family. His research eventually took him to Gambia in West Africa where his ancestor Kunta Kinte had been born. Blending Facts with fiction, Haley wrote Roots, the Saga of an American Family. Published in the fall of 1976, the work brought him prompt recognition.

The book has been translated into thirty languages, and the ABC television network telecast of *Roots* was one of the most watched events ever.

I have often heard people ask, "How much money is enough to make a person happy?" I can't answer such a question, but today there are many Black millionaires. Since the 1980's, the Black millionaire finds himself among hundreds of others like himself.

Madame C. J. Walker is believed by many to be the first Black woman to become a millionaire. However, this designation is disputed by supporters of Annie Turnbie Malone.

Both women were producing new hair care products for black women while developing their businesses at the same time. It is asserted that Walker worked as a salesperson for Malone. Both became very wealthy around 1910, but by 1927, Malone's business began to run into difficulties due to poor management.

I ran across a piece of Massachusetts history that appeared to be somewhat contradictory. In 1630, Massachusetts passed the first law that protecting slaves who had fled their master because of brutal treatment. However, eleven years later, Massachusetts became the first colony to legalize slavery.

Connecticut followed in 1650, and Virginia, in 1661.

In 1641, the first baptism of a black person was performed in New England. The name of the woman is unknown, but we do know that she was a slave in Dorchester, Massachusetts.

The first known Black Baptist was Quassey. He joined a church in Newton, Rhode Island, back in 1743.

The first known black Baptist congregation was the "Blue Stone" African Baptist Church located on the William Byrd Plantation in Mecklenburg, Virginia. The church's name comes from its location near the Blue Stone River.

In 1785, the first black congregational minister came on the scene. Lemuel Haynes was born in Connecticut.

Haynes joined the Revolutionary Army and was later ordained in 1785. He became the pastor of a White congregation in Torrington, Connecticut, and was the first black to receive an honorary M.A. degree in 1804. Haynes was granted his degree by Middlebury College in Vermont.

As a black man in America today, I often wonder how just the system was during slavery.

At that time, prejudice rained from the heavens into the lives of many whose complexion was shaded with dark skin.

How would I have adapted when the aggression of the white man was running rampant in the life of every black? Organizations such as the Klu Klux Klan initiated in the South after the Civil War during the Reconstruction Period. They created white supremacists and used any means available, including terrorism. This group was founded in Pulaski, Tennessee in 1866 and was organized on a formal basis in Nashville, Tennessee, a year later. Its activity began shortly after the Civil War up until the 1920's.

I have a younger brother who has been a member of the United States Navy for over ten years. Carl works aboard an aircraft carrier. I wonder if he knows that the first Black naval aviator was named Ensign Jesse Brown. A native of Mississippi, Brown received his wings in 1948 and thus his story was written down in the history books, (maybe not in *all* the history books)!

In 1919, in Los Angeles, California, Georgia Hill Robinson became the first Black woman police officer in the United States.

Those of us who currently live in Los Angeles know that the current Chief of Police is a Black man. I would be willing to bet that many of you don't know that Dorie E. Spears was the first woman Deputy Sheriff appointed in the state of California. She was approved in 1944. Yes, that right! Spears was a black woman who was once a student of the Los Angeles City College.

In 1962, Judge Edith Sampson was the first black woman ever elected to the bench when she became a judge on the circuit court of Cook County where Chicago is located. President Truman later appointed her as a United Nations delegate.

Time always makes us aware of just how far we have come from the past, or how far we still need to go to achieve our goals in the future! Today there are many interracial relationships. Needless to say this has not always been the case.

On September 20,1664, Maryland was the first state to take the lead in passing laws prohibiting the marriage of white women to black men. The preamble of the statue justified the prohibitions of intermarriage because "it prohibited freeborn English women, forgetful of their free condition and to the disgrace of our nation, to intermarry with Negro slaves."

The law was passed to remove this problem and deter "such freeborn women from shameful matches."

Our great leader, Malcolm X, once made the statement that blacks should "strive forward by any means necessary." This wasn't a new philosophy to many blacks of America. On Sept- ember 9, 1739, the first serious slave uprising took place in South Carolina.

Twenty to thirty whites were slain and more than thirty blacks were killed for alleged participation. The uprising, led by a black man named Cutp, began about twenty miles west of Charleston at Stono. The slaves killed two warehouse guards, secured arms and ammunition, and fled south, hoping to reach Florida. They marched to the beating of two drums and killed all whites who attempted to interfere. Armed whites pursued the rebels, capturing all but a dozen. Just think that today there are times when we cannot get black folks to come together to sing a petition!

In 1764, Brown University was named after wealthy New England shippers, the Brown Brothers, who made substantial profits from the African slave trade.

On February 12, 1793, Congress passed the first fugitive slave act, making it a crime to harbor an escaped slave or to interfere with his or her arrest. This act, like many others, was put into effect to help the white man monitor and manipulate the course and direction of the black man's life.

One of the first elements instrumental in the growth of the slave trade was the development of weapons. The use of rifles and hand guns helped to increase the white man's authority over the slaves. March 14, 1793, a man by the name of Eli Whitney changed the course of slavery by obtaining a patent for his cotton gin.

Whitney's invention strengthened the institution of slavery especially in the South.

The American government has allowed many laws that helped keep slavery alive and well in America. For instance, by 1836, the famous *"Gag Rule"* was adopted in the United States House of Representatives. Under the act, anti-slavery petitions were simply laid on the table without any further action. This denial of the right of petition angered former President John Quincy Adams, who was also an ex-congressman from Massachusetts. Adams fought vigorously against this rule, helping to arouse public opinion in the North. Anti-slavery petitions, began to pour into Washington, more than 200,000 of them in a single session. In 1844, the Gag Rule was rescinded. Its opponents said the gag rule was an effort to deny white men their right of freedom of petition and an attempt to keep black men slaves.

Guess Who's Coming to Dinner is the name of a very successful movie, starring Sidney Poitier and Katherine Hepburn.

It is a story about the interracial relationship between a white woman and a black man. The story revolved around the events of one evening and the young man who is invited for dinner. A similar situation happened back on August 14, 1862. President Lincoln called in a group of blacks to discuss public policy.

365

This was the first discussion by an American president with Negroes on public policy issues. Lincoln urged Negroes to immigrate to Africa or to Latin America. However, many Blacks denounced the President's suggestion. If anyone ever made a movie about this it would be called Guess *Who's Coming to The White House.*

Richard T. Greener was the first black graduate at Harvard University. Later, Greener was appointed to the faculty of the University of South Carolina. The University's white students and faculty temporarily left the college in protest.

On January 11, 1865, Robert E. Lee, with his army at low numbers, recommended the employment of blacks in the confederate forces.
He stated that it was " not only expedient but necessary." On March 13 of that same year, Confederate President Jefferson Davis signed a bill authorizing the employment of blacks as soldiers in the Confederate Army. The war ended before any drafted Blacks faced combat.

During slavery, the slaves were incorporated into two different systems to accomplish their duties. One was called the *Gang Plan.* Here, large groups of blacks, especially those on the huge plantations, worked in the fields for long hours. The second system was the *Task System.*

Here. an individual was given various specific chores to perform.

In 1956, the home of Rev. Martin Luther King was burned in Montgomery, Alabama.

Often, even the highest level of authority has a difficult time seeing the necessity of change. In 1913, United States President Woodrow Wilson rejected Oswald Villard's proposal to appoint a National Race Commission to study the social and economic conditions of the black man.

Whoops, There it is! 100 facts about the Black culture that many of you might not have been familiar with! I know that I promised you 101 facts so here is the final one. As I researched the different sources of material to find this information, I realized that many of us often lack the desire to learn about the countless accomplishments of our people. On many occasions, I came across reference books that had never been opened! Many of the pages still stuck together, the books were untouched by human hands.

This is something that has to change! If we are not willing to research our own history and become knowledgeable of who we are as a people, then how can we expect the rest of the world to become interested? To do this, we have to get back to the basics and this is Fact 101!

The one element that became increasingly clear to me while writing this chapter is that the Black man's past is full of tremendous accomplishments.

We have faced unmeasurable odds and overcome tremendous challenges. This realization has led me to believe that our present lack of growth has a lot to do with the fact that we are simply not pushing ourselves to achieve our best potential. Writing of this book has taught me that there can be no other explanation for a sluggish black America! The Black man has conquered many of his obstacles in the early beginning. This feat is second to none and the facts speak for themselves.

OPPORTUNITY

The pessimist sees the difficulty in every opportunity; the optimist, the opportunity in every difficulty.

L.P. Jacks

Chapter Eight

Black Man Don't Cry!

I decided to add this chapter to my book after the realization that I had not dedicated my writings directly to my Black brother. As I began to jot down my thoughts and insights, I came to the understanding that I wanted to make my feelings about you known to the world! There's no question in my mind that there's no other man like the black man.

It is important for black men to recognize that within our being lies our greatest resource. It's not until we arrive at this realization that we will manage to find our true place in America.

We must make an effort to look beyond our past to characterize how we act and think of ourselves. Instead, we must ponder on what the present and the future will bring us.

Educating Ourselves & The Nation

Many have tried to evaluate the black man. Now it's time for us to take control and make our own assessment. During this process, we must candidly unfold the truth about ourselves. This simple task has managed to allude us for centuries!

As a young black man, I have often been asked the question: "What is this country's opinion of you?" I always respond with the same reply, "It matters more to me what I think about this country than what she thinks about me." This response should be the general consensus. Many of us don't see it this way! It is the black man's opinion of this country that creates and stimulates progress.

Americans have their opinion of us, they have done so by their actions. As I have shown us elsewhere in the book, all of us, as Black people, must learn that the past is no longer our enemy but our friend. As Black men, how do we learn to do this, or better yet, how do we begin to do this? Like most things in life, the answers are found right in front of us. If this nation's opinion of the Black man was formulated by our past, then it is the actions of the present that will bring on the new hope for the future.

Change Our Perspective on the Past

At times, I feel as if I am looking at this nation through dark clouds of fog and pollution. The fog is representative of this country's injustice to my people and the pollution is the anger that I feel because of it. To put my feelings of the past into the proper perspective, I must first embrace my roots. As I squint my eyes to take a closer look, I see that my ancestor's only purpose was to serve, nothing more and nothing less! Accepting this fact puts me on the path of understanding who I am as a Black man. If Blacks can only look at the past in a different way, no one can ever deny them of the gifts which come with their inheritance and we can become an integral part of our society.

Trust me, you are going to love having the knowledge and understanding that these gifts are yours for the asking. I feel it is important for the Black man, to come face to face with this issue in order to gain entry to the next level of under-standing.

Throughout history, mankind has never witnessed a greater display of spiritual courage, as well as mental and physical strength. In our struggle to survive against all odds, we have submerged victorious. However, if the Black man does not acknowledge our beginning as positive, then here lies our first hurdle on the road towards success.

My knowledge of this early period comes from books and stories that others have told. There is very little film or video footage which captures the views and arrogance that were so prevalent in this period of our nation's history. What I do know for certain is that our Black forefathers had great courage, a quality that is rare in our society today.

Blacks tend to view their beginning as a difficult birth associated with long, arduous labor pains. Let us compare our country to a mother and the Black man to a child. Making this comparison helps us to understand that the child eventually grows up, most often happy and healthy, without any recollection of the struggles of the actual birth.

Today, the Black man spends too much time attaching himself to his mother's umbilical cord. We view our experience of birth with tremendous pain. In fact, this kind of mentality constricts our growth not only as a people, but also as a special part of the human race.

Again I am not saying that the Black man should forget his roots. Never. What I'm saying is the sooner we learn to put our birth in the proper perspective, the sooner we will find the strength and honor that lies within us. Even though I have mentioned this before, I believe it is very important that the Black man gains a sense of reparation.

The statement that I made previously, "It matters more to me what I think about this country than what she thinks about me," falls in line with President John F. Kennedy's words "Ask not what your country can do for you, ask what you can do for your country." This philosophy enables me to see my people's ordeal with slavery as the birth canal through which we were brought into this nation.

Many black men feel compelled to remind America of their struggle towards our deliverance of our existence. There is really no need to do this. Trust me. After three hundred years of slavery, I don't think Americans will ever forget our delivery. If you don't believe me, just ask any woman who has been in labor for more than a few hours. Any one of these mothers will assure you that it is an unforgettable experience! Therefore, there's really no need to carry a sign around our neck that says "America, I will never forget what you have done to me!"

My purpose is to reprogram the Black man's mentality. This way of thinking has kept us tied to a lifestyle that has been anything but acceptable. To create a solid content of character, we must reach within our depths and find the power that will make us strong. This is initiated by the simple act of organizing things in their correct order.

I believe that as the masses come to the realization of their own individual power, an incredible manifestation of positive change will overtake their consciousness.

Let me add that this type of change has no respect for color or gender. Its potential is at the disposal of all mankind. Those of you who are not black can initiate a change in your lives as well. You can follow these same principles.

Although I stated that I am writing this chapter for my black brothers, I by no means wish to imply that these principles of growth should be for one race of people and one race alone.
In doing so I would be repeating the same mistake our white brothers have made in the past!

The Principles Behind Power

Each of you will have different elements in your power. First, let me point out that with power comes great responsibility, regardless of color. In fact, the greater the power the greater the responsibility. If you're not a very responsible person, then the acquisition of power will be more of a liability to you than an asset.

The older I get, the more I realize that this world is really built around the simple things of life. For example, with the acquisition of power comes the understanding which enables us to learn the responsibilities that accompany it.

By now you must be wondering what is the foundation that will create such a powerful and responsible race of people? It is quite simply called the blessing of humility. This quality helps to open the power of understanding which enables us to perceive the responsibility that comes along with it. I believe this principle must be applied to any individual as well as any race of people or even a nation.

In the **Bible** there are many verses that speak of the blessing of being a humble person. One that stays close with me comes from the son of God in Luke, Chapter 14, Verse 11, "For whosoever exalteth himself shall be abased; and he that humbleth himself shall be exalted." This, my friends, is the first of many gifts I wish to make you aware of, throughout this chapter.

By the way, anytime that you see this * symbol, before any sentence in this chapter, please be aware that I am empowering you with another gift! My intention is to show you how to gain power in your life. Whether or not you choose to apply these principles will be totally up to you. If we are truly visualizing a change in our lives, then it is important to understand that the challenge that accompanies this change increases as well. Many Black men are unaware of the fact that the growth process is a continual procedure.

Redefining Our Goals

I often ask myself if the Black man will ever recognize the challenges that stand before him. The changes that have taken place have caused us to become jubilant in our accomplishment. However, we have failed to ask ourselves where these changes are taking us.

*The Black man's future is based on the primary principle of hard work and concrete effort. Instead of crying about the injustices that have been committed against us, the inability to get a piece of the American pie, let's gather the necessary ingredients and bake our own pie! I believe that many Black Americans are slowly realizing that the American pie doesn't really taste that great in the first place. If there is any credibility to what I am saying, then you can see we have wasted an awful lot of time and energy. For many years the black man has envied the white man's world thinking that his world was something of great worth. As the black man begins to experience some of the fruits of the white man's world, he is forced to realize that what we originally thought as something special was actually tainted.

As I see it, the ingredients that make up the American pie are unappetizing. The overriding philosophy that getting into a certain tax bracket and making a lot of money equates to success. is false security. It is this type of mentally that entangles us to our past. Most importantly, the growth potential regarding our ambitions decreases. It is our personal ambition that will determine the nature of our course and the direction we will take. This is the one lesson we can learn from our history.

Education & Wisdom.

Each man carries within himself his own set of desires and ambitions; however, these desires should be determined by certain realistic views not by our past programming. Keeping this principal rule in mind, the Black man must seek to continue his education. We need to embrace education as an ally. By this, I am not talking about the white man's educational system. This system has been tainted with contempt and arrogance. The education I am speaking about is based on the understanding of a simple knowledge: The kind of knowledge that man must acquire when he realizes he lacks it.

The one thing our past has taught us is this: education, is the key to real universal freedom.

Blacks must understand that since the White man kept us, from formal education there must have been some great advantage to possessing it!

Since our race has achieved a certain freedom of choice in the field of education, it is important for black Americans to dig new wells of knowledge. Wells that require greater challenges. The black man should understand that education alone cannot transform his ambitions into realities. *It is essential that our education be accompanied by wisdom. Without wisdom, education loses power. Wisdom is a gift from God and not every Black man will be able to acquire this gift. **First** he must realize the fact that he lacks this virtue and that it will lead him towards the right direction.

As this direction develops, we should be able to locate those who resemble leaders. These leaders will help open our basic understanding of education and teach us to embrace it with a hug of wisdom. In the white man's world, this kind of leadership has managed to be evasive. We must learn from their mistakes and turn things around. Let's offer them a helping hand towards gaining a worthwhile direction! After all, the goal for all men is to light the way for their fellow men!

Our Day Has Come

God's son, Jesus Christ, in Matthew, Chapter 20, Verse 16, preaches "So the last shall be the first, and the first last; for many are called, but few chosen." *At one time, the Black man was considered the last man on this planet, but God promised us that one day we will be first. This, my brother, is one of the greatest gifts of this present day. Simply look around you. The power of our calling is tremendous. There are very few things in America that the Black man does not have an opportunity to (take a dominating role in.) If we haven't done so, then we must ask ourselves why we have not accomplished more.

Let's take sports for example. We have managed to dominate more than sixty-five percent of the top sports in America, in some form or fashion. Of course, the White man still dominates golf and tennis, but this is because there are not a lot of tennis and golf facilities in the Black neighborhoods. Trust me, as soon as the Black man learns to make the proper adjustments we will make our presence known in these two sports as well. As the game of golf goes, I hear that there is a new kid around and they call him Tiger!

History clearly shows us that at one time the white man passed laws to keep us from competing in their world of sports.

Presently, you can rarely tune into a televised professional game and not be aware of our dominating presence. Don't be fooled! This is all part of God's promise. At one time the NBA had no Black athletes, yet all the basketball players who represented America in the 1996 Olympics were Black with the exception of one! Does this *fact* make us the better athlete? I'll let you answer that question, but this change tells me that the word of God is unfolding before our very eyes.

The Larger Prize in the World of Sports

We have often lacked the wisdom to understand this. The white man created the sports institutions and he also created strong avenues which will always keep him eternally locked into the structure of the games. I am fascinated with the fact that it's always the white players who manage to get the coaching jobs and the sports' casting jobs. If you have five basketball players, four black and one white ball player, you can be sure that the white ballplayer will be the first to get a coaching job. Many say the color of a man's skin is irrelevant, but we all know that it is not true! Maybe we need to begin to demand more of ourselves.

An example of a situation that needs our careful consideration is the Monday Night Football setup.

In football, the Black man can run, catch and throw the ball; however, there's a bigger question on my mind. Isn't the Black man good enough to broadcast the game? Al, Dan, Frank, Lynn and Chris, are names synonymous with Monday Night Football. Four white men and one black man makes up ABC's broadcasting team. Is ABC trying to tell us something? Mr. Lynn Swan is lucky if he is allowed to make two comments per game! It is no accident that Lynn's job is to follow the game from the sidelines. Like the mailman, Lynn is out on the field through rain, snow, sleet and shine. It's not unusual for him to go the entire game without saying a word. Is the white man saying that we can play the game, but that we are not intelligent enough to talk about it?

Many of us are aware of this situation and you can bet the white man is definitely aware of it. We must be willing to stand up and say, "No, we have had enough!" Instead the black man chooses to accept these terms. Meanwhile, time goes on and the Black man gains little progress. I say to you, "Black man don't cry, because nobody cares!" Until we are willing to initiate a change and make the sacrifices needed which will alter our situation, we must accept the situation as it is.

How we can turn these circumstances around is quite simple.

First, let's begin with an announcement to the American Broadcasting Company and put them on notice. Let's demand a response on this issue.

Let them know we will not accept this type of treatment any longer and that we are prepared to do whatever it takes to create this change. Believe me, if the black man learns to unify in numbers, we can fight the small battles and soon we will be able to demand whatever we desire!

The fact is that although the Black man has a strong presence in the world of sports, he has not learned how to take advantage of it.

Why you might ask? I'll tell you why. The black man is just happy to be there! They are happy to be making the kind of money that most people simply dream about. Quite frankly, the black man is content playing the game rather than owning the team that plays the game.

Unfortunately, the Black man has not learned that the talents he has acquired today can open the doors of tomorrow. Most black men do not know that they have the power to improve their future, but the futures of those who will someday follow them. Many of us are called to the arena of professional athletics, but few have the wisdom to move up from there. Because of this lack of wisdom, we are unable to see that we are merely pawns in a game created by the White man.

However exciting and majestic the sport may be, it's just a game that kids play. With that understanding, the Black man must come to the realization that there is more to the game than meets the eye! We must begin by setting the groundwork for this change to take place. We must first start to look within ourselves and ask. "How can we make these changes happen?" "Ask not what this country can do for you, ask what we can achieve for ourselves and that will turn our situation around for us." This decision requires a tremendous amount of sacrifice and motivation. These qualities are essential to change. If these elements are lacking in a person's character, then we can forget about this change taking place. This kind of change will require drastic measures.

It will demand that all Black athletes take a stand in a united effort. The key word here is united. Unfortunately, I have rarely seen the Black race united. The only time that I can remember seeing our people united in a common goal was during Dr. King's March on Washington, D.C. on August 28, 1963. If it was not for this massive display of unity, and the Million Man March, I would have little proof that my people could actually come together for any reason except to destroy themselves.

We can come together for events   which don't really matter, such as ball games and musical concerts, but for important issues, we stand alone.

Just for a moment, let's visualize the scenario I'm proposing. Let us suppose all Black NBA players would stand together and boycott the system. Today, basketball players are high-priced field hands playing their games on the white man's new plantations. As long as they continue to make their millions, they will continue to lose sight of the bigger picture. This picture sums up the fact that we are just happy to be in the game, so let's not rock the boat!

A few years ago, Michael Jordan proved to himself and the world that he could walk away from the game he loved. For that moment in time, the whole world stopped, sat up, and listened to what Michael had to say. Quite frankly, if Michael Jordan would represent himself as the spokesperson of a Black association, people would listen. Why would the public listen? One reason is that Michael speaks about the game with genuine love and affection. Secondly, he is very articulate! People actually listen when Michael speaks.

Imagine the NBA dominated by white players. Scary thought, isn't it? Especially after watching so many talented black athletes! The talent of the black athlete would be gone!

If you don't think this would make a major difference in the game, you are wrong. I don't think that Nike's tennis shoe, *Air Jordan,* would sell as well if it was *Air Bird or Air Walton.*
Somehow the image of a dominating athlete loses its intensity.

Now back to reality. The changes that so many of us have been hoping for will never happen unless we make them happen. Unfortunately, this is dependent on the black athlete becoming aware of his true power. Right now the black man will not stand united for this common goal. Therefore, when I hear the complaints and excuses, I want to shout, "Black man don't cry! You are the cause of the problem!"

My brothers simply do not understand that the power for change is at their fingertips. Perhaps they do realize it but they are afraid to make the sacrifices needed for this change. I think this is a good place to interject a point which is not easy for us to accept and I will share it with you. Like you, I am a black man proud to be a part of such a special race of people. We have been so busy trying to amalgamate with the White race that we have allowed our powers to dissipate. If we could learn to orchestrate this power towards a positive, unified goal, we could achieve tremendous accomplishments in a matter of months.

I believe that the White man recognizes this weakness in our character and uses it as a tool against us. Ask yourself, why are all the talented professional Black athletes represent by white agents and managers? Better than ninety-eight percent of them have white representation.

The White man is smart enough to understand that even though we can earn the high price salaries, he can always have a hand in the spending of the black athlete's high salaries.

Could this lack of understanding be attributed to an absence of leadership? No, I don't think so. One key factor that impedes our advancement are the many distractions in our path. A large number of blacks have never had great wealth: Many of them lack the knowledge on how to make that wealth work for them. Many get distracted, living for the moment. They lose sight of the fact that a lot of effort is needed to keep this elevated lifestyle an everlasting reality.

Sports Vs. The Big picture of Life

Since the black man is unwilling to implement whatever power he has for his own benefit, professional sport's really not a vehicle for the advancement of our race.

We have allowed ourselves to be corralled into a section of American society and have learned to dominate nothing more than a simple game. In the process we have taught our children that the only option they have to get out of the ghetto is through professional sports.

The reason I feel strongly about this issue is that I am guilty of allowing myself to be indoctrinated by this same principle. Like many other Black kids, I have spent the greater portion of my life training for the honor of becoming a professional athlete. If the Black race continues on this course, it will find itself once again bound by the chains and shackles of servitude.

Do you think America cares about our actions? We have allowed this to happen to ourselves. Let me put it to you this way, do you think that the sponsors of Gatorade frown at paying thousands of dollars to an athlete like Michael Jordan when his endorsements create ten millions of dollars of revenue for Gatorade? Do you think that Nike cares that they are promoting a stereotypical image of the black male athlete?

I could go on and on, but I think you get my point. The truly sad thing is that less than one percent of the population achieves this level of success.

It is no wonder the white man is unselfishly giving up a small piece of the American Pie. How long will it take for us to realize that we have allowed ourselves to take second place to our white master?

Don't get me wrong. I don't believe that this should be considered a racial issue. It is natural for all men to want to compete against our fellow brothers. It is vital that the Black male not lose sight of the fact that our presence in this country is an ongoing issue. Sports and athletics are institutions that contribute to the well-being of our society. They should not and cannot become our only link to success. We must learn to take advantage of whatever resources are available. If athletics is considered one of these resources, then we must milk it to the maximum, or lose out all the way around.

In one of his speeches, the great Dr. King emphasized the fact that whatever our position in life we had to learn to be the best we could be. "If your job was that of a janitor, then be the best janitor you can be!" We should apply the same principles of courage and fortitude that enabled us to survive the arduous years of slavery to our present-day dilemmas. We must learn to take the advantageous position within the sport's political arena.

I am afraid that we have allowed sports to become a distraction that obstructed our view of the overall big picture. Success is said to be measured by the number of obstacles that one has to overcome. I'm hoping that our struggle in the sports world is just another of the many obstacles my people will overcome. We have spent the last two hundred years being taught by others. It is time to teach ourselves.

No Tolerance for Cry Babies

It is simply a human trait to cry out and complain about the circumstances that are wrong in our lives. It takes more energy than most people want to put forth to initiate a change. It is easier to cry about the fact that someone has slapped you then to make sure it does not happen again. One thing that I have learned living in this society is that we have little or no tolerance for cry babies (of any color.) This nation shuns whiners. It seems that we have more respect for those who take control of a situation. As a people, Americans have become indifferent to the struggle of others. There are so many different sob stories that most Americans simply have become callous to them.
This is not to say that these problems are unimportant or lack legitimacy.

390

There's an overall consensus that everyone has shit in their lives, we just don't want to smell it.

Action, action and more action is what generates the people's attention, not inaction! Americans have little or no patience for crybabies that complain about being mistreated.

Any homeless person will tell you that for every two people that offer assistance, fifty will pass them by and ignore them. If you want to get this nation's attention, you better know how to play the game. Of course, not all Americans think this way, but I wouldn't be exaggerating if I said that seven out of ten couldn't care less about anyone else's situation.

Black Men & Prison

In some sense, I feel that many Black people understand there is a need for change.

Unfortunately, many find themselves locked up in prison so they find it difficult to do anything but cry about it. They can only shed tears of sorrow for the realization that an injustice exists within our system. Fifteen states in this country have correctional institutions that have more than a forty-five percent black male population. Will this wrongdoing always be apart of the Black man's plight? In some areas the numbers are even worse.

Mississippi, South Carolina, Alabama, North Carolina, Maryland, Virginia, Michigan, Illinois, New Jersey and New York each have more than a fifty-five percent black prison population. Greater minds than mine have tried to analyze this issue; but the bottom line is that the black man is a scapegoat. America has managed to create an element of callousness that has grown thicker and harder over the years.

My message to the black brothers who are incarcerated and have become one with the walls that surround them, is to have hope. Many great men have had to survive years of imprisonment. Prison is the community's solution to the criminal element of society. For the black man the word "prison" denotes years of persecution and neglect. The Black man has been mentally. physically, spiritually and emotionally abused through history. Guess what now? America doesn't want to hear these woes. Despite this country's lack of empathy we must continue to strive forward. Our cries against this lack of justice go unheeded. How many of these men have been incarcerated for no other reason other than the fact they are Black?

The mentality of most blacks is that the white man wants his revenge, and in fact, there are still white folk who believe that the black man is "guilty until proven otherwise."

Since our government is made up of mostly white people, then it is safe to say that it is the government's policies that are unjust. Many of those that are incarcerated are simply bad people. But how many blacks in prison are victims of a society that has ignored, forgotten or simply doesn't care about their existence? The sad thing is that if the white man doesn't care and the black man doesn't care, then who else is there to care?

Investigating many of the crimes that have been committed by our black brothers, we discover that the white man was in many ways the instigator. The drugs currently found in the black community were not smuggled into this country by Black people. The guns and arm shipments that permeate this country didn't find their way here on black owned ships. Yet, our judicial system does not take these things into consideration. When the justice system decides to lock up a young Black kid behind bars, this issue should be taken into consideration.

We want to believe that the mentality of white America has changed. This is not the case. A while back I was coaching a group of ten year old basketball players at the Beverly Hills YMCA. During the middle of our game, a black transient walked into the lobby and confronted a white woman.

I didn't witness the incident, but I overhead someone say he had grabbed her posterior. From the corner of my eye, I saw the father of one of my players attack this helpless man. Everyone became very defensive. I quickly ran to the lobby and found this man on the ground, in the fetal position. I kneeled over him. I could barely understand what he was saying. It was obvious that he was disoriented and did not have all his faculties about him. I suggested that he remove himself from the property. The crowd in the background was shouting, "call the police!" I hurried him outside, but one of the bystanders called 911. In a matter of moments, the crowd had become agitated and angry. I was one of only three Black men in the gym. I didn't realize it at the time, but that evening I realized that perhaps the attitude towards Blacks has not changed much through the years. Granted this person's actions were wrong or misguided, but they should not have warranted such a strong reaction.

My point here is that although many transformations have taken place throughout history, the basic mentality of most white people is to fear the black man. Generally speaking, white America has not begun to address this issue and certainly hasn't taken any responsibility for its involvement in this unjust system.

It was not a black businessman who infiltrated millions of dollars worth of cocaine and automatic weapons into L.A. streets. According to a recent news reports it might have been the work of certain U. S. agencies. However, there are many Americans safely sitting at home supporting the current system. They feel that everyone in jail is a criminal and deserve to be there.

Unfortunately, this is not always the case. Many black males are caught up in a world of prejudice and unfairness. At one time, it was considered legal to incarcerate a black man regardless of the reason. The correctional institution is often less sympathetic towards the Black male.

I mentioned earlier in this book that my mother raised four kids without a man in the home. Her sister, Bobbie, raised five boys single-handedly. Today, my aunt is no longer with us. She died watching her eldest son being incarcerated. Because of her death she didn't have the opportunity to witness the same fate befall her second son. He also fell prey to the same system. A system based on incompetent American judicial laws. Aunt Bobbie's oldest son, Dwight, was always in some kind of trouble. It was no surprise to any of us that he made a career of going in and out of correctional institutions. Rodney, her second boy, was a soft-spoken kid who always had a smile on his face.

The laws that America created to protect us, turned against him. He was charged with drug possession because of his association with an acquaintance, a drug dealer.

This man, in an effort to plea-bargain with the police, sold Rodney down the river. Rodney had no drugs on him at the time of the arrest, but he is still serving time today. Rodney was a native Texan, The state of Louisiana managed to take twelve years of his life. After the trial was over, my mother called to say that Rodney's co-workers and friends testified on his behalf that he was not a drug user or dealer! The fact that he had never been convicted of a crime was not taken into consideration. Rodney's underpaid, court appointed lawyer left the courtroom with tears in his eyes. He knew the system had failed and another innocent black man had once again been wrongfully accused!

The number of Black men in prison today is staggering. The real sin is probability in the future these numbers will increase. It is important that you ask yourself, what does it take to make a change?

In my opinion, as a member of the Black race, we must begin to take control of our lives. We must begin to become more aware of who is being incarcerated and why! This can help us to learn if someone is being unfairly incarcerated.

What we need to do is to start monitoring this process which consumes so many of our people. This sounds good, but how do we initiate a project like this?

First of all, we must learn to utilize our current resources. Let's take a look at the NAACP and see how they would take charge of the problem.

A division within this organization could be set up to monitor every case in which a black man is accused of committing a crime.

With today's communicational technology this task is simple. This data would help to establish certain guidelines regarding the length of term per crime committed. I know that many of you will criticize this suggestion and question the matter of funding. I think a worthwhile cause such as this would warrant funding through philanthropic means.

I would even be willing to bet that the NAACP membership would triple if the effort was set forth towards making a real difference in the lives of these men. Besides, if the black man would put his money into an organization such as this, opposed towards a pair of hundred dollar Nike tennis shoes, then we could finance this project with ease! Priority is what is missing in correcting the black man's world.

Is our society out to persecute the black male? I really would like to think this is not so.

The one thing I do know is that it is not there to help us! What steps can the individual black man take in order to protect himself? First of all, the more knowledge we have, the greater our chances are for survival. Knowing the perimeters of the law will arm us against ignorance and provide a better basis for communication. Granted, in the past, the white man created laws to serve his own purpose. It is because of this reason that the education of our children is key. Education is the instruction booklet for life. Without it, we will miss many important details regarding our existence.

Understanding our rights is one of the main ingredients of my formula for growth. Even with this understanding, there is one important issue that presents itself in the face of every person, the respect for authority. Without this element in our society, chaos is inevitable.

Fathers, Authority & God

Many Black men have been forced to grow up in a household with little or no male guidance. This missing link has given the Black man an excuse for his slip ups in American society. Is this a viable excuse or is this just another way to justify our lack of success?

My theory, however humble, is that unless a father can provide you with the proper guidance, wisdom, respect and understanding, what is the point of having him there. I have seen just as many two-parent families with kids who are troubled and misguided. Not having a father has never been a major issue with me.

I made a conscious decision at an early age that I would have to learn many aspects of life for myself. If you really stop and think about it, many important lessons in this world are learned through one's own experiences. *Of course, it helps to have someone guide you, but the course you will eventually take will be determined by your own free will.

In spite of the progress that has taken place, we must still face one of the biggest hurdles of our lives. The lack of male leadership in the black community. This problem is an enormous one. It is a tear in the fabric of our lives. There is no question that the structure of the black family has been weakened by the lack of a male figure. This situation is not only a black issue, it is a human issue.

Many black men have had little guidance regarding the role of authority. At the risk of sounding like a preacher, I must say that the true understanding of authority comes from God.

Americans have attempted to take away His authority. It is our fear of God that initiates the beginning of discipline and control. In many ways this explains the state of America today. Authority doesn't come from the government, the laws of the land, our mothers, fathers, teachers or law enforcement officials. A lack of respect for God, the creator of this universe, impedes or hinders our efforts for change. Because America is still too damn arrogant to realize this fact, this matter will get a lot worse before it will improve.

Most prisoners that find God while in prison and feel as if they have a fighting chance for survival. This is the first step in controlling the beast within. Asking God's help places them on the road to recovery. It is a small act, yet it is one that has a dominoes effect.

Once we control the entity which runs wild within us, we have achieved an inner peace. Nike has a very powerful slogan that says, " Just do it!" The way it is portrayed seems a little arrogant, but we should apply this concept to ourselves. Use this slogan to control the beast which roars inside us. Just ask God's help! It is really that simple.

Another problem I would like to address, is the issue of anger. There are many ways to help the black man deal with his anger of unjust treatment he has received from society.

First of all, let me say that there are many who care about your plight. If you are lacking direction or opportunity, there is help! Quite honestly, I think Black Americans can feel better about themselves knowing that we stand united as a race of people. More importantly, I believe this type of reaching out can create the basis for a new beginning.

There are so many different issues that affect the growth of the black male, it is impossible to broach each individual topic. I have touched on several that are pertinent not only to our growth but to our survival as well.

When people sit back and make their assessment regarding this nation's moral decline, rarely do they conceive the role of fatherhood is at the crux of the problem. Within the authoritative structure of our society, the role of the father figure is second. God is at the top of the list, the father is next, followed by the government. However, since there are so many who question the presence of God and because of the corruption in government, many Americas have very little or no respect for these sources of authority. For this reason, the family, with the father as a figurehead, is elevated to the top level. If authority is lacking here it is easy to see why this country is sputtering.

The high crime rate in this country and the lack of respect that exists in today's youth is a symptom of this disease.

What many of us do not understand is that the top two authoritative positions need the third to provide a channel of communication. The father as the head of the family is there to give direction and guidance to his children who will in turn grow up to be strong and productive instruments of society.

More on the Father Issue

The absence of fathers in our home has created children that are ill-prepared for life.

A consequence of this dilemma is the gigantic responsibility that falls upon the shoulders of Black mothers. This creates an imbalance which cannot rectify itself. The result is that many black brothers are being incarcerated.

The number of single-family homes in this country is astounding. In 1993, fifty-nine percent of black children were living in homes run only by mothers. The love of a mother is no doubt great, but the presence of a father is imperative for a child's self-worth. Some of you are probably questioning how I can feel this way when I never knew my father.

It is exactly because I lacked a male role model in my life that I have such strong feelings on this issue. It is imperative to have an adult male in the house during the formative years. A pat on the back, a comforting word, or an acknowledging smile from an adult male can be the most cherished moment in a young man's life.

Unfortunately, the lack of a father figure in most single-parent families has created children with low self-esteem. Today the Black male doesn't understand his role in society, therefore he uses the lack of male guidance as an excuse. Quite frankly, excuses are the one thing that the black male can do without.

The absence of a father figure is the one factor that prompts Black men to enter athletics.
Sports allows young men to understand the transformation that takes place from boyhood to manhood.

Fortunately for me, between the years of four and twelve, I had the opportunity of having a stepfather in my life. The lessons I learned from this man still stand strong in my mind. I was twelve when Otis passed away, but my little brother was only six at the time. Whenever Carl is going through a rough time in his life, I remind him that this is not an excuse for failure.

One lesson that Otis taught me was that it is important to recognize the things you have and not to focus on what you don't have. He used to say that embracing a positive approach was the first step in acquiring more. I've always made a point of passing that little bit of wisdom along to my young siblings especially when things looked desperate in their lives.

I find it hilarious that the government attempts to intervene in this situation by forcing fathers to accept their financial responsibilities. The father's role is taught by example, not by force! Of course I don't expect the government to understand that the true bond that exists between father and child is one from God. If you have to force a father to be a parent, it is simply better for that child to grow up without one. Besides, isn't the pot calling the kettle black. The American government hasn't set a great example for its people. A father's financial support is important to all mothers; however, it is better not to have a father than to have one that does not want to be there.

Since I didn't have a father, I compensated by adopting various male figures as role models. Ward Cleaver the father on the *Leave it to Beaver*, and Andy Oppy's dad on The *Andy Griffin Show* became my imaginary dads. The lessons I learned from them had a great impact on my life.

Parents don't think it is important what kids watch on television. My point is that kids have a psychological need for a father figure in their lives.

It should be considered child abuse for a child to grow up without a father figure in the family. However, if this happens, the child must learn to deal with it. I'm sure that even the most well-developed child has experienced some kind of psychological scarring as a result of this situation.

As this problem escalates, its deteriorating effects will be felt throughout this country. The impact will be intensified by many overwhelming situations. As long as one cannot contribute to the discipline and guidance of their children, the black male will begin his race from behind the starting position. This is a truism and it would be foolish for us to be in denial of this fact.

We must learn the importance of running a strong and hard race despite our shortcomings. Preparing ourselves with a new psychological mental awareness will help us make the adjustments which will ultimately give us a new starting position in America. The strength of our black male is hidden in the understanding of who we are. It is this understanding that should be passed down through the bloodlines of our fathers.

I hope that as the development and naturing of the Black male occurs, the whole world will see a great change in the status of the black community. This change will ultimately add to the quality of the American agenda. Boys that grow up without fathers can throw a huge wrench into the workings of this metamorphosis.

The Black family must learn to meet the challenges of the future. We cannot allow the nonchalant ways of the past to continue into the future.

*It is important for all Americans, but especially the black man, to remember that God brought us here! It is our personal relationship with God that allows a constant flow of knowledge and understanding and brings an awareness of who we are. The black race has been an integral participant in this country's development. From the first moment that we set foot on American soil, we became a part of the soul and strength of this country. It takes all of our efforts to make this country strong. We cannot ignore the number of black kids that are growing up without the love of a father or positive male figure.

To assume the role of the head of the family is a responsibility that males must take on, (whatever their personal situation might have been.) The school system should incorporate a course on parenting as a part of its basic curriculum.

This human aspect of education can benefit all young men on the importance of family values, commitment and responsibility. This one simple solution, to such a complex problem, could resolve many of today's problems.

I fear that twenty years from now we'll still be trying to analyze this same problem. Eventually society will be forced to look at all the possible alternatives and create a change, but until then, we must all suffer the consequences of our procrastination. Along with the procrastination comes the lazy behavior that is said to be a part of the character of the black man.

Unless the black man formulates a plan to create a change, he will find himself with his head in a noose. He will be praying and hoping that the rope will loosen and give him one more day to live and breathe. How can the black man change his direction in order to become strong enough to motivate his family?

* First, we must direct our focus towards the heavens. Secondly, we must ask One that is greater than ourselves to teach us the way. Thirdly, we must stay away from sin. Sin dims the light of progress and shuns those who want to follow the path of God. We need to be unified as one. It is very important to start our change one family at a time. The power of the masses will help to create change.

Changing Course

The first step in creating change is the awareness
of an ultimate power and how it can be
instrumental in helping each of us reach our desired goal. *One of the great mistakes of our
generation is that we have been trying to emulate
the white man's way of life, instead of trying to
understand the real power of the universe. It is
easy to become entangled in the white man's
world: his wealth, his power, and his corruption.
Frankly, both races have lost sight of the source.
It is through this source that we will gain the
power to understand and embrace the challenges
of the future. This strength of character will
deliver us from our present condition. The source
is from God.

Although our race has witnessed many reforms
in the last fifty years, do not assume that all of
these changes are for the best. We have created
the illusion of success based upon someone else's
ideas and concepts. We have allowed ourselves to
measure success by someone else's standards
rather than our own. The irony of all this is that
most of the population in oblivious to this fact!
We owe it to our race of people to sever the ties
that bind us. Over the years, we have fought hard
to gain admission into this very private club but
we have come to the realization that the price of
admittance has been too high!

No, I am not condoning segregation. The pain
and suffering that our people have gone through
because of prejudice has left us with many scars,
but I am not saying that we should separate
ourselves from those that are good and pure.
Black, White, Red Yellow and Brown, all of us
should distance ourselves from those whose
actions and behavior are circumventing the aspir-
ations of all Americans. All of us, but especially
Black Americans, must learn to segregate
ourselves from the scrutiny of the watchful eye of
the white world.

Our purpose is to strengthen the moral fabric of
this country. Those of us who are willing to stand
alone will eventually persuade the masses to
reform. In order for this to happen, we must admit
that something is seriously wrong, assess the
problem, and create a plan of attack. Once we
establish the right course of action, everyone will
jump onto the bandwagon and create momentum.
Simple, isn't it? Most things in life are. It is only
man's arrogance that complicates the situation.

In a greater sense, this change is most crucial
for the black man. We have neither the time nor
the united resources to get caught up with the
notions of a misguided nation! Our energies must
initiate a real effect towards change. Unlike the
white man we don't have the luxury of making
mistake after mistake.

At the beginning, it is possible that our efforts will
be misjudged and assumed to be anti-American.
This fact cannot discourage us because the
character of this nation is such that it will
recognize genuine progress and the efforts directed
towards it.

Through these efforts, the Black man will better
himself and become a more efficient American.
Eventually he will be able to change the course of
this nation. American people are slowly acquiring
hunger for change and soon they will be willing to
step outside the norm in order to acquire it. *Many
times I find myself using this slogan, "We are all
in this together!"

The understanding of the power of the black
man can only be instigated directly by the black
man. Others will assess us but it will be up to us
to ultimately decide how others will judge us.
Today, being a successful black man means
learning to be many things: a diplomat, a
preacher, a teacher and arbitrator. We wear many
hats, but we must become selective in choosing
the hats we wear. A great way to do this is to learn
to take the championship blood that runs through
our veins and use it to our advantage. If the black
man was to take what he has learned in sports
and apply it to other facets of life, we could jump
start our cause!

We can turn America around, and in the process, display a characteristic that has been hidden from society.

Understanding these times we live in will give us the ingredients needed to bake our own American pie! It is this pie that will bring together the dreams of our ancestors. These dreams survived in the midst of hatred and ignorance by those who held us captive. The ingredients to create our own pie are within our reach. If we choose to ignore this fact, then our ancestors will surely have died in vain. This is a responsibility that all blacks have inherited whether we chose to accept it or not! We don't have any other choice. It is something that runs through our bloodline.

We cannot create this change on our own. It will take divine guidance. The black man will have to find favor in God. The same God that delivered us out of the hands of slavery. We can achieve this with the confirmation that He still exists. We should put our personal needs aside in order to seek God's guidance. We must begin to open the channels of communication and understand that which God has already given us. If we delight in his ways, the desires of our heart will be answered. These are not my words, but His words that I am relaying to you. Please see Psalms, Chapter 37, Verse 4.

We can never understand the tremendous role a
father plays in our lives if we can't understand
God's role as our Father!

God will teach us what He expects from us and
we will be able to teach our kids what is expected
of them. Our continued effort in understanding
God will prepare us for the future. It will show us
what to look for and what to stay away from.
Understanding this fact is the first step in falling
into God's graces. I understand what the *Bible*
means when it says, "the spirit is willing but the
flesh is weak." Staying away from sin is a battle in
itself. However, through Christ, this battle has
already been won. We just have to learn how to
accept the victory!

Today's Battles

I am calling for all black men to stand up and be
counted. Never has the need been greater than
right now. As a matter of fact, the calling for all
American men to stand up and be counted is more
crucial now than ever before. Many of you think
that since there aren't any wars going on, we don't
have any battles to fight. This is a misconception.
Today, this country is fighting battles of greater
proportions. What are these battles which are
eating away at the heart of our American male,
especially our Black men?

They are manifested in many different forms. One of the most basic is taking place against our manhood. If affects who we are and how we present ourselves to society. *In America today, it is acceptable for grown men to dress up like women in order to promote their careers or whatever, and guess what? This should give you a clue of what time it is.

We are very naive if we think that this doesn't have an affect on the balance of our country. More importantly, the balance of the world. If you think this situation represents a small number, then you are truly unaware of the magnitude of the problem. What is at stake is the salvation of an entire human race? If you see nothing wrong with guys being girls and girls being guys, then drive through West Hollywood, California after a gay pride parade or after a Halloween parade. A bell should go off in your head.

If adults have a difficult time keeping this essential matter in perspective, how can we expect our kids to have a comprehension of such things? I was just listening to a news program where a group of high school kids were trying to fight for their rights to cross-dress at school. This situation has been embedded deeply into the foundation of our society.

I am not going to get into a debate of whether this should be considered right or wrong. I will leave that issue for those of you who advocate that this will have little to do with the salvation of our nation. Thank God we live in a country where we have the freedom of choice. Let's not forget that too much freedom can be considered bondage. It is time for Americans to examine every facet of our lives and select a path that is truly best for us all. We must learn to separate the good from the bad and eliminate anything that destroys the substance of man.

The black actor, Wesley Snipes, recently acted in a movie and played the role of a transvestite. Although I would not endorse this movie by paying to see it, I realize that misguidance has no color boundaries. Again, the black man does not have the luxury of time or the resources to present himself in a society that already thinks less of him!

Considering the many internal battles one needs to fight within a society, it's apparent that there are more important things to deal with than to cry about how the world is treating us. We cannot afford to bring this kind of negativity upon ourselves. The black male, has been running a race against time. Many have complained about the conditions of the race, crying every step of the way.

There are also those of us who view our struggle as an indication of growth, the results from our will to survive. Regardless of race, color, we can expect to encounter many obstacles in life, but how we deal with life's unexpected hurdles is what makes us survivors. We can compensate by making the necessary adjustments. For many years, our cries for freedom went unheard. Our tears of disillusion flooded our vision with resentment and disappointment.

Another battle that men are fighting in this country is the battle of the sexes. One of the man's greatest assets is a strong, supportive woman at his side. One of the disadvantages of today is the confusion and misguided opinion surrounding the role of men and women in society. A lot of the chaos is attributed to our own lack of understanding and who we are as men.

This cross falls not only on the shoulders of black men, but all who call themselves men!

If men are having difficulty with their identity, then it stands to reason that women will be perplexed regarding their identity, and more importantly so will our children. This is especially true for the black man. The distance that has been created between the black man and black woman does nothing to help our efforts in becoming a stronger race of people.

The black woman's attitude towards the black man has a great deal to do with our present.

Under these conditions, we are allowing the future of the Black race to deteriorate. Many of our present day challenges stem from the earlier years of slavery. I am not one that believes in excuses; however, it is important that we acknowledge the origin of this bewildering situation. Acknowledgement is the first step in healing the afflictions that exist between black men and black women. Notice that I used the word "challenge" instead of "problem." The word "challenge" denotes a willing approach towards a solution and a constructive way to deal with an issue. On the other hand, the word "problem" signifies an impossible result. *It's the small adjustments in life that make the difference in the final outcome!

When did this challenge begin, and how do we begin to take control of the situation? The relationship between the black man and black woman dates back to the days of slavery. In those days, men and women were forced to separate. We were considered to be nothing more than livestock. Husbands, wives, children and parents where torn apart from one another. I believe that we are still feeling the repercussions of that injustice! These practices helped to destroy the fabric of the black family of that era.

A psychological stake was driven into the heart of our people which has stayed with us to this day! Unlike other traumas which have occurred throughout history, there wasn't a period of healing for the black man and his woman. As with our bodies, if a sore does not have a chance to heal, it can never truly be expected to get better. To add to this, in his effort to emulate the white man, the black man lost sight of the fact that he never healed the wounds of his other self the black woman. This distraction has been instrumental in the continual disintegration of the black family.

Any type of injury requires time to heal or it will grow into a cancerous sore. This is what has happened to the black family today! We have allowed this affliction to grow into a tumor.

With all the educated minds of our time, this little prognosis has managed to elude us. The result has been a lifetime of disruption which hasn't allowed us to fully appreciate the incredible wonders of our heritage.

We can justify anything in life, but we must also recognize the truth about our own race of people. The black man claims that the black woman has an attitude. Do these men ever ask themselves why she feels this way? The black woman feels that the black man is lazy and that he prefers white women.

Does she ask herself why ?

My suggestion is for Black men and women to start by viewing each others as allies, not only in the present and the future, but in the past as well. We can initiate this with a day of acknowledgement, a day of recognition for our race of people. This will be the first step towards stitching a wound that has been left open for many decades. Again, the Black man has to learn to choose the right battles. With each battle, one must gain the strength, power and knowledge to move forward. With this power, we can enlighten the darkness around us.

Let's begin by showing our black sisters love and compassion. Without their courage and strength we would have never survived the past. Show our women the respect they are due, and show them that their sacrifices were not in vain. This new attitude will help to tear down the hostile attitude that many black women project towards black men.

Many of our paths have taken us towards other avenues, women of other races, but deep in our hearts we must always recognize the fact that every black woman carries the noble blood of great warriors, the wonderful spirit of survival, and the regal beauty of ancient queens.

I hope this will lead us to understand the importance of the Black woman in the history of the Black man in America!

We must keep our focus on addressing the real challenges in life and begin to build a foundation for the future. This structure will be so strong and majestic that the whole world will be in awe of it! It is our responsibility to construct a structure that will withstand the perils of time.

Final Thoughts on Black Man Don't Cry!

In closing this chapter, I want to discuss in further detail something I feel will help the black man's outlook towards his future. Once we condition ourselves to stop crying about our circumstances, we will understand that our crying was a hopeless, wasted energy.

To be frank, a lot of the attitude the Black man has, is the result of the mentality that "the white man owes us." This is a very wrong assessment. The fact is that many White people would rather turn and look away in our time of need, than offer a helping hand. Of course, it would not be fair for me to say that all white people are this way. Many of my greatest opportunities in life have come from the white race. In fact, I believe that a lack of support is something that all mankind is guilty of.

Ask yourself when was the last time you walked by someone who needed a helping hand and pretended that you didn't notice them?

Many young black males feel that the White man is obligated to help us because of the past and their mistreatment of our race. Not so, my black brothers. Your advancement in life is just that, your advancement. It is in your control, not your family or your friends, nor your white brothers. This leaves us with one alternative and that is to face the next issue of what we are prepared to do!

Almost eight years ago I to walked away from the nation's top-rated syndicated television show, *Star Trek, The Next Generation.* I had worked on the show for two and a half seasons as Michael Dorns' stand-in. He played Lt. Worf, the ship's chief security officer. Occasionally, I also appeared as Lt. Hudson, a re-occurring role on the show.

My character had limited dialogue, nothing to write home about. At this time, I had the opportunity to study and watch nine of the entertainment industry's finest actors.

I felt that it was time to initiate a move towards the advancement of my career.

I decided to make an appointment with the executive producer, Rick Bermin. Gene Roddenberry had recently passed away and Rick had become the top producer.

It is imperative to go directly to the top when dealing with decisions that control your well-being and success. Remember that!

A few days later I had a meeting with Rick. I was professional and to the point.

I asked him direct questions, "Does the show plan to do anything with my character?" His reply was vague. He stated that there were only a few shows left that year and that his objective was to finish up the season. "What about next year?" I asked eagerly. He replied that there might be a possibility of something happening in the upcoming season. The meeting lasted twenty five minutes and as I walked out the door, I thanked him for his time and knew exactly where I stood.

Later that evening, I saw the Line Producer on the stage and I personally gave him my two weeks' notice! My decision was based on something that Emmett Smallwood, my high school football coach taught me. The lesson I learned was to always look directly in the eyes of the person you are talking to. This simple act helps to determine the person's true feelings. Throughout the entire meeting, Rick didn't make any eye contact with me whatsoever. He wasn't involved in paperwork or anything that would distract his attention, he simply didn't address me man-to-man.

At the termination of the two weeks, I had finally given my good-byes to all who had claimed to be my friend: Oh yes, by the way, the entertainment industry allows very little room for real friendships. The only real friend you have is your mother, that is, unless she is your agent too! As disappointed as I was to leave the show, I understood that I had to. I felt that I deserved better. I shared this story with you for two reasons. One to make you aware that you can control your own destiny. Sometimes that means walking away from something or someone, because you feel that you deserve better. Secondly, you may have good intentions; however, those around you don't necessarily feel obligated to help you to move ahead. When this happens, don't cry about it, but continue to move forward, regardless of those around you. If we learn to expect from life only those things that we earn for ourselves, then we will realize that the only person who owes you is yourself! Not your family or your friends. The fact is that you never know who your friends are until you ask them for help.

Recently I called an old friend from Star Trek The Next Generation. You know him as Commander Riker, Captain Picard's number one officer on the *Enterprise.* I had heard that Jonathan was about to direct *The Next Generation's* movie, *First Contact.*

I thought, "What the heck, I'll see if I can get a reading." I called him a number of times, I stopped by the studio, and sent him a registered letter, addressed to "Commander Riker." I didn't receive one call, so what do you do? Well, you don't cry about it. You just keep on keeping on! Remember this, if you don't remember anything else in life, know that very few people care about your success as much as you do.

If the doors don't open, for whatever reason, then go through a window. If you can't find a window, don't be afraid to take out a wall.
Trust me, you will think a lot more of yourself, than if you stand around crying about the lack of opportunity. Besides, the greatest opportunity is the one that we make for ourselves! Think about it!

Blacks must realize there is no one on this planet who is more or less important than themselves. We truly are in this together! All mankind! Our white brother has shown us the results of his negative behavior and its effect on society. Can we not benefit from his mistakes?

Making ourselves aware of our future needs as a *unified* race will be difficult. We must find a way to incorporate this philosophy into our constitution. Unification, however, does not include segregation, it includes motivation.

I believe that our society is hungry for a way of life that will give us a chance for survival. Who better to show us the techniques for survival than the black man? Our accomplishments in this area have been documented on the pages of America's history.

We must not be afraid to take the lead in showing all Americans a new way of life. We can do this by pointing ourselves in the right direction. The responsibility of leadership will fall on all of us who are not afraid to stand alone. We must be the race that assures justice for all mankind. As a matter of fact, the white man has come to the conclusion that his lifestyle needs a major over-haul. This is one of the many reasons why so many Americans are shying away from voting.

The stage is being set for anyone who is willing to assume the role of real leadership, regardless of his race. That is why there is no better time than the present, for the black man, to gain control of this power and make his presence felt throughout this nation. This will be achieved through the unified effort of us all. The time to make this happen is now!

Chapter Nine

If I Were President!

As I sit at my computer gathering my thoughts for this chapter, I'm trying to think of the best way to start it. Suddenly, an element of sadness crosses my mind. The reality is that it will take countless years for a black American to become the President of the United States! I ask myself if there is a possibility of this happening in the next twenty-five or thirty years, and I know that in my heart even though this country has made many changes, we are a long way from something happening of this nature. Even if it were a possibility, knowing this country as I do, it is hard to imagine a script that would surround that particular set of circumstances.

This nation attempted to scratch the surface with the Rev. Jesse Jackson running for vice president and with the possibility of Colin Powell running for office.

I personally believe that America's consciousness has not developed to a level of understanding needed to elect a black man into this highest branch of office.

Taking all this into consideration (with all these feeling on my mind) I decided to become the first black President of this country. It doesn't really matter how I got there. The fact is that as of January 1st, 1998, all my friends will began to call me Mr. President. Before I take the oath of office, I have two stipulations. I will be president for one year only and any policy that I implement cannot be changed for any reason, it can only be expanded upon.

Moving Into the White House

Before we can create any real changes in this country, Americans have to do away with the degradations of the past. The first thing that must go is the White House! I find it fascinating that this country can still boast of being fair and equal and at the same time, call the President's home the 'White House'. This is an insult to every minority and every American of color.

It is my opinion that if a previous president wanted to make a real difference regarding racism they would have initiated this change long ago.

So the first act of business is to change this subliminal message. From this day forward, the place were I will be living as the first black president is going to be renamed " The Heartbeat". This new name will symbolize a place where all understanding flows. It will be a constant reminder that the color of the blood that runs through all of us is the same. This will eliminate the possibility of any American feeling that any race of people is dominant. Why this issue has never come up before is a surprise to me. If you question whether or not the white man is still arrogant, it can be viewed here! It is time for this nation to understand it is not the things that you say that are important; it is those things you do that make a difference.

Countless of leaders have stood before this nation and claimed that they wanted to be fair and just. These leaders seemed to overlook the fact that it is the little changes that can make a difference.

What can be more simple than to change the name of the building that is the symbol of all American people. I believe real changes are not that difficult and they don't take a whole lot of time.

I have decided to change the system starting with the head. I have decided to do something that should have been done a lone time ago.

I am going to hand Congress a three day notice! That's right! I am firing Congress. This electoral institution has to be the poorest excuse of representation that exist on the planet. It's frightening to think that this group of individuals are actually paid to misguide, stagnate and manipulate the nation. So, from this day forth, each member of congress has exactly three days to notify its constituents and let them know that they will no longer be a symbol of representation to this nation! They can tell the people that the new president doesn't see their efforts as an asset. The internal arguing and bickering between republicans and democrats is no longer acceptable. The President feels that the American people simply deserves a lot better than they have been receiving.

Wait a minute, Mr. President. If you fire congress, what about the representation of the people? I'm glad you asked. I have decided to replace congress with a congress of two representatives from every race. These representatives will be voted into office by the members of their own nationality. I will create the United Nations of America.

428

Black Eye On America!   **Mr. President!**

It is from this nucleus that I will set up American policy from now to the end of our existence.

The countless, special interest groups will have to learn that they are going to have to lobby all Americans and not just the ones that benefit their interest.

Addressing the Nation.

Before I go any further, it is important to address the nation! On this evening I fully expect time to stand still. For one hour everything in this country will stop. No football games or tea parties will take place during this time. Never again will the President of the United States have to take second place to insignificant social activities. It is high time that Americans learn to respect the words of the president of the United States.

Granted, previous presidents have lost the respect of Americans by being inconsistent.

I will open my first address to the nation by claiming back this vital element to the presidency. Lies and scandalous behavior will no longer be tolerated in the executive office. For the entire year that I am in office, I will ban anything that is negatively said or written about the President; (unless the individual has been directly involved with the president personally.)

429

My purpose is to teach Americans the importance of any individual to respect authority. I do not believe Americans fully understand the power of words. At first, I realize this will be a little hard for Americans to adhere to. Because we are so caught up in this freedom of speech thing, we allow freedom to impede the efforts of others.

The theme of my address to the nation, will be "Time to Clean up America". We will begin this process by creating new agencies and dissolving old ones. Any existing government agency that in the past has been associated with two or more scandals will be dissolved and replaced with new blood. Whether it be Congress, the CIA, the FBI, or the Attorney General's office, they will be terminated. It is time for this country to create a new attitude. We must develop an attitude that includes an element of trust for these agencies that serve the people. Why and how this country has allowed important government agencies to represent this nation, after the cancer that as grown within, is beyond my comprehension. This will no longer be accepted in my administration. Enough is enough!

I will not allow this country to keep pouring countless tax payers' dollars into organizations that continue to show signs of a lack of integrity.

Black Eye On America!   **Mr. President!**

One of the issues that I will attack in my address to the nation is my two-fold plan to rid the country of the uncontrollable drug problem that is rapidly growing in this nation.

The first part of the plan includes an apology to all Americans. I feel that this is necessary because this problem should not exist. If this country cannot control the drugs that are being produced inside our own borders, then maybe we are not as advanced as we would like the world to think.

If every year drug smuggling is on the rise, then maybe our defense department needs to start taking a closer look at this problem. This issue definitely imposes a great risk to the security of this nation! The drug problem is an internal challenge. I say this because drugs can only be imported to this country if access is available.

My administration will deal with this issue by redefining the "legal" and "illegal" drugs. Personally, I think anything that cannot be grown naturally without synthetic alloys should be considered illegal. However, I will create a committee to help me evaluate this issue more thoroughly.

This country seems to be stifled with the challenge of doing away with the drug problem. Why? There are two elements that create a drug problem. One is supply and the other is demand. It makes common sense to place all our efforts in deleting these two components.

First, in order to do this, we must genuinely have a desire to change our habits.

This is a lot easier said than done. I don't think so, America! This is how simple the situation is. Let's start by eliminating the suppliers. It is simply that easy. Gather all the data on both the individuals and the countries that are supplying the United States with drugs. With today's technology this can be done in about two weeks' time. America will then deliver a personal ultimatum to those individuals and will make it clear that she will not except their actions any longer.

This ultimatum will be accompanied by two certificates, one an unconditional pardon and the other a death certificate.

The unconditional pardon is to let those individuals know that this country has forgiven them for their role in the destruction of so many American lives. Up to this point there won't be any repercussions. The death certificate will serve as written notice to, any individual, group of individuals or government agency, responsible for supplying this country with illegal drugs will be destroyed by any and all means necessary! I will create an agency that will carry out these actions.

I realize that many of you don't believe it is that simple to delete the supply of illegal drugs, but it is! Now, to address the demand aspect of drug warfare.

I believe this can be resolved in six months to a year's time. I will create two agencies to deal with this challenge. They will start to collect all information on any Americans that have a drug problem. Each individual will be placed on a six month detoxification program. They will not be ridiculed or ostracized because of their drug problem, by their community or by society. After completing the program they will be given an opportunity for financial support to rebuild their lives according to their personal situation. During the six months this administration will have deleted a major problem. It can be accomplished by dissecting the core of the problem. In the past, America has allowed the escalation of drugs to exist because of her lack of willingness to reach within and destroy the demons behind its existence. It has been this country's weakness that has allowed this situation to continue to rule us.

Crime and Violence

Now that America doesn't have a drug problem any longer, sixty percent of our crime problem has already been wiped out. I fully understand that as long as there are people there will be some form of crime and violence. In order to eliminate crime we will need to eliminate the need for it and that is virtually impossible.

The only way I can see attacking an issue of this magnitude is to create a Crime Prevention Commission. This commission will be authorized to implement an immediate educational program which will teach young people how to handle certain situations and how to recognize the signals that accompany them. It is my opinion that crime and violence should be a required course in the elementary, middle school and high school levels.

Learning to understand the basic principles behind crime and violence will be the only realistic means by which we can begin to rid society of their presence. Although I firmly believe that my generation might be lost when it comes to these issues, I don't feel that future generations have to be condemned.

Americans often complain about crime and violence. We sometimes lose sight of the fact that we condone this type of lifestyle. To say we are intrigued by these two elements is an understatement. Sixty-five percent of all Americans (including children) in their everyday lives advocate some form of violence. Granted, most of the programing that is introduced to us is on a subconscious or subliminal level.

In most cases, Americans are allowing themselves to send mixed signals regarding these issues.

If we are ever going to change the state of crime and violence in this nation, we are going to have to start by asking ourselves whether we are for or against this matter. The answer to this question will be the deciding factor which will determine the potential growth of crime and violence in the future,

As in many other issues, Americans control the bottom line. America's problem cannot be diminished unless we are willing to completely remove crime and violence from our daily diet. The reality is that we live in a society which serves these elements for breakfast, lunch and dinner. Our children wake up to watch cartoons whose characters are being mutilated and decapitated. Yet Americans consider this normal and acceptable. Americans often cheer the violence in sports. I personally cannot recall a top box office smash in the last twenty years that didn't include a substantial degree of violence. This tells me two things: Americans have been programmed to desire and acccept both crime and violence.

Whether this is a human issue or not, I have not yet decided. What I do know is that it's definitely an American one. It is very obvious that you can either be for an issue or against it. The difference in the choice will give you the direction for change.

If we condone crime and violence in our society (which it appears that we do by our actions,) then all we need to do is continue on our present course. Trust me, the manifestation of this country's crime and violence will triple in the next ten years. It is my guess that we must accept that fact.

If this country sincerely decides to change its course, which can be determined by a majority show of hands, then as your President, this is what I propose. First of all, the viewing of crime and violence for many who lack the moral substance will eventually be manifested into reality. Watching crime and violence will result in negative results. I will begin by decreasing the amount of C and V that Americans are allowed to watch on T.V. My purpose is to slowly wean the public in a twelve month period. After creating strict laws and regulations, these matters will be enforced. Next, I would implement a ruling regarding the amount of news coverage devoted to reported crimes. The evening news will report positive information. As it is, Americans work all day only to come home to an evening full of negative and pessimistic news reports.

I believe that in order to change this country's attitude regarding C and V, we are going to have to stop glorifying it.

Have you asked yourself why so many cop programs have bombarded the air waves lately? I don't
think it's an accident. I believe that this is the
writing on the wall. It should make this country
aware that things are way out of control.

I believe that C and V will always be a part of
society; however, I also believe that it doesn't have
to be glamorized. The sacrifice to create change is
minimal. We simply have to make up our minds
and lean towards that issue. We must stop
sending mixed signals to the institutions that are
force-feeding us with a C and V diet. If you have
noticed, I refer to crime and violence to C and V. I
believe this is what it would be reduced to if
Americans would cease to support it.

Putting an End to the Homeless

The homeless challenge in this country is one of
the most hilarious situations that I have ever
come across. The only reason that I choose to
laugh is to keep from crying. The fact is that we
live in the greatest country on the planet. I might
appear to sound arrogant, but we do. How this
situation has escalated to this level, is beyond me.

First of all, for someone to be considered
homeless is to say that someone doesn't care.
Unfortunately, that someone is you and I.

437

What I would like to do here is to show you how easy it is to change this situation. Secondly, a person is never homeless unless this country runs out of land. Hello America! Has this country's land mass started to disappear lately? There is too much undeveloped property in this country for the problem to exist.

The first step in creating a home is to have a sky overhead and ground down below. The last time I looked, this nation had plenty of both. Now, since we have plenty of both, we must ask ourselves, how can an increasing number of homeless people escalate each year? The answer to such a question is often incriminating to all Americans. This is why I say this. It is my opinion that the homeless should be redefined. The new definition should say, " the space that is created between those who have and those who have not". The problem arises because society has managed to create a monopoly on the available land that we all call America.

The challenge with America's homeless is all about shelter, the land and money needed to construct that housing. Those who have, have created many fine lines, preventing those who have not, from having the opportunity to acquire what they have. The residue of their actions results in the homeless situation.

The fact is that this country has created a system where those in a less aggressive society have not been given the opportunity to survive. Not to mention competing in the game of prosperity. Our system declares that in order to play the game one has to be gainfully employed and have the financial means by which to buy a home or rent a property. If own a home, then you must pay yearly taxes. Along with the opportunity of owning a home, a number of vendors must be employed to make this home livable. Gas, water and electricity are mandatory if you wish to hang out there. Not to mention the surplus amenities, telephones and cable, which help make life more exciting.

Creating affordable housing for Americans is quite simple; however, it seems to be an issue that has managed to elude countless politicians and government agencies. Many of the people who find themselves homeless simply lack the motivation or the ability to create and/or provide shelter for themselves. Question, does this make them less American or less of a human being?

No, it simply makes them less fortunate. As their numbers increase (and you can bet that they will), so will the callousness of American hearts towards them.

It is my opinion that the homeless challenge in this country can be a temporary situation; therefore America's efforts should encompasses that approach! So, as your President I am going to create temporary communities in every city across the nation for the homeless.

Wherever there is vacant property (abandoned buildings), there will always be a home for those who are less fortunate. These communities will be monitored by each state's capital city.

The principle behind this alternative system is to give these communities a second chance to be a part of society.

Anyone entering these government-funded communities will have to adhere to a number of mandatory rules. This is by no means a free ride. It is simply an opportunity to be a part of the American dream in a positive, constructive way. Each member of this community will be educated on what is expected and how to survive in the real world. The primary goal of these communities is to help people to understand that they must learn to create a standard for themselves in order to move forward in this country. There will be mandatory attendance of such courses as Self Respect, Job Training and The Principles Behind America's Economic System. Cleansing the body of alcohol and drugs will be a part of the principles and philosophies of each community.

Each resident will be responsible for themselves as well as one other person. They will be taught the principles involved in operating a small community; therefore, upon entering the real world they will have a basic understanding of how the system works. Each community will be equipped with a clinic, police station, grocery store and a court house, to address internal problems. This project will create an opportunity for the residents to play key roles in the everyday workings of the community.

I stated earlier that these are temporary communities. Each resident has only one year to be a part of this particular program. After graduation each resident will enroll into another program which will allow them to be a greater part of our society. The ultimate goal is to create strong American citizens. We must never forget that inside every homeless person is an American that has given up on America!

Foreign Policy

The foreign policy which I choose for this country, during my year in office, is one that I believe will put back the integrity in our nation and how other countries view us.

I believe this country's current foreign policy can be summed up in two words, *need and greed.*

This will not be allowed to exist in my administration. First of all, concerning the issue of import and export. I feel that it is important to implement a policy which states that if we cannot make in America then we are not allowed to buy it elsewhere. There is no doubt, that this country's present policy is pro buy it cheaper elsewhere and sell it at a higher price here. This is no longer acceptable!

How we can continue to take food off our own tables is a mystery to me. An example of this is the hard times that our farmers are going through. Each year, this American institution dwindles away as if it were a small tree in a harsh storm. Quite frankly, to correct this problem is very simple! We can do it by implementing one law. We cannot import more than fifteen percent of a country's goods. In my opinion this forces us to produce and buy from our own.

For example, eighty-five percent of this nation's corn crop must be grown here in the United States. This policy will include all products from corn to automobiles and will be enforced to the limit. It has become increasingly clear that one of the reasons this country has an unemployment problem is because we have lost the commitment to take care for our own!

In an effort to implement this country's capitalistic concepts, America has lost sight of the fact
that we are cutting off the hand that be should
feeding us. Whether are not this situation as been
created by the government or other special interest
groups does not matter. What does matter is the
fact that this kind of behavior will no longer be
acceptable.

One thing is for certain, I will not allow this
nation to continue to supply other countries with
our technology, arms and biological weapons
simply to see them show up in the hands of our
enemies. This type of foreign policy does not reflect
the idea that Americans are of sound mind and
possess basic common sense. I firmly believe that
any country that has been to war with us in the
last fifty years should be considered a threat to
national security; therefore, under my administration they would be treated as such.

Another very important facet of this country's
foreign policy is an issue that must be evaluated
with great wisdom and confidence. This is the
issue of war! Often, war has been used as a tool
for capitalistic gains or as a distraction to the real
problems of this country. My personal feeling
about this topic is very direct and to the point. If
our nation goes to war then it must be prepared to
totally destroy the enemy.

I don't believe that a country should go to war to flex its muscles or to bully their adversary into their way of thinking.

Balancing the Budget

This is an issue that has baffled our government for countless years. Politicians, election after election, have proposed their ideals and game plans for resolving this situation. Still, each year this nation is faced with this challenge.
I believe the inability to balance the nation's budget is a direct reflection on the character of this country.

In order for this country to correct this problem we need first to change the scale by which we have been measuring ourselves. This alone forces us to take a long, hard look at the possibility that we are in fact a gluttonous and voracious society! The fact that this nation continues to struggle with this problem tells me there are few who are willing to make the sacrifices needed to correct the situation.
The scales of high finance do not lie. In fact they are a direct reflection on how spoiled this nation has become. From high on Capitol Hill to the playgrounds of our schoolyards, Americans have lost the desire to appreciate what a truly blessed nation we are!

Instead, we have increased our desire to want and demand more material things even if it means going into debt to acquire them.

From every home in America, to every government agency, this entire nation is guilty of this attitude. This, my fellow American is the reason we have and will continue to have problems balancing our country's budget.

I have given this situation much thought and I have come to the decision that there are only two things that can be done to change the course of the problem. First of all, I want every American, every company, agency, and institution to write down five ways that they have been wasteful. This list must be posted in sight for one whole year.

This requires a true and honest accessment of ourselves. On a separate piece of paper I want all Americans to write down five ways by which they can correct the problem. These five corrections are to be kept for a one year duration. At the end of that year and before I leave office, I will perform an act whereby I will cancel and nullify all debts within the United States of America.

You heard me right, the moment that I leave office, no one in this country will owe anyone anything. I will call this *"starting from scratch day"*. This will be a day where all debts are annulled and no one in this country will owe anyone.

No one will collect anything from anyone, starting from the family of four, to the United States government. All debts will be cancel. I believe that we have currently gone past the point of no return when it comes to balancing the budget. The only way to correct this is to totally start from scratch. This will give everyone a new and fresh opportunity.

As your President I feel that all Americans should have an opportunity to turn this situation around for the best. Some loses will be greater than others, but we must start somewhere! I hope that this country will learn from its mistakes. If we are to continue to grow as a world power, then we must be a nation of honor and integrity. This my fellow countrymen cannot and will not happen if we continue to be in debt.

America's Environment

This wonderful nation we live in has managed to put a number of very important issues on hold. One such issue has to do with the environment. Oftentimes we loose sight of the importance of a particular situation because of its gradual deterioration. If you are not aware of the severity of this problem, then let me be the first to warn you that we have a monumental challenge before us!

The thing that makes the environment such a major challenge is that there is a chain reaction which accompanies its progress.

I believe the air we breathe is one of those issues and it will continue to be placed on hold until we have destroyed the very air that we breathe.

A very large contribution to the problem is the element of waste. This is actually quite frightening because waste is a part of everything that is created in this world. How we choose to discard this waste will determine whether are not this world will be able to survive future generations. One thing is for certain, this country cannot continue to go on with this nonchalant attitude. The fact that there is such a great demand for something as simple as bottled water should tell us that something is evolving out of control.

Today's current regulations to cut down on the amount of toxic gases and pollutants which are being emitted into the atmosphere is like putting a band aid on a open-heart patient. This simply is not going to cut it! The thing that has slipped by most Americans is the fact that when it comes to this matter we aren't allowed a second chance.

As the world continues to shove this important issue aside, we are forgetting that there aren't a lot of other planets where we can hop to and start a new life.

Once we pollute this planet to the point of no return, that is it! Because America is considered a world leader, we must take a larger step towards making our environment a better place. In the next few years, when someone starts to market fresh air to breath, then the writing is on the wall.

I see that most of our pollution problems stem from transportation, industry and radioactive waste. Because we have created the elements in these three categories, then we should be able to reverse the process. One issue that seems to register regarding the environment is the cost factor.

There are two alternatives to the transportation problem. Because the automobile requires fuel which emits toxic vapors into the air, then we must either find a better source of fuel or a different form of transportation. It is basically that simple. If we cannot find a better form of transportation, we need to take all the automobiles off the road, including large trucks and buses.

This might be an inconvenience, but I believe with our backs against the wall we will be able to come up with a workable solution. The fact is, America has become too complacent with the means by which we do things.

It is time we create a new attitude for ourselves as well as our children! The industries that don't meet these new standards will be closed down permanently. It is time for this country to stop vacillating with an issue that will eventually effect the well-being of our existence!

As for toxic waste, who in their right mind would manufacture a product that creates a byproduct that cannot be disposed of? Whether these are people, industries or government agencies, they will be immediately shut down. This is how simple the solution is. I promise you, this nation has both the technology and the means by which to change the way we do things. If America is to make drastic changes; then, she must be willing to take drastic measures in implementing those changes.

It is important for this nation to begin to clean up the waste that it has created. Since this is an important issue it must be implemented in our schools. Our kids need to be prepared to deal with the problem this generation has created. Our kids must not allow government agencies and special interest groups to pollute their planet. Quite frankly, it is our responsibility to lead them towards that direction. As your President, it is my responsibility to set the stage for that possibility.

The changes that this nation is going to have to make cannot begin unless we are willing to make some major adjustments in our lifestyles. Whether or not we are willing to initiate this process will determine our future. When these challenges are placed on the table, only then will we be forced to choose an ultimatum. This is oftentimes a situation that can be suicidal for a society. Whether or not this country is willing to make the right move is debatable.

Change is based on whether or not society is capable of cutting to the chase. This country hasn't decided whether or not it is willing to make these sacrifices. We often blame our leaders for the state of our nation. It is time to decide if we are ready to make a difference.

Final thoughts on my term as President

I wonder if this nation is ready for a President that will not tolerate the old way of life. Rarely do we ask the question "what does America want in a president?" I don't think this question is asked often enough. Americans have become too complacent. Granted, this is partially the fault of our leaders and their inability to motivate and stimulate the best that lives inside of us. The reason leaders lack this ability is that they fail to tell Americans what is expected of them.

450

I believe the content of this nation is such that it will rise to any challenge. Before we clean the White House we are going to have to clean our own home. The President of the United States is merely a reflection of our nation. We can't expect greatness from our leaders if we do not find it within ourselves. If we accuse our President of lacking character there is a great possibility that our nation also lacks character.

The reason I wanted to be in office for one year, was that it would take that period of time for the people to realize that this country's problem is not the President, it is the people. I believe that it will take three hundred and sixty-five days to make you aware. The policies and suggestions I have created are quite simple. However, I believe it is simplicity that will enable us to get back to the basics. Whoever this nation chooses to elect as their commander and chief will reflect on us as Americans and those things that are most important to us.

I hope that I have given you the opportunity to clear up some of challenges this nation has been stumbling over for countless years. Again, the methods are simple, how we have managed to let things get so far out of control has always been somewhat of an enigma to me. I don't want to see this nation continue to fall. There is no need for it.

What we have failed to realize is that we have turned our backs on many possible leaders, simply because they have not been in the mainstream of what we believe leadership is. Let me leave you with these thoughts.

Always be aware of those around you. Oftentimes you will find that the average man and woman will somehow be the greatest example of true leadership. America cannot continue to let leadership be only one color. If we do, we will only get one result. This nation will never know the qualities that a black president could bring to the table. I'm sure there are countless minorities that would love to help better serve this nation. Maybe one day this country will grow to that point and allow this to happen. It was truly an honor to serve you, America.

The President

Chapter Ten

Black Men

□ □

White Women

The challenge of tackling a topic of this nature is not going to be easy. In many ways, this subject is one that has changed the face of America. I believe that at the root of America's racial tensions lies the thought of the black man and uniting with the white woman. While gathering research data at the local library, it became perfectly clear to me that the topic of the Black men and white women is a concept that has not been written about. I first tried to find statistics that would give me an insight on this situation. There was very little written on this topic, in contrast to the available information on the black man.

Unfortunately, I could not locate one single reference book that had any information on this subject. Suddenly, it occurred to me that this subject is still considered taboo in America.

History of the Topic

The beginning of this situation is very hard to document it encompasses thousands of episodes. Thousands of personal, one-on-one relationships that have created the stories that will never be retold. Although history didn't record these incidents, it did document this nation's disapproval of such behavior.

Throughout history, the white man has made it perfectly clear that this type of behavior would not be tolerated. In 1715, Maryland enacted laws designed to guard against interracial marriage. There are many reasons for the white man's insecurities. You can bet that the possibility of his white woman lying down with the black man was at the top of his list.

In order to impose his will on the rest of society the white man created the illusion that there was a major difference between himself and the black man. In the 1880's the white man went to great measures to prove that the black man was in fact inferior.

Many blacks were subjected to physical and mental tests, (measurement of the head and brain.) They also examined the difference in the anatomy. However, the studies were based on inconclusive data. The studies reflected the opinion of those who conducted the test rather than the actual scientific data.

Once the black population increased, so did the challenge of keeping the black and white race separated. After the Civil War, the South, in order to lessen the chance of racial conflict declared that any contact between blacks and whites would be restricted. The South felt that blacks were a different breed of mankind, biologically inferior to whites. Of course, they were not alone in this kind of thinking. Many Europeans shared this belief as well.

Racial separation was enforced in travel, theaters, restaurants, churches, schools, industry, in the political and social structures. A more subtle and cunning racial barrier arose in the Northern part of the United States. Blacks could not buy or rent houses outside the areas generally reserved for them. In a sense, it was at this time in history that the lines of segregation were drawn. The black man had but one alternative and that was to stay within those perimeters or be persecuted.

At the root of all these precautions and restrictions was the fear of one common issue, The black man and the white woman.

Only time has been able to answer the primal question of whether or not the black man is an inferior being. Time has also given mankind an opportunity to witness the extent that the white man has gone through to maintain his illusion of superiority.

One can only question the mentality of the American people at that time. The method by which she justified her social actions were nothing less than barbaric. During that period, there was very limited documentation of the gross mistreatment of our race and the mentality of the white man toward the black man. We can only assume that the lack of documentation is an acknowledgement by most Americans that the past had better be left alone.

If in fact this is true, then underneath the foundation of this country ferments a sleeping giant which will someday awaken to continue its destructive past. The one thing that history can guarantee, is the fact that it will always repeat itself. Unless this nation learns to take on the wrongs and the misconception of the past, it is most likely that we will see the same troubles become a part of our future.

I often wonder if the countless black men that are populating our nation's correctional institutions are not the product of the white man's mentality from the past. Maybe the future will give us a better idea of this possibility.

Very few people ever acknowledge the possibility that behind this racial struggle is an underlying motive: the issue of the black man and the white woman. The propaganda of the myth that the white man must protect the white woman from the horrible African savage has instigated countless laws, policies and the psychological attitudes of white society.

I purposely didn't introduce this topic in my chapter on racism because I wanted to keep that chapter clean and simple. The relationship between the black man and the white woman will always be one that is entwined with harmful egos and attitudes.

Why do White Women like Black men?

For many white women, their thoughts which are enhanced by the image of the black field hand going through his daily chores. Unbeknown to him, the master's wife is staring down at him from her bedroom window.

Her mind is imagining his strong hands next to her pure white skin. His stature resembles that of his ancestors, the chiefs and kings of exotic tribes. The sunlight reflects on his well-defined torso and her heart begins to race. In a sense, her thoughts were part of the natural course of humanity. It was the time period which made her thoughts look like a thorn in the side of society.

Her desires were not tolerated by the times, but after weeks and months of being ignored by her husband, (who by the way, has been satisfying his needs with one or two of the slave house servants), she succumbs to her greater passions within. As the days of summer get hotter, so do her thoughts, her needs and her desires.

She puts aside any and all fear. All elements of reason and sanity are overshadowed by the months and months of coveting this physical statue of a man.

One, hot, summer afternoon the Madame of the house instructs one of her house servants to make up a pitcher of cool lemonade. She sits out on the large porch swing moving back and forth and becomes intoxicated from the thoughts of the field hand. He diligently performs his chores. She battles the demons that have manifested them-selves inside her.

Each passing day, the lust inside of her is the only thing that can feed the hunger of the demons who cry from within.

Suddenly, her train of thought is broken by the opening of the front screen door. A young, perky, house servant emerges carrying a tray with a pitcher of cold lemonade. She tries to initiate the Madame in conversation. The Madame becomes annoyed and the house maid is told to quickly return to her chores. The Madame tells her to take a glass of lemonade to her dark fantasy, the one who invades her every thought.

Maple slowly carries out her orders. Upon her approach, she startles the field hand. She reaches out the cool drink, so as as not to get to close to him. Maple realizes that she too is intimidated by the size of this strong and large specimen. She finds herself looking away. The man that stands before her is a sculpture, resembling the statue of a Greek God. For a moment, Maple is caught in a trance, as she watches a drop of lemonade fall from the bottom of the glass. She follows the drop with her eyes as it lightly lands on his bare chest. The drop appears to become larger as it rolls over his muscular terrain, working its way through a light layer of soil that seems to be embracing his body. Maple continues to follow the drop as it begins to disappear towards the front of his tight-fitting pants.

Maple is so caught up in the moment, that she fails to realize that Kumanda has finished with his drink and is handing the glass back to her.

She still imagines herself following the drop of lemonade on his chest where the perspiration has gathered around the area of his groin.

The excitement is too great, she quickly turns around and runs back towards the porch. Intentionally, she leaves the well-defined slave, standing perplexed with the empty glass still in his hand.

Maple runs up the front steps and flies past her master. The Madame of the house smiles to herself, she enjoyed living the fantasy vicariously through the house servant.

As the field hand puts the empty glass down on the ground, he momentarily glances over at the master's wife. She responds with a slight nod. She realizes that the passion growing inside her cannot possibly be quenched by a single glass of lemonade.

All over the North and the South, the same scenario repeated itself. Yes, the faces and names have changed, but the content of intrigue between the black man and white woman has developed into the situation we see today. Although there is little written, on this topic, it is a fact that in many European cultures it was the norm for rich, wealthy, white women to have black lovers.

It appeared the wealthy carried their own set of standards and didn't care less what the rest of the world thought. Over the years, the residual effect of interracial relationships has stained the fabric of society. Currently, it is being witnessed across the country. Yet, if we were able to read the true thoughts and opinions of those who look upon these situations from a distance, I often wonder what type of true voices would be heard. After all, what people say is often a far cry from what they think.

The question as to why white women like black men is one that never seems to be asked. However, it is a question that society doesn't really care to address because of the response. You see, the answer to this question reflects a decision of choice. A choice which refers to the preference of one race over another, in this case, the black man over the white man.

Though the answer to this question lies in its foundation, it rarely has the opportunity to come to the surface. One would think that this choice would be simply about preference. Yet, the implications that follow often result as a strike against the ego of the male gender.

At one time, the choice to be with a black man was perceived as a direct attack on the white male population.

In many cases, the white woman's decision in choosing a black mate became a reality check that forced the white man to admit his limitations. He had to realize the fact that he was not the 'crem de la crem' of society.

Many white women say that the black man has a different type of energy from the white man. They claim that the black man carries an internal rhythm from within and that somehow enables him to view the world around him in a slightly different light.

Today, in a free society, the individual will of both man and woman have a much greater opportunity to come together as one. Although, for the black man and white woman, the passions of old have been replaced with new desires that are fueled by a modern generation. The increasing possibility of this union has a lot to do with the great physical connection that is placed before our society. Today, white women are integrated into America's melting pot. They have a greater opportunity to differentiate between the white and black man's content and character.

This, added to the highly visible dominance of the black man in the area of sports and entertainment, has given the white woman an opportunity to have more than an ample chance to taste the juice of a much darker berry.

We often see that the black male and white woman cycle repeats itself over and over in the sports world. The plantations of old have been replaced with arenas, stadiums and field house today. The Black man is still on display, for the white woman to admire, but she can now view his majestic splendor in a much more comfortable and delightful manner.

The white woman can continue her fantasy from the court side of any basketball game. She can enjoy watching the tall and graceful thoroughbred prancing back and forth in front of her, as if he was being placed on the auction block, to be sold to the highest bidder. The next time you watch a professional basketball game on T.V., closely look in the eyes of any female spectator and you'll recognize the look of appreciation for the players that are playing before her. Ninety-eight percent of sports fans are white men and women. Because of this opportunity the white woman can fulfill her subconscious desires.

By the way, if the black male athlete had a command of the English language, he would become an instant commodity. This would not only increase his charisma, but the value of his sex appeal from those who lust after him. A great example of this is the very talented M. J.. You can bet that when Michael Jordan walks on to a court, the eyes of every white female look in his direction.

And guess what? You can bet that their lustful thoughts are in full gear and these thoughts are magnified when he speaks.

The white woman not only sees a well-spoken, articulate man, but the 'crem dela la crem' of manhood. It is no accident that M. J. is such a marketable product. Not only do many Americans aspire to be like Mike, but I imagine a large number of white females would like to be with Mike.

Despite the many reasons as to why white women prefer black men, I would like to devalue this issue with the simple observation that it falls under the category of freedom of choice. Is this not what this country is all about? Having the freedom to make decisions that will enhance our lives to be more enriched and enlightened. Shouldn't we accept a mixed couple as two unique human beings that have chosen to walk together for the length of their relationship. Let's discard the possibility that one race of man is better than the next.

What Does the Black Woman have to Say about this Issue?

When we look at the black man and white woman, we often push aside the black woman's presence to the corner of society.

There it can be out of harm's way.

In many ways, the black woman has the greatest right to evaluate this situation more than anyone else involved. Unlike the white man who initiated this mixed situation throughout history, black women simply didn't have a say about the matter.

If anything, it is here where we might be able to understand, if not empathize with the attitude that the black woman is said to have regarding this matter. Let's for a moment review the ordeal that the black woman has had to endure since her embarkment upon this continent.

Her arrival in America was anything but a luxury cruise, to say the least. She was treated like livestock, just as her male counter part. The black woman was *forced* to bond with the black male. *Courtship* and *romance* were not a part of her vocabulary. In most cases, she was ordered to spread her legs regardless of love or understanding and take unto her any and every black male which the white master had chosen for her to procreate. Let's not forget the countless number of rapes that went on by the white man, which in turn created thousands of mulatto offspring.

After the birth of her offspring, she had the displeasure of standing by as her child was plucked from her arms and sold into slavery.

As years followed years, she sat idly by as many of her fellow sisters experienced the identical episode after episode. Families being torn apart. She realizes that at the center of this curse, is the color of her skin.

Still today, the black woman continues to find some sense of understanding to her controversial beginning. One thing is for sure, the attitude of black women is in many ways warranted. In fact, in my opinion, if this attitude is portrayed in the right way, it can be displayed as a crown on her head. I say this because only a queen could have survived the difficulties of the past and still stand tall carrying both the pride and dignity of character that makes her the woman she is today.

It is no great revelation that most black women have very little tolerance for black men and white women being together. On the surface, it would appear that the black man has preferred another over her. This situation harms their fragile ego, The one thing about the ego, if it is abused without justification or reason it often becomes bitter with animosity. It takes a very wise black woman to understand that the union of the black man and the white woman is not a reflection of her character. Only wisdom and understanding can take away the anger and animosity. Within these gates of wisdom lies an internal peace.

At the core of that peace lies the true essence of the black woman.

Inside that core flows a river of understanding, not only of the things of this world but of many worlds that are to come.

As black women (need to) make sense of their place in America, I believe they will someday realize that it isn't the black man that has made them feel complete. God is the one that has given her the jewels which she has placed on her crown. No man, black or white, has that kind of gift. Man is simply the instrument by which God chooses to plant His seeds. Woman is the instrument by which God watches (what He has planted grow.)

Once black women understands that black man and white women were part of the seeds that were planted long ago, they can find the heart to understand this complex issue.

Just as the white man took what was not his, so has the black man. Only through the pages of time can we understand this. The black woman is guilty of allowing this situation to determine the outcome of her livelihood. This cannot continue to be the case. The black woman must learn to move forward and carve her place in society. Others will recognize her as the queen whose ancestors she was once apart of.

Once she begins to do this, she will realize that the only men in her life should be kings.

In a sense, blacks must not see this issue as anything more than what it is, an integrated relationship. Why did I make this statement you might ask? Because if black women see it in any other way, then they give away their power rather than keeping it.

With our current communicational resources, it will be easy for all of us to view the black woman for ourselves. Once the confidence of the black woman grows so will the black man's need to place her at the altar of his desires. Today, this has already begun to happen. The black woman shines brightly. She must never allow anyone's choice to dim her luminosity which is meant to be enjoyed by the entire world.

Why Black Men like White Women?

In the case of the white woman and the black man, the relationship seems to provoke a spark that ignites a moment of negative energy in the hearts and minds of many in society.

And like the white women's decision, the black man's decision also carries with it sharp edges that seem to constantly keep society in an awkward position.

One of the reasons for this personal choice reflects the black man's need to be a part of a different culture. Another reason seem to fall under the category of pure lust, but this is not always the case. Oftentimes, it is simply the ability to communicate with one another that creates the groundwork for countless relationships.

I often hear it said that the black man's interest in the white woman is simply do to with the many years of programing, enhanced by watching countless hours of, television programs and commercials. A format that displays the white woman as the physical desire of every man's heart. Years and years of watching white women prancing all over the television screen has created a false illusion of her allure. The black man finds himself trapped in the midst of this fascination. This has some merit, but can it be enough to totally justify the black man's desires?

To really understand the black man's decision details more than meets the eye. In some ways his decision is based on countless elements that make up his past, present and future.

If we were to start with the beginning, I think that it would be very easy to pinpoint the black man's initial interest in white women.

Let's not overlook the possibility that the black man was disillusioned by the image that the white man had created for himself.

What I'm trying to explain to you is that the black male was able to view the existence of the white female only from a distance. Psychologically the black male was programmed to believe that the white female was some heavenly goddess whose beauty was only worthy of the white man's touch.

In a sense, this enforced separation (of the black male and white female) created a passionate mystic which eventually grew into the countless relationships that we see today. Ironically, it was the white man's early actions which created this situation. The black male was (programmed to be this nation's laborer.) In a sense, unbeknown to him, the white man had created a stronger, much more attractive black man. Ironically, the white man allowed his physical body to remain dormant, which in many cases resulted in a poorer specimen of man (at least phsycially anyway).

Generation after generation, the white man helped to create a black man who quite frankly was much more physically desirable. And you can bet that the white woman was the first to recognize the evolution of the black male.

Another factor that helped to peak the white woman's desire was the fact that the black male was used for the purpose of breeding. Oops! That was a very big mistake! The white man saw the black man as a piece of livestock but he didn't realize that his woman saw the black man as a sexual animal.

The white man would pick out the biggest, strongest black male on his plantation and have him breed for the only purpose of reproducing a strong offspring to add to the inventory of his plantation.

At this time the message permeating throughout the country was that the black male was a more sexual being, simply because he was more sexually active. Lets face it, the white man was giving it to everybody but his woman; therefore, he helped to create a very frustrated female. Human nature will run its course. Unfortunately, in this case it simply forced the white woman to search elsewhere for her sexual fulfillment. Guess what? She didn't have to look very far. Right in her own backyard she found her afternoon delight.

The black male in this case was between a rock and a hard place.

He understood that the white woman was off limits, but the sexual willpower of most men can be measured by nothing greater than a teaspoon.

Imagine for a moment this situation.

A white woman enters the barn and quickly closes the oversized door behind her. Looking around, her eyes survey a number of livestock. Finally, she comes across the large black male that had entered ten minutes earlier. Quietly and slowly she walks toward him. Each step brings her closer and closer to her desires. Feeling lightheaded from the blood that is quickly racing through her heart, she calls out her servant's name. He turns around quickly. His face is dark with panic, as he realizes that he is alone with the master's wife. Sensing his fear, she begins to assure him that everything is all right.

As the woman walks closer and closer toward him, his mind is filled with mixed thoughts. The panic in his face becomes more evident and he finds himself looking everywhere but in her direction. The Mistress is standing less than a few feet from him now. Her eyes are fixed on his large body. She quietly assures him that everything is going to be ok. She tells him that the master will never find out what is going to take place. She also tells him that if he leaves the barn, she will tell the master that he looked at her the wrong way.

Out of fear, the black man stands motionless. He feels the Mistress slowly press up next to his body. Still, the servant is making no effort to look at her.

He is becoming aware of the difference in the way she smells. Clean and flowery, pleasant to the nose. His eyes are forced to look at her hair, which looks different that of the black woman from which he has been forced to reproduce with. His passion comes to the forefront and the seeds of passion embrace themselves, leaving no room for any other thought, just the inevitable.

Weeks later the lady of the house is sharing her story with a cousin who is visiting from up North. Here the seed is planted and it begins to run rapidly and out of control, all across the nation. Suddenly, every frustrated white woman has a newfound view of the black male that serves her daily needs.

The white man's biggest fear came to fruition. Without taking responsibility for the situation, he tries to find a solution by setting an example to all black men. Blacks are hung from trees in public view, and others are castrated. This only adds to the complexity of the situation and the hatred between the two men increases.

As America liberated herself from her conservative beginnings, the relationships between the black man and the white woman began to grow; however, they have always been accompanied by feelings of animosity.

The mere fact that the black man would choose a white woman, segregated him into a category that questioned his worth and the degree of his character.

This choice would often invite controversy and self-inflected turmoil into his life. Many times fighting his own race of people, as well as the white race.

If we take a closer look at what this relationship implies, I believe what we would find is really nothing out of the ordinary.

I believe that in many cases we lose sight of the basic principle that this is simply a matter of preference. I think if you were to take a look at the situation without the racial overtone and the negative energy, again you would find a (**basic matter of choice.**) Why do some people prefer chocolate ice cream, while others prefer vanilla? If you saw a white man walking around eating a chocolate ice-cream cone, would you dislike him? I don't think so. I think that society forgets the fact that mates are selected by choice.

What makes something as simple as this, an extraordinary situation in the first place? I believe that one's desires versus another is what causes the friction, this ultimately changes what is considered normal into something that is unwanted and undesirable.

In many ways our, society is one that is extremely phsycially oriented. The more we see black men with white women the more we become accustomed to it. In many of the major cities in America, this trend is growing rapidly everyday. The more it is viewed the more it is accepted. At least on the surface anyway.

Times are changing and so are the attitudes by which Americans view certain subjects that are considered taboo. I guess in some ways we have grown up a little.

What Does the White Man think Today About This?

There is no doubt that throughout the pages of history the thoughts and ideas of the white man make up the content of what the world perceives as America. The history of the white man pretty much speaks for itself. I believe American history books reflects the white man's perception of history. They overlook a considerable amount of important data which simply reflect a number of facts that are best left unsaid.

I for one, don't think that this is such a bad thing. However, it is not a very realistic approach either.

The fact is that there is very little that any of us can do about the pages in history that have already been written. Although many facts can be considered inaccurate and biased, I feel that any and all corrections should be made at the present time and the future.

In order to correct the problem we must understand the mistakes and the failures. For many of us, this is an issue that is not easily resolved, especially if these mistakes and failures affect countless lives in a very negative way. Unfortunately, the white man is guilty of this. Throughout this book I have tried to express my views in a candid and nonprejudicial manner that would not infer hatred and animosity.

I purposely did this because we cannot grow as a people if we use these elements as fertilizer. Tackling issues that many would rather you left alone, can evoke energy by the writer or the reader. I hope this is not the case here.

I have often said that American history is about the white man, his accomplishments and his disorder. Although there is not a lot of information regarding the attraction between the black man and white woman, you can bet the white man is fully aware of its existence.

You won't have an opportunity to read about the countless black men that were hung because of the white man's disgust and fear.

In fact, it is easy for this country to roll right along ignoring these atrocities. As in the case of O. J. Simpson. Behind this gigantic trial was the underlying message that it is still unacceptable for the black man (even a sports's hero) to be with a white woman.

To this day, countless Americans are oblivious to the fact that this trial was not about a black man getting away with murder. It was about a black man being married to a white woman and the white man having to take it. Times have changed many issues in this country. But this issue, is not one of them, at least not as far as the white man is concerned.

In fact, I can sum up the whole situation in two words *(more tolerance)*.

Today, the white man has simply learned to tolerate this situation, his views have not changed. Like most men, his ego is damaged when he isn't the preference or choice of the day.

Frankly, it is not a matter of whether or not the white man has a right to feel this way, because I believe that he does. However, it is the method by which he continues to consummate his beliefs that I find fault with.

Unless a man is secure within himself he will never be able to accept the fact that his woman is attracted to a man of a different race.

Black or white, red, yellow or brown, this is a fact which involves the characteristics of the male species. In fact, the real mistake the white man made throughout history was the methods by which he choose to voice his disapproval. The reality is that many negative chapters in America's history can be attributed to a little seed called *insecurity*. To think that the devil can place an obstacle in the path of man and cause him to stumble, is a very sad thing.

Whether or not the white man accepts the relationship between the black man and white woman doesn't really matter. Like it or not, this relationship stands before the whole world to see. They will also witness the new pages of history and let's hope for the sake of mankind that they do not read like the pages of the past.

Putting it all into Perspective

Whether or not the issue of the black man and white woman will ever have any major effect on American society is something that can never really be documented. This situation affects the family and friends of those involved, We'll never really have an opportunity to view the social changes that might occur from all this.

Maybe the solution, lies in the interracial offspring. Perhaps, one day we will be able to document the result of the many black and white interrelationships.

When these pages are recorded in history, there is one important element that must accompany them. That is the element of *truth*. Often times it is this element of truth which breaks through the hatred and anger that permeates throughout this country.

As a matter of fact, I believe it is this honesty about the things I have written that will give you the truth and knowledge to understand that it is our individuality that makes all of us special. I believe that truth helps us see the mistakes of the past. There is a great possibility of this happening, unless we are unwilling to face our truths with an honest desire to make the necessary changes.

Since we are discussing this topic, let me share with you what I feel is the truth regarding the relationship between the black man and white woman. The truth is that if you take the black and the white out of this issue, you would be left with a basic man and woman. The truth is, this is all you need in any real relationship. Think about it.

HOPE

The thoughts by which we seek to change yesterday.

Dexter Clay
Author of Black Eye on America!

.

Chapter Ten

Hope for Survival

This final Chapter is a recapitulation of some of the chapters in *Black Eye on America!* The main prevailing theme throughout this book can be summed up in one word *Hope.* The topics I have touched upon, each has the ability to inspire us to remain hopeful. At times, hope is all we have to hold on to. Rev. Jesse Jackson has often spoken of the need to keep hope alive. It is this element of hope that will generate a movement towards a better tomorrow. Hope is the catalyst for change. We owe the next generation of Black Americans the hope for survival.

I realize that some may misinterpret part of the information in this book, which is unfortunate. Others will disagree with certain sections of the text, and that is their prerogative. My wish is that my readers will at least remain open to what I have to say.

481

This country has been crying out in pain and it is imperative that we pull it out of its misery. In this final chapter, I will take a last look at all the chapters and the views previously shared with you. This book is not about my grievances towards this country. It is about my desire to see the U.S. as one of the greatest nations on this planet. I believe this nation's progress is being monitored by a source greater than ourselves.

Leadership in America

In the chapter "American Leadership, Live or Let Die," I gave an introspective look at today's political affairs. I tried to give an honest assessment of this country's leaders and political parties. I hope you will recognize my genuine endeavor to initiate a change by giving you positive solutions and explanations to many of today's dilemmas. We often complain about the state of affairs, but do we have the knowledge or wisdom to rectify these problems?

Why is it so important for our leaders to exhibit qualities of honor, integrity and candor? It is quite simple. Our leaders are the head of the body, figuratively speaking. It is the head of any organization that gives the body it's direction.

Why do we make leaders take an oath before they take office? Because we expect the very best from them that they can offer. The reason the quality of a leader is of the utmost importance is that good leadership eliminates any possibility of failure.

A very important thing for us to understand is our role as Americans. Make no mistake, the role we play as individuals is vital to the country in accomplishing success. A parent's commitment to the PTA will ultimately make a change that will affect the school and community. However insignificant our actions seem they are never unimportant.

Our nation is slowly and sadly taking a back seat to other world powers because of our lack of leadership. I wonder if Americans are aware of this change. If we do not understand this fact, then we are unlikely to comprehend the importance of leadership in America. As I explained in the leadership chapter, changing the direction of leadership from the people up, rather than from the leaders down, will give the power back to the people. Those of us who learn to ask the right questions must also demand the right answers.

By taking a closer look at America's leaders, we force ourselves to begin to monitor the characteristics of this country's leadership. This will cause us to become more aware of the lack of quality we have been settling for.

Many Americans can be described as "arm chair quarterbacks." Many of us think we would be quite capable of leading this country. It is easy to feel this way, sitting at ease in our recliners. Once the game ends; however, it forces us to rethink our position.

During the last presidential election, I could see that we were on the same course as the past. Once the presidential conventions began to honor their candidates, each party chose their best quarterback to play the big game. As the game got closer to the playoffs, each party bombarded television viewers with negative campaign ads. I was watching the same old game, but with different players.

In my opinion President Clinton was re-elected President simply because of a lack of choice. He projected the closest image of what we perceive as the stereotype of an American president. Like most other elections, the country provided us with little choice; therefore, many Americans voted for Clinton simply out of despair.

Ross Perot didn't have a fighting chance, Although he possessed all the qualifications of a leader. He is a successful entrepreneur and could have led this country out of financial chaos. Unfortunately, he is an unattractive little man! Our society has become very superficial and looks play an important role in politics!

It is ironic that Mr. Perot was probably the hands-down best candidate for leading this country, but he never had an opportunity to convince America of his potential.

The election proved to be one of the Republicans' biggest downfalls. The horse they chose to run as the winner of the big race looked as if he had been put out to pasture. Many of those attending the Republican convention looked like they were related to their candidate. The Republican party is a very white party! Its policies resemble the arrogance of the white man of early America. Their attacks on affirmative action and multiple assaults against the welfare system affirmed the fact that the Republican party still condones an antiquated way of thinking.

The best and wisest choice for president would have been General Colin Powell. He was smart enough not to run. He understood that in a corrupt system his efforts would have been in vain. He would have been used by a system that is already corrupt.

Hope is kept alive by the individuals with the potential of becoming true leaders. We must realize that by looking behind the facade we will see the beast behind the mask. Our only hope is to find an individual who will bring to the table the best possible qualities.

His character must have elements of fairness, equality, truth, communication, patience, guidance, and most important of all, forgiveness. Since our society is so eager to put our leaders down, then let any American that is without sin cast the first stone. Last, but certainly not least, Americans must realize that only God can provide us with the real blueprint for great leadership. Let's keep this in mind as our nation continues to push God out of its environment!

Combating Racism.

Every seed of change carries with it the element of hope. Without the power of change, hope cannot come alive. Nowhere is this more evident than within racism. Racism in America is alive and well. It exists because many of us have failed to apply the principle of putting action or works to create our hope for change. The *Bible* calls this *faith without works.* This simply means that if we do not put forth the effort, we can forget about wishing for things to happen. Every single American has the power to make a change in their lives.

I feel as if I have been fair and honest in my assessment of this subject. I wanted you to see how easily racism can become a part of our lives. We need to be constantly aware of how it grows and generates.

In my research on this matter, I have found that racism's greatest asset is fear. Fear begins as a seed which once planted grows rampant. Since most of us fear the unknown, chances are we carry within us the seed of racism. This seed will grow wild and out of control if left unattended. All of us must ask ourselves, "Am I a racist?" If you respond truthfully, then your answer will hit you right square in the face.

Many of you will not be able to ask yourselves this pertinent question simply because you will be afraid of the response. This country has made a few attempts at dealing with this issue, but you can't put a band-aid on a cut that needs stitches. Many of us have learned to overlook what we don't want to deal with. In this case, if we ignore to address this issue, we will pay for it for several generations.

Americans cannot be deluded by the coalition of the different races that are portrayed on television and in films today. We have some very real challenges when it comes to racism. In my opinion, our educational system should have a required course on the subject of racism. I believe this would help to destroy this growing weed before it spreads and takes over the field of our life.

With all the progress that this country has made, we cannot continue to tiptoe around the issue of racism.

It is wrong for us to feel that if we ignore the topic, it will just go away? Unfortunately, racism doesn't disappear simply because we want it to. It is better to attack it while it is in its dormant state. Don't wait for it to raises its ugly head and bite us with its fangs of venom. When that happens, Americans will be too emotionally caught up to see things clearly.

Racism can be likened to a sleeping giant. It is wiser to attack a giant when it is in state of slumber. Once it awakens, it has the potential of destroying everything in its path.

The O. J. Simpson and Rodney King incidents brought racism into every living room of America. We will never be able to totally get rid this beast, but we can change the opinions on this subject.

The fact is, America is a melting pot. Our country of origin or ethnic descent may differ, but we must learn to respect each other. Racism will always be an integral part of the American way of life. There still can be a ray of hope. With God's help, we can gain the knowledge and wisdom to overcome our feelings of prejudice. In whatever fashion this country tries to deal with its different issues, it will always fall back on the shoulders of God. I guess that is the reason why I am annoyed at Americans. Their diligent behavior in severing the ties with the one source that can help them overcome all of their challenges.

During this process of healing, it is important to surround ourselves with love, understanding and patience.

Suddenly, something miraculous will happen! We will realize racism is not something that we are born with, it is learned. Let me share this image with you, one that will show you how simple dealing with this issue can become. Racism, can be compared to someone running through a giant pasture. Once they run through it, they look down at their pants and see all the different items they have collected along the way. Somehow, all kinds of objects have managed to attach themselves to their pant legs. In the field of life, we must recognize those items, that for whatever reason, manage to attach themselves to us. This is especially true in situations that cause us to mistreat others. I want all of America to understand that racism will only continue to be a severe problem if we try to pretend that it does not exist.

I believe that if this country is aware of racism's presence then we will be able to keep it into the proper perspective and avoid repeating the mistakes. Everyone has the opportunity of contributing positively in this regard. It is just a matter of deciding when we want to get started!

The Issues in Education

A, B, C, D, E, F, G. These symbols mark the beginning of education for all Americans. Today education is more complex than when we first learned the alphabet. In my chapter on education, I tried to give you an alternative view. We should never underestimate education's power to influence our growth as a nation. We can incorporate the power of knowledge and change the conditions around us.

The complexity of our ever changing world has created a never-ending challenge. We must keep up with this world's infinite quest for knowledge. Our nation is increasingly intertwined with other countries. At this stage in history, we can no longer implement the old methods of teaching. The more technically oriented education becomes, the greater the responsibility for teachers. Our kids must become wise enough to understand that they must lean towards the direction of knowledge. As adults we must show them the way.

The survival of this country, is in part, dependent on the abilities of those who will one day take the reins. If our children are not prepared, then everything we have learned in the past will have been in vain. What makes us foolish has a lot to do with what makes us smart.

Many Americans think that education makes it impossible to be foolish. Unfortunately this is not so. An increase in knowledge does not guarantee that we'll gain wisdom. Nor does it insure that we will have the common sense to use it. Americans have two choices. The way I see it, when it comes to education we can either replace the element of wisdom in our school or we can learn to adapt to a system that is heading us towards disaster. The fact that we have taken God out of our educational system has in a sense guaranteed a catastrophic outcome. The evil element of this world is allowed to grow without God's involvement and wisdom. God's infinite knowledge can open our hearts and minds and allow us to overcome the many obstacles that are in our path. Some of you will understand what I am saying, while others may not.

Face it, fellow Americans, in order for us to get back on track, we must keep pace with the changing needs of our society. The goal of our schools should be to meet the individual needs of the child. Our school system must adapt to a new technological era.

We must strive to decrease our class size, hire qualified motivated teachers, and increase parent involvement. It is the parents' involvement and leadership, that will inspire the teachers and administrators to do the best job possible.

The longer it takes for us to see the errors of our ways, the longer we will lack control over the situation. But there's no time to waste, our educational system cannot survive without new and improved guidelines. Authority and discipline are two key elements that must be implemented. Both of these are God's principles.

Our country boasts of the level of education it offers. We are a self-proclaimed nation of intellectuals. Although many of us have been educated to achieve a professional status, we fail to see the simple solution to our educational predicament.

We have the power as individuals, as a people, and as a nation to demand that God return to our schools, The choice is ours and so is the aftermath of our decisions! There will be those who will argue that God and education don't have anything to do with one another. I assure you they are wrong! Go back and reread the chapter, "Fools of Education". We have become too educated for our own good! We may have knowledge, but we lack common sense.

Beyond Blacks in a Corner

I wrote "Blacks in a Corner" to describe the struggles of the black man in this country.

As I began to make an assessment of the black man's situation and potential, it became evident that I had to view the position from a corner of American society. What's wrong with this picture? This country belongs just as much to you and I as it does to any other race of people. How can we have allowed ourselves to be pushed into a corner? After all, this is the country of our birth!

The only response I have is that we have allowed this to happen and we have no one to blame but ourselves!

There are many reasons why we are where we are, in a country that has so much to offer. Our progress has been slow and tedious. There is still a huge disparity between the two races. In some respect, we are no further along today than we were one hundred years ago. Our men are still burdened with a stereotypical image. It is foolish for us to think that we are not haunted by our past.

Our hope for survival must begin with the Black male. We need to reinterpret our place in the world. I will be the first to agree that the past has a lot to do with our present circumstances.

However, using the past as a crutch will not change the situation. Let go of the anger and dissatisfaction! Remember the past as a process towards survival, one that has given us great courage. We are who we are because of the struggles of our past.

We have to learn to be proud of our beginning and to use it as a lever for the future. There is power in recognizing the fact that this proverbial corner of life we find ourselves, is something that we have created for ourselves. Let's begin from this moment on to knock down the walls that surround us and keep us imprisoned. Once we begin to free ourselves, we will come across an astonishing revelation. We will find that we are not confined to a corner of this nation, but we are at the very heart of this country and we are in a position to create a change!

One of our primary responsibilities is not to make the same mistakes that our white brothers made. As we move forward, we can begin to open up our hearts and embrace all those who come in our path. We should never consider ourselves better or greater than any other human being. This philosophy is not idealistic, it is a goal that we must strive to achieve. My point is that it really doesn't make any difference if we achieve the same accomplishments as the white man, especially if getting there means scarring our existence!

In order to initiate this change blacks must begin to examine their own lives. Pop singer Michael Jackson wrote a song called "Man In the Mirror." The lyrics have a great message for our people. Our greatness will ultimately come from within ourselves. We must start with the man in the mirror. The sooner we can identity with the person that is standing before us, the sooner we can propel forward.

The Black Man & Sports.

One of the most enjoyable chapters for me to write was the chapter on sports. I believe that it was so much fun because of my own experiences. The desire and hope to succeed has given me inspiration throughout my life, especially with my involvement in sports. Back in 1981, during my training with the New York Jets, I had a broken big toe, bruised ribs and knees, and a broken wrist. Despite all the injuries, I ran my fastest time ever in the forty-yard dash.

It is my desire to win, the belief in myself, and the hope for a better future that gives me the power and courage to strive to beat the odds. And if I can do it, so can you!

Oftentimes, we fall short of our dreams, but as long as we have hope, we can keep our dreams alive.

In this chapter, it was my intention to give many of you the opportunity to view the world of sports in a candid, realistic way. I wanted you to realize that however majestic and popular any sport is, it's still just a game! I tried to do away with the pageantry and glamor surrounding these events. If my thoughts on the subject cause you to think about sports, enlighten your views and give you a new perspective, then I am pleased!

Although each one of us reacts to any one sports game differently, it is what we learn from our individual experience that is important. We must take away the distractions and focus on the reality of the situation. Society judges the amount of time given towards any achievement as a testament to its credibility, whether this proves to be true or false is debatable! I believe these judgments are false. The importance of the things we do is measured by the amount of time we dedicate to them. For many young boys, the game has become so crucial that their energies are focused entirely on this arena of life. In my chapter,"Sports, They've Created An Idol," I wanted you to see how big business has distorted the world's view of sports. For many young black men, athletics is the only way out of an unfortunate situation.

One of the ways that few black men can achieve recognition is through sports.

For this reason, many young athletes spend most of their formative years trying to achieve sports' stardom. Unfortunately, many realize that they'll never reach that goal. There's no doubt that athletics have given the black man a great many opportunities, and for this, we are very thankful. Let us consider the price the black man has had to pay for this privilege. The black man has become a pawn in the white man's chess game of life. If our primary contribution to society is through sports, then we have been short-changed and have lost sight of a much greater reward.

It is obvious that we dominate the sports world, but we shouldn't stop here. My purpose is to plant the seed of awareness, challenge yourself and reach new heights!

By the way, I'm by no means foolish enough to believe that my book will initiate a massive movement towards the unification of the Black man. Our race of people have been programmed for years, and it will take time for us to de-program ourselves.

I simply want to leave my brothers with this thought: athletics can offer us many rewards, but the salvation of our people will not be achieved through athletics. We must reach a clear understanding about our role in athletics so that the rest of the world can change its perspective about sports and athletes.

Sports is big business and it offers many young athletes the opportunity for financial independence. How many athletes have the courage to bite the hand that feeds them? Should we pity those who worship athletes, or those who think that they deserve to worshipped? The first commandment states, "I am the lord thy God and thou shall not have strange Gods before me." I don't recall God making any allowances for athletes.

Religion & God

The hope for survival encompasses every element of this country's future and religion is no exception. This institution is supposed to teach and guide us towards a better understanding of God.

We must ask ourselves, does today's religion nurture our spirit, or is it simply the by-product of our once personal relationship with God? Time has kept the faith of hope alive, but in this century, there has been a deterioration in the area of religion. Those of you who have any reasonable understanding of this knowledge also know that this adversary has the power to confuse and control our thoughts and actions.

Those of you who follow religious studies will know that there is a foretold prophecy that speaks of great changes that are to come to our society.

These changes will cause our world as we know it to transform. Some of you are asking yourselves, "What is he talking about?" Well, the Bibles tells us that many will be destroyed for a lack of knowledge. If you find yourself among those who despise God, it is important that you quickly understand you are playing a crucial part in bringing about your own demise.

I am wondering if there is anything that I can say to you that will spark an interest in God and provoke a desire to be closer to Him and His divine goodness? Every life experience has either drawn me closer or farther away from Him. I understand that there are many of you whose circumstances have destroyed your love and trust for one another. I am also aware that certain words may be right for some to hear and wrong for others.

My hope is that you will stop and look towards the direction of God. I have accomplished something very special, if after reading this, just one of you can reach out and become closer to Him. Most religions teach us that someone or something much greater than ourselves governs our life. We learn that through His presence we will be guided towards a more profound existence. In our journey, we will achieve God-like qualities and a greater awareness which will bring us closer towards Him.

Our life becomes a lot easier when we acknowledge God and His goodness.

This simple statement should have the power to change the mind of the most atheist or anyone who scorns religious studies.

In the hearts and minds of many Americans, God's light has slowly begun to dim. What effect will this attitude have on this nation's goodwill? These are the kinds of questions that we must ask ourselves. Soon it will be too late for us to respond. This nation is being polluted by a spiritual virus that is destroying the core of our existence. We must be aware of the fact that much of our society is advocating the total absence of God's love. The result of such thinking is described in the "Book of Revelations." Here we find the great predictions and prophecies that warn us of the outcome of such actions.

As we continue our struggle for survival, we must be mentally, physically, emotionally, and spiritually ready. The spirit of this country must be based on greatness, not on false pride.

The purpose of our religious leaders should be to help us understand and guide us towards this purpose in our life.

Before I leave you with my final thoughts on this subject, let me candidly share with you my feelings toward God. First of all, God is real!

I also believe that He has the power to appear anytime, anywhere, in any form. He can come to us as a stranger on the street corner or as a bird flying high overhead. God is the ruler of this universe and countless other worlds that we might not beware of. God is the master of all human and alien forms. God can be happy or angry. I believe that when our forefathers drew the blueprints for this nation, God was pleased that this country had a desire to create a foundation that was built on His trust! I also believe that God was displeased when we took Him out of our school system. Religion is only the means by which to find God. Lastly, God is the first and the last of all things, and we will all be given a chance to stand in His presence.

In closing, I would like to leave a very clear message for a special race of Americans. I would like to tell all black men not to cry, for the hope of survival truly belongs in your hands.

Throughout this book, I have attacked certain issues, but have tried to express myself honestly in order to give all Americans an opportunity to candidly view our nation without prejudice or rancor. I graciously proclaim, "this is my country!" This declaration should be made by the entire black race!

When it comes to the black man, my conclusions are quite simple. We must not allow ourselves to become disillusioned with who we are and where we stand. The black man has earned the right to call this country his own. Because it is his nation, he has the inherited right to make any changes which will increase the success of its growth. Throughout the years, we have been programed with the notion that this nation is the white man's America. It has taken the white man several hundred years, but he has managed to create a nation of violence, full of rage and hatred. It is time for us to say, "Enough is enough! We will not be witness to the white man's arrogant and selfish actions any longer!"

To be fair, I do not place the blame for all our problems on the white man. However, the white man's track record speaks for itself. There is no need to carry a sign that says, "Hey, you fucked up!" If this country is to survive, we must understand that healing is going to take a united effort. A united nation has no place for egos, Black White, Red, Yellow or Brown. Not only will egotism get in the way of the healing process, but it will ultimately delay the progress of our nation.

It is imperative that the Black man understands the challenges that face him. Our actions will make all of us and this nation stronger than ever. So how do we do this?

First of all, we must never underestimate that which opposes us. It would be very foolish for us to assume that the negative attitude towards the black man has changed. Although each generation brings about positive change, we must realize that the white man's hatred still exists. Often this hatred is replaced with tolerance.

Secondly, the Black man must unite with other races that are also impatiently waiting for a change. This will obviously come from the unification of all minorities and can be achieved through the power of the vote. I decided to register to vote on my fortieth birthday. Although I don't have much faith in American politics, I compare voting to having a gun. If you must use it, it should be to defend yourself. It also helps if the gun is loaded. We must arm ourselves with the power of our vote and demand a change instead of begging for table scraps!

Realizing that the power is in our control will help us to obtain the changes we need to acquire.

Again, I must emphasize the fact that the black man does not have the luxury of losing sight of the real prize in this country. That prize is the freedom to help create a better America. We must create new "sports areas" to dominate. Our hope for the future is not found in our great performance in American athletics.

It is through our involvement in the mental and spiritual growth of this country that will achieve our greatest heights.

Through athletics, we can utilize the countless doors that have been opened to us. However, in order to thrive, the black race must understand that athletics can become a means towards a new beginning. We must create new dreams that will take us much further than the field of athletics. We must accept this philosophy and teach it to our children so they will not be disillusioned by the system. Of course this is not an easy task. Kids today have the ability to adapt easily, but they lack the wisdom to foresee the outcome these changes will have in their lives. We owe it to our kids to give them an opportunity to achieve the very best.

The last thing that I would like to reiterate is that we must draw positively from our experiences. Look to your ancestors' for the strength and character you need. Let's open our hearts and give our support to Africa, the land of our fathers. Our Jewish brothers have taught us the importance of strong ties to the motherland. Their unification as a race of people has been the catalyst to their success. Will we close our eyes to the needs of our brothers in Africa? The cry for food in Africa must not fall on deaf ears in America.

You see I believe that this is the real reason that we were taken from our homeland, so that we could be made strong enough to help those that were left behind. If we respond to this challenge we will continue to be blessed as a people.

I am truly thankful for having had the opportunity to write this book. I sincerely hope that it will help give all Americans the opportunity to see the black race as a very special race of people. As black Americans, we simply want what is best for this country. We must be willing to demand it and claim what is rightfully ours. I hope that *Black Eye on America* will be a good place to begin this change for a better tomorrow!

~~THE END~~
The Beginning!

What's Up Next?

Check out our Web Site
@Http://www.blackeyewp.com

<u>Under Books</u>

<u>*Only For A Season:*</u> The story of a black woman born in 1937 and the struggles that taught her how to love. Available September 15, 1998.

<u>*Black Man Don't Cry!*</u> A in-depth look at the Black male; his past, present and future.

<u>*Three White Shepherds,*</u> A wonderful story of a young Black man who moves to Beverly Hills and adopts three young boys. This is a story of their struggles, triumphs and the moral that love has no color!

Under Audio

Black Eye on America! Available July 15, 1998

Under Posters

Black Eye on America!

Only for A Season

Three White Shepherds

Black man Don't Cry!

Under T-Shirts and Caps

Black Eye on America!

Order Now!
Toll Free

1-877-BLK-EYE1
1-877-255-3931

Black Man Don't Cry!
(Poster)

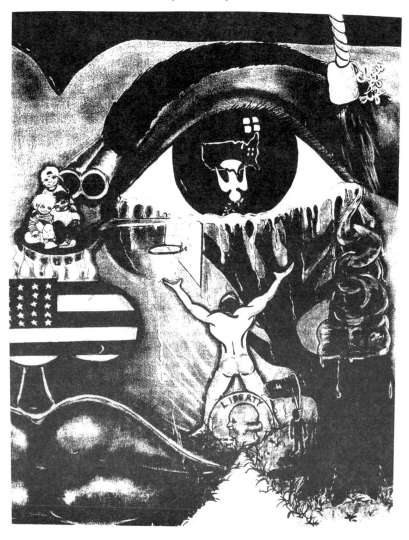

Created by Robin Tavaris

O

O'hair, Madalyn pg.
Oilers pg.
O"Neal "Buck" John pg.
O'Neal Shaquile 148
Ozone pg.

P

Pairie View A&M pg. 127
Path, pg. 236
Pee, Wee pg 99
Peck, J. David pg. 349
Pepsi pg 148
Perot, Ross pg. 484
Pete, Calvin pg.355
Philadelphia pg. 333,
Pistons, Detroit pg. 129
Politicians pg.
Powel Colin pg. 335,426
Portier, Sidney pg. 340
Principalities pg 300

Q

R

Racism pg. 103,
rap music pg.

I must say, one of the many pleasures in writing this book was the need for countless hours of research. To those authors whose works I have drawn upon, my sincerest thanks.

Academic American Encyclopedia Volume 14 & 15

An Atheist Epic.

Alton Hornsby Jr. Chronology of African American History.

Been In the Storm So long (The After Math of Slavery)

Bible, King James Version.

Britannica, Micropedia
Volume 7 & 8

Dr. Cormier, Ruby. White man Paradise, Black mans Prison, Published by Progressive Press.

Colliers Encyclopedia Volume 14

Coslett Publishing Company William Sport, Pennsylvania, Leaves of Gold

Colliers Encyclopedia Volume 7, 11, 16

Diagram Group the Sports Fan Ultimate Book of Sports Comparison

Ed McCabe, Ozone Theraphy's

Encyclopedia Britannica
11th Edition Church History.

Harley, Sharon - The Time of African American History.

Neal R. Pierce, The Deep South States of America 976.03 Beverly hills Public Library

The New Book of Knowledge Education.

115th Edition, Statistical Abstract of United States.

The Black Resource Guide 10th Edition.
Harper & Row, Publishers, New York, Philadelphia, and London. The Treasure Chest.

Simon & Schuster. Avenue of the America.

Malefic K. Asante & Mark T. Malton Historical and Cultural Atlas of African Americans.

Joan Potter, Constance Clayton African-American First.

Payne, Betty. The African American Encyclopedia. Volume 5 Published by

Marshall Cavendish Corporation.

Lee, George, L. Interesting People (Black Americans History Makers)

McGraw- Hill Book Company Encyclopedia of Black America

Maeroff Gene, Don't Blame the Kids. Mcgraw-Hill Book Company The Trouble with America

Ploski, Harry and Williams James, The Negro Almanac- Fifth Edition.

Kohl, Herbert, Rethinking Schools An Agenda for Change. Copyright 1995.

Book of Data.
World Almanac
Book of Facts 1998

World Book Encyclopedia Constitution of the United States

115th Edition. Statistical Abstract of the United

States 1995, The National

Smith, Jessie Carney 2000 years of Extraordinary Achievement

John Hassan, Sports Almanac

Morgan, Bradley J. Sports Fans Connection
Sports Illustrated

Wilson, H. W Current Biography 1977 Year Book.

World Book Encyclopedia
Volume 12